Marginal Organizations

Marginal Organizations

Analyzing Organizations at the Edge of Society's Mainstream

Dennis W. Tafoya

palgrave
macmillan

MARGINAL ORGANIZATIONS

First published in 2014 by
PALGRAVE MACMILLAN®
in the United States—a division of St. Martin's Press LLC,
175 Fifth Avenue, New York, NY 10010.

Where this book is distributed in the UK, Europe and the rest of the world, this is by Palgrave Macmillan, a division of Macmillan Publishers Limited, registered in England, company number 785998, of Houndmills, Basingstoke, Hampshire RG21 6XS.

Palgrave Macmillan is the global academic imprint of the above companies and has companies and representatives throughout the world.

Palgrave® and Macmillan® are registered trademarks in the United States, the United Kingdom, Europe and other countries.

ISBN: 978–1–137–37946–7

Library of Congress Cataloging-in-Publication Data

Tafoya, Dennis W.
Marginal organizations : analyzing organizations at the edge of society's mainstream / Dennis W. Tafoya.
pages cm
Includes bibliographical references and index.
ISBN 978–1–137–37946–7 (hardback)
1. Informal sector (Economics) I. Title.

HD2341.T34 2013
330—dc23 2013036137

A catalogue record of the book is available from the British Library.

Design by Newgen Knowledge Works (P) Ltd., Chennai, India.

First edition: May 2014

10 9 8 7 6 5 4 3 2 1

Jay Tolson, CEO, member of various corporate boards, a long-time supporter of the disadvantaged, the arts and academics. A person of vision, always willing to give of himself in order to be of benefit to others. He has always found time to be a mentor, resource and supporter of me and my efforts. I am grateful and completely in his debt.

Contents

Illustrations

Figures

Tables

Preface

This book is a product of my research and teaching in both academic and organizational settings. The marginal organizations discussed in this book are sometimes described as part of a society's shadow economy—the informal, gray or black market that is often recognized and even praised as a source of employment for the often unemployable, as an example of street-level creativity, innovation and adaptation in the face of depravation, scrutiny or intolerance and a means for moving or creating streams of money in an otherwise impoverished or depressed population of society. This is one view of the marginal organizations examined in the present book, but another view, as descriptive, is of organizations that avoid paying taxes, skirt labor laws and regulations, engage in outright criminal activity and, in sum, often put those working in the organization or members of a society itself at risk of injury or loss.

Most books and articles written about marginal organizations or the sector in which they operate are descriptive accounts of what the researcher observes after studying them in the marketplace. This research reflects the work of professionals from strictly academic arenas like economics, sociology, psychology, political science and anthropology and applied fields like law, law enforcement and criminal justice or a fresh and growing field like investigative journalism. The material provided through the studies produced makes for interesting, informed reading and fodder for additional studies in the area.

In this book, I hope to advance research aimed at understanding the operations of marginal organizations and the informal economy in general by illustrating how different tools, models and theories often used in the examination of organizations in society's mainstream can be applied to studies of marginal organizations, those existing outside, but often operating in and around society's mainstream organizations and population.

The book is written for practitioners and scholars who are looking for ways to advance their thinking and understanding of the organizations in this dynamic sector of society, or the sector itself. These professionals will see that applying materials developed through the study of society's established mainstream organizations isn't always a neat, linear process. In fact, many commonplace tools, for example, in planning or developing a mainstream organization, are seldom used in marginal organizations and, in some instances, simply don't apply in any meaningful way.

Researchers experienced in studying organizations in the sector will be quick to see why this can occur because many of the organizations operating in society's margins—its terrorists, organized crime, the petty drug pusher or bootlegger, the smuggler or prostitute—don't have the time, resources or, importantly, cannot afford the risk and exposure brought on by successfully employing business or organizational tools used in the mainstream. Few of these organizations market their products ("Buy your organic, field-ripened marijuana here"), divide their sales efforts to cover, say, national or regional, accounts or when they do think of their organization's brand, conceptualize it the way a mainstream organization might. Marginal organizations exist in a society's shadow and grow and operate in ways that reflect the environment from which they come and the challenges brought on by the mainstream that seeks to control, often regulate and sometimes destroy them.

Material in this book reflects more than 35 years of research, study and work helping to design and operate effective organizations—in the mainstream. One can't think systemically about an effective mainstream organization, however, without a sense of the challenges brought on by the very active energies of the marginal organizations that share the society in which they operate. So a significant amount of the material for this book is drawn from existing studies, interviews with people "familiar" with marginal organizations from a variety of perspectives and direct (albeit often unobtrusive) field research and observation.

The observations and conclusions drawn and presented in this book are my own. However, like the organizations examined, we as researchers seldom exist in complete isolation; so I do want to recognize the help and/or ongoing support I've received from a few key people. Dr. Mark Stearns has been an excellent resource when talking about material related to the book. His knowledge of retail, chemistry and his experience as a biochemist made him a credible person to whom I could present material from the book in order to gauge its reasonableness or just to get his impressions of the material vis-à-vis one whose business, while embedded in the formal, mainstream economy, is so often copied in the informal, marginal sectors of society. I appreciate the time and perspective he has always been willing to provide.

Jay Tolson, to whom this book is dedicated, has been a long-time source of support and encouragement of my work and research. The use of succession planning, institutional use of "skunk works teams" in manufacturing, strategies for bridging and improving relationships between labor and management are just a few of the areas from which I've benefited from his progressiveness and openness with respect to new ideas. He is a person of vision and one who, when his own view is impaired or incomplete, knows how to source the people and resources needed to gain the perspective that may be missing. I am grateful to know him and having worked with him.

I am especially grateful to Eileen Ware, a long-time friend, who always made time to listen to various thoughts related to my work and encouraged me and supported my efforts. Eileen's friendship and keen intellect were helpful in broadening my thoughts and capacity for innovation and invention—traits that proved particularly valuable for this book and the new theories it launches. She is a perfect example of a person who always adds value, regardless of her role or the extent of her involvement. I am truly indebted to her and her friendship.

This is my second project with Charlotte Maiorana, my editor at Palgrave Macmillan. She and her team continue to be a solid resource for me. Charlotte's openness to new ideas is a key feature of her professionalism that makes our work together especially rewarding. I look forward to many more projects with her. With this in mind, I want to also mention the fine assistance and support Sarah Lawrence has added to this project. Sarah was new to this effort but she knows how to look at the heart of the matter, is willing to make suggestions or offer her assistance and truly makes publishing a manuscript a team effort. She and Charlotte are the personification of two key concepts in this book I find central to any successful organization: teams and individual contributors. It's a pleasure to work with them.

Finally, I truly want to acknowledge the constant help and support I receive from my wife, Nancy. I value what she brings into my life and work. She is a trusted friend and one of the finest people I know.

CHAPTER 1

Introduction to the Concept of the Marginal Organization

People invent opportunities. Sometimes these opportunities result in a business venture, at other times in a means for escape from a difficult or dangerous situation or in an opportunity for advancement, and at still other times in a simple chance to eat, to survive. Whatever the result, if necessity is the mother of invention, invention is the nexus of opportunity. In this book, we explore a by-product of human efforts to construct opportunities for themselves and others; it is an investigation into the ways an individual's or a group's bond with society translates into action that leads to the formation of an economic way of life that exists outside of the society's mainstream.

Invented opportunities do not always produce good or legitimate outcomes. Prostitution, drug sales, undocumented aliens or crime in general may be opportunities for one to earn a living or to gain wealth, but that does not mean they are acceptable pursuits. These are activities on the fringe of society, not at its core. Likewise, there is a panoply of other occupations or endeavors that, while generally viewed as acceptable, are still constrained to exist in society's margins. The food wagon is a great place for a quick lunch but it hardly offers the convenience and certainly not the luxury of a good, sit-down restaurant. Likewise, the team that shows up to mow the lawn, the subcontractor who installs a new dishwasher or the fellow hired to paint the house all provide needed services but still aren't mainstream; they offer limited, sometimes "cut-rate" services and typically without the splashy range of features as their full-service mainstream counterparts. They are probably not legally incorporated organizations, they are just people who do needed work. The yellow pages or the local coupon mailer do not feature them; they make their contacts via word of mouth, perhaps through a friend or a friend of a friend. These dynamic subsystems may comprise facsimiles of a larger, formal economy or a broader society but, however metamorphosed, as street vendors, backroom shops, legal or illegal labor, corruption or any number of other organizations, they are not the same as organizations in the mainstream (Sassen, 2009).

Taken at face value, these organizations are described in ways that make them seem like vanguards of a liberated mentality. Indeed, some have labeled these collectively as part of society's informal sector (Thomas, 2001), others as informal situations (Sabatini and Farnsworth, 2006) and still others as the informal economy, a "low cost, grassroots and potentially revolutionary way to create jobs in the context of overregulated states" (Henken, 2008). However they are labeled, in the absence of grand sentiments or euphemistic titles, these organizations are motivated by more mundane pursuits than providing quality products or services. Their aim is to construct opportunities that earn money to pay the bills or at best to "get by," to avoid taxes, dodge social security payments and generally skirt, where possible, labor laws (Andrews et al., 2011; Williams and Round, 2009; Hart, 1973, 1990).

Yet, these organizations merit study or examination for many reasons, not the least of which is that in some parts of the world they can account for nearly half of a country's gross national product (Becker, 2004; Schneider et al., 2010). Our approach begins by conceptualizing them as existing in the margins of a greater society. To this extent they are not in the mainstream, which defines most of the organizations in a society but, rather, they operate on a society's fringe, periphery or edges. So the state-controlled lottery or casino are mainstream organizations while the unsanctioned, online gambling or the person "running numbers" on the street corner are the marginal operations seeking stakeholders willing to risk some money in the hopes of winning more. The store selling beer, wine and liquor can find itself competing with a group operating an illegal distillery making moonshine, and the concession stand in the sports arena selling team memorabilia competes with the street vendor hawking similar but contraband items.

Our view of marginalized organizations is that they are illegal operations. The aforementioned street vendor may not need a license to sell the goods offered but the vendor is expected to collect and pay sales taxes, to adhere to labor laws and to ensure that the merchandise sold is legal and not in violation of trademark or copyright infringements. The owner of a lawn care operation may pay personal income tax while paying those who mow the lawns, rake the leaves and trim the hedges cash "under the table," thus avoiding payroll and social security taxes. Parts of the lawn care operation are legitimate and some others are not (La Porta and Shleifer, 2008).

Organizations in the marginalized society are not necessarily set up as profit entities either. A "charitable" organization may accept donations to support its soup kitchen or "outreach" programs but may not seek classification as a particular type of for-profit or nonprofit entity. Indeed, some of these organizations are notorious for using the income they collect to support a lavish lifestyle or to provide extreme compensation for the organization's leadership.

History is filled with examples of organizations characterized as offering goodwill or charitable services while really operating as a front for illegal activities. The organization that offers "protective services" to local residents, businesses or whole communities is one example. The scam here is simple: if you don't pay us for "protection," we won't protect you from us... if "you don't pay, you can't play." At other times, marginal organizations operate as fronts for more nefarious activities or missions. Vigilante groups organized to promote or "protect" a particular way of life are an example. Societies such as the Ku Klux Klan or even organizations classified as terrorists, like al-Qaeda, frequently claim to exist to perform protective functions on moral or religious grounds. Whatever their claims might be, when they are not performing in ways that are sanctioned by a society, they are examples of organizations operating out of the mainstream and are thus included within the scope of our research and this book.

A key feature of marginal organizations is autonomy; they see themselves as independent, self-sufficient and often self-governing entities. One result of this orientation is that marginals always have the attention of two groups: their patrons who want and sometimes need their products and services, and elements of the mainstream who watch, observe and sometimes scrutinize marginals as potential trouble or threats to established order. Many marginals look like mainstream organizations in that they have structure, hierarchies and control mechanisms, but their structure, functional nature or overall design is often fluid, capable of quickly adapting to the conventional norms and organizations of the society with which they are associated. Their relationship to the mainstream is important to understand. On the one hand, they are often dependent upon the mainstream for their livelihood; mainstream citizens and consumers are often primary stakeholders in a marginal organization's social and economic network. On the other hand, however, mainstream organizations and institutions often are a marginal's primary adversary. The mainstream comprises organizations who may see marginal organizations as threats or competitors to their own operations, those whose job it is to regulate and enforce rules, regulations and laws a marginal organization may violate and those who simply don't see marginal organizations or those associated with them as appropriate for the "mainstream way of life." In the end, these threats of mainstream attacks or action often serve as a catalyst for a marginal's inventiveness or general desire to know and capacity to adapt to the mainstream environment around which they function. As suggested above, this does not mean they have to behave in manners or ways prescribed by the mainstream; it just means marginals have to be capable of adapting their organization so that they can operate *despite* the mainstream's rules, regulations or prescriptions. Think about it. Puppy mills, illegal gambling, smugglers, drug operations or prostitutes can all operate within the same geographic region, the same political or legal environment as each other *and* their legitimate, mainstream counterparts.

So the mainstream is an inescapable backdrop against which marginals operate and the foundation that defines a marginal's intrinsic nature. It's as though the marginal is a hybrid organization—a close copy of mainstream organizations but just different enough to be distinguished from society's economic and behavioral standards. However, while the structural makeup of mainstream organizations may serve as a template for understanding a marginal's operation, these features alone do not provide enough perspective to help understand marginal organizations and their operations. For example, Becker (2004) directs her readers to three theoretical approaches she believes summarize most of the literature explaining links between marginal and mainstream relationships: those promoting a legalist interpretation of marginal organizations, the structuralists who focus on the marginal organization's makeup and the dualists who approach marginal organizations as separate from the dominant mainstream and its organizations. The legalists see marginals as entrepreneurs who rebel against overregulation by mainstream, government organizations (11). Like the other two theories, the legalist approach has its merits but it's the inherent nature of this theory to restrict its scope to some of the smallest of marginal organizations, and that's too great a limitation for us.

Dualists see marginal organizations as separate from the mainstream. Dualists may acknowledge that the marginal and mainstream populations are a spectrum containing a range of organizations defined in terms of, for example, their degree of legality or the formality of their structure, but in the end, the dualist perspective is a "black or white" orientation; there may be gradations within the mainstream and its margins but organizations are either in one or the other. This doesn't mean an organization can't migrate from one side to the other, just that the two segments are independent and it's the nature of the organization that ultimately determines if it is classified as marginal or mainstream. Finally, the structuralists often approach marginals as subordinate to the mainstream (Castells and Portes, 1989). This view clearly sees marginals as being on the lowest rungs of an organizational hierarchy. This view might work if marginals were being judged by their earning power, and then only if the earning power of marginals was, say, always in the lower 5–10% of the hierarchy. But some marginals are economic powerhouses earning hundreds of millions of dollars. Drug-trading organizations, Somali pirates or those who deal and trade in illegal weapons or armaments are among the wealthiest organizations in their countries of origin. The number of marginal organizations worldwide or within most countries also makes them a major presence, to say nothing of the number of people they employ. Other times the marginal may be a dictatorship or a military tribunal that controls and directs an entire population or country. A structural theory bends when these types of organizations are accounted for; so, while there's some validity to the orientation structuralists take, it doesn't offer a single best theory accounting for the relationship between marginals and their mainstream.

In fact, there's probably no single best theory to account for marginal organizations, but just effective definitions or parameters stipulating the scope of one's study. In this book, any organization, for example, economic, social, political, religious, military or cultural, can be classified as operating in society's margins. Our approach is to simply include any and all organizations that operate outside a mainstream's set of laws, rules and regulations. The literature seems to support this criterion and, as importantly, it avoids the romantic notions like those that approach marginals as ventures or entrepreneurships that create employment or economic opportunities for their membership or society.

Our orientation doesn't use an organization's motivations as a delimiter; if the organization operates outside the law, rules and regulations, it is a marginal, not a mainstream, organization. This approach also rectifies an ambiguity created in some existing studies. For example, some treatments of marginal organizations muddy the relationship between the marginal and mainstream when they approach marginals as being defined by exceptions: as organizations that may not operate as mainstream organizations (e.g., pay taxes or adhere to local labor laws) but provide goods and services that are otherwise perfectly legal (Becker, 2004, 11).

Given the scope of this book, as presented above, we are open to including any and all organizations that operate outside of society's legal, rules and regulations parameters as examples of marginal organizations. We take this approach because it seems in line with general treatments in the literature and, more importantly, it provides us with coherent populations to use when seeking to understand if and why marginals are successful, why they may be perceived as a burden on the mainstream or how and why they operate in society's margins in the first place; it also is important to understand the ways in which these organizations "behave" and act in their environments. Simplifying our notion of what is and isn't a marginal organization greatly facilitates our understanding of what particular features are needed for marginals to survive and sometimes flourish without creating unwanted ambiguities or confusion.

We take this orientation for several reasons, beginning with the fact that society's margins include a mix of organizations with economic, social, political or even cultural motivations, and also that too narrow a focus or definition of what is a marginal organization is both misguided and misleading. Let us consider the following observations.

First, a marginal's role in society should never be discounted. These organizations can have significant influence in every society and they do so because they meet the needs of people, stakeholders, that are not being met by mainstream organizations. Marginals emerge to capitalize on opportunity; it's often a win/win situation. The marginal and the stakeholder gain from the relationship, and whether the relationship is defined by drugs, sex, politics or religion it's the opportunity for a relationship that fills one's needs that counts.

Marginal organizations are opportunistic. If there is an opportunity for easy money, an opportunity to gain needed followers or an opportunity to enhance the organization's position, even if those benefits antagonize mainstream organizations, do it. Why not? Marginals know they're already on the outside, so some see any opportunity as only a means for gain and, at best, only resulting in nominal increases in the discrimination, hazing or harassment they may feel they experience.

Some marginals provide stakeholders with the recreational fix or outlet they need and can't get in the mainstream. In this capacity, the marginal provides an escape, a release point for the stakeholder in need and, of course, willing to pay the price for pleasures received. All organizations exist to meet some stakeholder's needs; it's just that marginal organizations often handle needs mainstream organizations seldom see as important or worthwhile in addressing.

Organizations emerge outside the mainstream because there are low entry requirements in the marginal sector. Anyone can steal, sell one's body or join a gang, and that's because almost anything can be ripped off, almost anybody can be sold and there's always a gang somewhere looking for a new member. In these instances, the individual has all the equipment needed to participate; it's that simple. Some characterize this as an example of an entrepreneurial spirit, but in many instances, choosing to move into the marginal sector is more a last resort than a planned opportunity.

Marginals are ubiquitous; they are the perfect universal opportunity. Crimes can occur anywhere, anytime. So if there's a way to access the mainstream, there's a marginal organization seeking to capitalize on this opportunity. One should be careful, however, not to associate commonality with competence or even to assume competence to be a marginal's prominent trait. The opportunity to act, more than the possession of particular skills or competencies, is what facilitates the marginal's capacity to act, to travel within the mainstream or to multiply. Marginals also benefit from their simultaneous capacity to engender a social dimension that both nurtures the organization and gives members another reason for being involved in a sometimes dangerous environment. This is a powerful feature many organizations seek to possess but it is perhaps most pronounced in marginals because it serves as a binding agent for both the organization and its members. The marginal that is set up as a business enterprise may experience greater stakeholder bonding than a given business enterprise operating in the mainstream. A marginal's membership knows that both the organization *and* the membership are excluded, are outcasts, from the mainstream; it's typically not one or the other.

The margins provide a place for organizations engaged in criminal activity to exist, where they can recruit, orientate and train new members in the organization's rites, rules and procedures. This is an invaluable opportunity and one critical for a marginal organization's survival. There's a level of privacy, cover and concealment the marginal may not be able to secure in the mainstream. A society's margins may not offer the same comforts as regions within the mainstream but it is home to many outcasts. Indeed, while the marginal organization is familiar with moving back and forth between the mainstream and its margins, most mainstream organizations would not know how to begin these types of excursions even if they wanted to make them.

The mainstream is only a partial opportunity for the marginal. The mainstream is an economic resource to be mined and, at times, a unique learning opportunity for the marginal. But the marginal must be on guard and constantly vigilant. Some mainstream stakeholders use their position as guardians or vanguards against the marginal to use and interpret the law when it's convenient, to engage in illegal activities like wiretapping if necessary or to restrict or unlawfully detain a marginal if this seems warranted. These behaviors and experiences teach the marginal to be cautious, to be prudent. But, despite the dangers, what marginals need is a place where criminal activity can be consummated. Places where money can be laundered, goods can be fenced and police can be avoided, uneven or unenforced regulations can be used to the marginal's advantages. When possible, marginal organizations rely on their own territories outside the mainstream to fulfill these needs. If, however, it's not possible to stay within the safety of the marginal's own environment, they must move into the mainstream to meet their needs.

Anyone can be a leader or important person in a marginal organization, provided they "fit in" and embrace the organization and its mission. Once in, however, there seldom is a need for a formal education to participate or advance. It is a self-governing, self-ruled environment. The mainstream doesn't dictate who or what the marginal should value; that's for the marginal organization's membership to determine. This is more than a self-evident factor. It also serves to provide the marginal's membership with a unique sense of destiny. The marginal's membership chooses its own path and pursuits. Marginals frankly don't listen to the dictates of the mainstream—otherwise they'd be part of the mainstream.

Marginals learn that whether in the margins or mainstream, people allow criminal activity to exist; society or citizens "look the other way" if what's occurring doesn't impact them, or if they benefit in some way. The marginal is the organization that avoids paying fair wages or sales tax, but the enabler in these instances is the individual who pays cash in a deal to avoid paying the extra tax or the homeowner looking for someone to mow the lawn for a cheap price. Society will target the marginal but, in actuality, there are two thieves. It's fair to say this type of situation reflects a double standard, but most marginals accept these conditions as just another feature linked with operations associated with or at the convenience of mainstreamers.

Marginals know that some level of crime meets the average citizen's needs. The average citizen runs red lights, avoids paying tolls or taxes, cheats when completing income tax forms. The marginals know this, so they create parallel opportunities to benefit from this profile. They enable illegal gambling, the sale of drugs or illegal alcohol, the service of prostitutes and the ever-present opportunity for a "good deal" in the purchase of smuggled cigarettes or bulk items "right off the truck." Marginals seem to know that crime makes everyone guilty, so who's going to report it? If someone in the mainstream takes drugs, buys stolen goods or uses a prostitute, then the mainstreamer is compromised and becomes a part of the problem. Since people don't tend to incriminate themselves, the crime goes unreported.

Marginals also benefit from the fact that crime and criminal activity are too big, or at least perceived to be too big to be completely contained. It's easy for mainstreamers to decry the fact that the "crime problem" is too big, that's there's no controlling it, that it doesn't involve "us." As a result, marginals have a way out of punishment or lengthy incarcerations. After all, what's wrong with spending a few months in jail if it's possible to get decent food, to catch up with old friends or associates or to learn new skills or techniques for use once released?

Potential victims or opportunities are everywhere for the marginal, so there is always an employment opportunity. This keeps marginals going and on the go. Marginal organizations are society's entitlement program or, for the individual, an annuity. Marginals exist for many reasons, but one of the most significant is that they are a destination for large groups of individuals who, for whatever reason, cannot function in the mainstream.

Finally, deriving rewards from one's work or affiliations often is a matter of perspective. It's possible to make a lot of money as a marginal, so while the marginal's members may have to sacrifice a place in mainstream society or certain perks, position and status that only the mainstream can offer, there still are benefits. In and of itself, this is a powerful incentive for involvement and risk taking. Many mainstream organizations are notorious for not hiring "an ex-con," but marginals aren't likely to discriminate in this way. For the marginal that person may be someone with the type of job experience needed.

Analyzing Marginal Organizations

The description, examination and evaluation of marginal organizations are this book's focus. It's the primary focus because there's value in broadening our understanding of how marginals function as organizations in pursuit of a vision and mission.

The tools and materials provided and discussed below illustrate ways for seeing that beyond the products that are sold or the services offered there are many significant differences between one marginal organization and another and between marginal and mainstream organizations. In fact, the possible insights gained from the material that follows may stimulate some writers and researchers in the field to reexamine existing studies of this unique segment of society.

Marginals face a number of challenges as organizations. For example, when approaching marginal organizations as proactive entities seeking to shape and not merely react to the conditions defining their environment, it's possible to see that marginals have stakeholders with needs to be met, external adversaries that aim to challenge or engage the marginal organization when possible and, all the while, a need to secure, produce and distribute products and services in order to continue operations. Now, obviously, these are pursuits of all organizations whether marginals or in the mainstream but the world is not the same for a marginal organization when compared to an organization in the mainstream. Marginals lead a harassed and, in some instances, pursued existence. Many are branded with stereotypes and face prejudicial behavior when seeking to move out of the margins and into the mainstream. For some in the mainstream marginals are expected to know their place and to stay within certain boundaries if they want to continue to operate.

Finally, most organizations in the mainstream have a sense of the future, an idea that their organizations can be sold to continue operations or may be passed on, for example, to other family members. There isn't a sense of the future for many marginals. Mainstream organizations can think in terms of a succession plan while marginals often don't have the time for, or any sense of, the future. "Live for today" is more than a way of life for the marginal organization; it's a reality. The same can be said for those working in or supporting a marginal organization. Most workers in marginal organizations don't think in terms of retirement, and if they are lucky enough to live to a retirement age, many can't turn to their government for retirement benefits because the organizations of which they are a part never participated in, nor were able to participate in, programs that fund Social Security or Medicare resources for them. They simply don't qualify for these benefits.

Operating Styles and Organization Profiles in Society

Understanding what today and tomorrow can look like for the marginal organization is a major theme in this book. For example, it's not uncommon for marginal organizations to be a focus of mainstream scrutiny but it is not just the products and services marginals offer that contribute to this condition. Often it is a marginal's customs or rituals or, simply, the way these organizations act, that the mainstream finds objectionable. Prejudice, profiling or a general intolerance are additional issues for many marginals already labeled as potential competitors or organizations that are viewed as less than simply unwanted.

The debate around the use of mobile food wagons in Columbus, Ohio, is an example. Ferenchik (2006) wrote, "A year ago, Northland community leader Chuck Parker asked Columbus to crack down on the mobile food wagons popping up in parking lots along Rt. 161." Ferenchik noted that code enforcers had already cited a Hispanic-owned stand and another was under investigation for code violation. He quotes Parker as saying, "We're concerned if they set up shop anywhere. What's to prohibit another 50 of them to set up in any parking lot?...I personally don't want to live in little Tijuana" (April 29, 2006). Later, in 2007, Ferenchik, referring to the food wagons as an example of the "cultural change sweeping through Columbus," noted that Julia Arbini Carbonell, president of the Ohio Hispanic Coalition, felt these types of movements against food wagons was "unfairly targeting Mexican vendors" (December 6, 2007).

As a result, many marginal organizations behave in a reactive manner within their own and the mainstream's environment. Everything about the way they are referenced in the literature illustrates this operational tone. Marginals are labeled as part of the "informal economy," or as members of the "shadow economy," the "dark side" or the black market. These are more than mere labels, however; they are ways to describe or profile organizations and people who are different and who appear to drift, to coexist at a distance or who shift in the current of more "legitimate" mainstream organizations. Marginal organizations don't set the pace for a society; they drift along the mainstream like small boats in the wake and stream of socially acceptable mainstream organizations. In many ways, marginals only exist "at the convenience" of the mainstream status quo.

However, while the behavior and positioning of most marginals may best be described as "reactive," others are definitely defined by a very proactive behavioral style. These organizations, while not truly confrontational, are often willing to go "head-to-head" with their mainstream counterparts. Criminal, paramilitary and terrorist organizations and certain religious cults and sects set a standard against which their mainstream counterparts react and respond. The same is true of political factions that see themselves as competing for the rule of a territory or country. The proactive, assertive style these marginals display may not occur by design or plan but, rather, is forged out of the confrontations and tempestuous interactions the marginals experience in pursuit of a vision or mission and grounded in a sense of right. These organizations believe they have a role or purpose in society to fulfill, and they resist attempts to limit or prevent them from achieving their goals.

This distinction between reactive and proactive natures surfaces throughout the book. As discussed in the early chapters, the foundation for a marginal's operations and behavior focuses on the role that structure and process factors play in the ways goals are defined or set, plans are conceived, work is organized or tasks assigned and executed. These are salient characteristics when studying organizations because they offer important insights into the ways they operate and people behave. So beginning our review by looking at the role that structure and processes play in marginals gives us early insight into their potential strengths, weaknesses and vulnerabilities.

For example, an organization with a reactive profile may be just as autonomous, self-reliant or driven as one with a proactive style, but reactive organizations often seem to operate in order to merely survive while the proactive organization often appears to search for ways to promote and advance itself.

Each carries out or executes plans or assignments in response to its mission and environment but the reality of the day often translates very differently for these organizations. Prostitutes and drug addicts often demonstrate reactive profiles when they agree to follow health and safety patterns that limit the spread of diseases associated with unsafe practices. In these instances, the marginals don't resist efforts to change their behavior but rather go along with the change as a way of appeasing those in authority. Even the moonshiner operating an illegal distillery deep in the woods who stops using lead-based solder when building the distillery, is reacting to demands of the environment. A mainstream, "legitimate" producer of alcoholic beverages might promote this type of change in a production process as a commitment to quality and customer service but for our moonshiners this behavior may be best approached as a need to prevent sickness that could draw attention to the product made and distributed. For marginals, a reactive introduction of change often is just another process introduced as a way to keep mainstream regulators at arm's length.

Marginals that promote a proactive operational style behave differently. Terrorist organizations, for example, operate in terms of their vision and mission for the environment or society and not in terms of how society or a cultural environment expects or wants them to operate. A measure of visibility and exposure for these marginals fits into their plan; it's part of the organization's image or brand. This is why a school or playground is just as likely to be a terrorist target as a government building or a military installation. Anything and everything that falls within the terrorist's mission is fair game for the organization with a proactive behavioral style. These organizations are sensitive to the efforts of their adversaries but overall they are guided by inner prescriptions rather than those imposed on them by the mainstream or the environment in which they operate.

To be successful reactive marginals develop skills and competencies that help them "read" and react to their environment to improve their changes to "get along with" those in authority. So it is necessary to understand the nature of the environment within which a marginal operates. What is the nature of the mainstream environment where marginals are concerned? What is tolerated, or what are the tolerance levels in an environment? The ways in which different geographic regions of the United States approach current social issues like same-sex marriages, abortion or the use and sale of marijuana illustrate the variable nature of the potential environments within which marginals can operate. Sometimes there even seems to be a "seasonal" nature to the limits a society places on what are acceptable or unacceptable practices. A "spring break" or Mardi Gras often are times when prescriptions regarding drinking, drugs and sexual behavior are relaxed in certain operating environments. Migrants are often tolerated when crops need to be harvested but frequently find their welcome fades with the harvest and shouldn't expect to stay on beyond that time.

The interface between organizational style and an operating environment illustrates that while marginals may use the same operational practices as mainstream organizations that doesn't mean they are used in the same ways. Direction and control, communication, information and evaluations strategies are as important in marginals as they are in mainstream organizations; however, each can be expected to use these strategies in different ways simply because the organizations operate in two different societal streams. Consider the following discussion.

Types of Marginal Organizations

We approach organizations by looking first at the vision and missions they pursue and then, much later, at the products or services they offer. For example, mainstream states, cities, college campuses and the like have learned to tolerate the food truck that appears each morning and leaves by mid-afternoon. These food vendors offer employment, product diversity and an efficient way to get a quick meal as long as they don't "disrupt" the local mainstream way of life. Now some researchers might bristle or object to the comparison but put a prostitute or drug dealer in the environment and, generally speaking, one sees a very different response to these marginal organizations.

Why? All three are small, entrepreneurial ventures, staffed by usually no more than one or a few "employees," and are legally permissible operations in different parts of the country; yet the overall reactions to each differ largely, we believe, because of a conflict between the visions and missions of the marginals involved and the mainstream stakeholders where the marginals hope to operate. Structurally, too, these three marginals are very similar; each is a simple organization with low overhead and a narrow and sometimes fixed product mix, but here again the conflict between the marginal's and the mainstream's vision and mission about what's acceptable or appropriate signals the root of the conflict that can unfold around their operation.

Sometimes it is useful to lump all marginal organizations together and to treat them as a class of organizations, for example, when engaged in statistical or economic analysis, but if one wants to truly understand the nature, function and purpose of a marginal in a mainstream environment, it's best to study it as an individual operational entity. One of the tools offered in this book helps meet that approach. It's a classification scheme that allows the researcher to approach all organizations as belonging to one of four distinct categories. It's a typology developed and tested among mainstream organizations (Tafoya, 2010, 2013a,b) and it holds up when used on marginal organizations as well. This means it's a useful tool when looking at marginals alone or in comparison to mainstream organizations. The typology is discussed and illustrated in chapter 2.

Measured Influence

In this book, we do not just compare and contrast marginals with organizations in the mainstream but rather we describe and examine marginals in their own right as found in cultures, countries and societies around the world. Marginals may be on the periphery of a larger mainstream society but they are, in many ways, truly self-sufficient organizations capable of disrupting, sometimes even destroying, the larger mainstream society of which they are a part. Their role and potential effects should not or cannot be dismissed or ignored. Our approach is to examine and to seek to understand marginals in terms of their capacity to influence, to stimulate or to precipitate change. It's an interesting feature of the book that allows us to examine the small, speck player that tries to be more influential than its limits can enable it to be; it's a means for examining the role pride, ego or self-assuredness can play in crafting strategy in the absence of a plan or, worse, simple common sense; and it's a way to examine instances when imagination and inventiveness, without the perspective of sound management or leadership skills, can result in stress, distress or tragedy. Influence may be an attribute of all organizations but it's also a matter of degree.

A Marginal Organization's Impact on the Mainstream

Impact on Policy and Procedures

Marginal organizations can affect their mainstream neighbors in many ways but six are especially notable. Effects on policy matters are an area where marginals can affect society from the local to national levels. Obviously, these effects emerge in part because of the tendency of marginal organizations to function outside traditional or expected policies, laws, or conventional routines. Sometimes the effects are nominal, like stimulating the enforcement of existing rules, regulations or laws. Enforcement of laws may be relaxed for any number of reasons; hence, when a marginal organization becomes a target of the establishment or mainstream, enforcing previously unenforced laws can be an expedient way to address unwanted activity (Thomas, 2001). Much of the attention devoted to managing the activity of undocumented aliens is an example. Many undocumented aliens contribute to mainstream and marginal sectors in a variety of ways but fear of terrorism, the perceived burden these people place on schools, health care or other community services or, simply, racism, have led to demands that existing laws be enforced regarding this segment of the marginal society.

Undocumented aliens are also at the center of discussions regarding the development of new or current legislation, a second way marginals can impact policy. In these instances, the "need" for new legislation may be tied to the efforts of some special interest group seeking to draw attention to a "growing problem" or a "problem that's out of hand" (Ferenchik, 2007). Other times the focus on marginals is a convenient way for a politician to rally the sentiments of a constituency. Prostitutes, drug pushers, even organized crime are reliable election-time targets. This isn't meant to imply that the committed politician isn't concerned with these elements of the marginal society at other times; it's just that marginals are often most useful calendar tools, as when an election is imminent.

Health, safety and security matters linked to the existence or operation of marginals can trigger the implementation of legislation or rules or, can simply drive policy reforms that are linked to their existence or operation. Unfortunately, the emphasis and implementation of some legislation, rules or policies can place an unusual burden on enterprises that have small profit margins or unique operating platforms. Health and safety rules, for example, directly impact some marginals. The ubiquitous food wagon, a street symbol in many cities around college campuses, sporting arenas or special events is a natural target for the energetic local administrator seeking to launch preventative programs in the interest of public safety. The stimulus for change efforts aimed at this segment of the marginal society are designed to protect the public, but at what cost to the marginals? Consider, for example, the treatment and impact of legislation aimed at controlling lunch wagons in parts of California.

Lunch wagons can continue operating in "Lodi [California] without following city rules that otherwise would force them to move every 10 minutes and forbid them from setting up on private property." "Those regulations, however, apply only to lunch wagons selling from the public right of way. Wagons in Stockton [California] can operate on private property as long as they have proof of consent from the property owner, do not set up tables and chairs, and the wagon's workers have access to restrooms and comply with other state health regulations" (Anonymous, 2006)—an interesting set of requirements for trucks that operate from parking lots that typically don't have restroom access. Wrote Thigpen (2010) about Lodi regulations, "In 2007, the city approved a set of rules for lunch trucks, which require vendors to register for special permits, submit to background checks and comply with regulations." One wonders if restaurant workers in the same area must also submit to background checks before they are allowed to make or serve food!

History also documents those times when fear of disease or influenza influenced policies associated with entire groups of marginals perceived as related to these potential threats. Immigrants, cultural groups like gypsies or, the gay or drug-dependent communities have been the focus of rules leading to policy changes or procedures regarding the interaction between members of the marginal community and mainstream. It's now common practice, in some instances, for the police and emergency responders in certain areas to put on protective gloves when dealing with the homeless or other disenfranchised members of the marginal society. These policies may be local but the perceived need for them can be linked to populations or organizations in the margins of society.

Sometimes the impact on policy can touch the physical structure or makeup of a society or government. If the need seems warranted, the role of existing government agencies may be expanded to deal with the issues brought on by particular marginals, as when the budgets or roles of the police or groups like a town's animal protection department are expanded to deal with puppy mills or the illegal sale or housing of animals (Johnson, 2012). Still other times the significance of a marginal organization and its activities may lead to the emergence of special "watchdog" organizations set up to monitor or regulate activities of a marginal organization (Holt, 2008).

Impacting the Economics of an Area or Its Organizations

Effects on policies and procedures often reflect the impact of marginals on society or government generally or agencies established to support mainstream operations and activity. Sometimes the impact of marginals is measured by examining ways they affect other organizations, like those perceived as their competitors. Food wagons on a college campus, the entrepreneurial cook who sells her tacos, enchiladas and burritos from the trunk of her car in the parking lot of the local grocery store or the enterprising street vendor selling hats and T-shirts near the stadium or clothing store, have some impact on the economics of the area in which they operate—on the amount of money available to the mainstream organizations in the area offering the same types of goods and services.

In other words, simply thinking about the relationship between a marginal and mainstream organization doesn't add as much clarity to our understanding of their true nature of impact as when we compare and contrast patterns between marginal and mainstream organizations to ferret out differences among them. Establishing a simple dichotomy defining organizations as being part of a society's mainstream or not is a start, but this doesn't contribute much to our perspective or understanding of these organizations and their nature. Both are, in fact, connected by the very fact that they are all part of a larger, dynamic system comprising numerous different organizations each pursuing its own and sometimes competing missions and goals. Both marginals and mainstream organizations have a stake in what happens to each, whether they support the other(s) or not, whether they realize it or not.

In short, marginals are part of an intricate societal stakeholder network comprising their own vested stakeholders as well as organizations from the broader mainstream. Stakeholders in these networks affect and are being affected by the others to a greater or a lesser degree. Economics is an example. From the perspective of the local merchant, the issue may be one of market share, while a consumer might look at the same situation as an opportunity for diversity in price or product availability. Regardless of the stakeholder perspective, the results can range from simple annoyance with "nuisance activity" (e.g., surprise searches and inspections, licensing or overt policing or monitoring) to tensions among the stakeholders that result in incidents of brinkmanship leading to the use of force, violence or other unnecessary actions.

The underlying issue that links these organizations is competition—for customers, market share, space, money, alliances or, simply, opportunities. The introduction of marginal organizations into the mainstream's network brings it into competition with mainstream stakeholders, whether they offer the same goods and services or not. Entry into this network means that established value streams are affected, sometimes only stressed but at other times broken or disabled. The impact of these types of stress or change is significant. A value stream is composed of a number of different stakeholders each with his/her own mission and needs (Tafoya, 2013a,b). When a new organization enters the stream the stage is set for a potentially dynamic set of effects to occur.

But the effects, while manifested in the economics of the stream or the larger society, are not easily predicted or anticipated. Some effects may be reflected in changes to traffic (foot and vehicle) around the stream, shifts in the geographic makeup of the stream, changes in facility or building use and, of course, the logistics associated with peripheral matters like parking or simple conveniences (e.g., "restrooms are for customers only"). What makes the impact of the marginals an issue in these instances is that while loss of business, market share or sales are direct effects on the economics of a mainstream "competitor," the secondary effects on traffic patterns, convenience, image or visibility are residual effects that can affect both competitors and noncompetitors in the mainstream. Food wagons or street vendors hawking hotdogs may be in direct competition with local restaurants, but when the same food wagons contribute to the area's traffic congestion this also can lead a consumer interested in shopping at a nearby clothing store, a business not at all in competition with the food vendor, to seek out other places to fulfill his/her needs—places that offer easier access and lesser hassle.

Finally, the economic activity affected in an area may not be restricted to those expressly linked to a value stream associated with competing mainstream and marginal organizations. Travelers in different parts of the United States or those sitting down for a nice meal in some parts of Europe can find themselves confronted with signs that warn of pickpockets operating in the area or warnings about thieves operating around camp grounds or other vacation areas. In these instances, the darker side of the marginal society seeps in, launching a different aspect of a marginal's influence on the economic activity of an area or the organizations operating in them. We've grown accustomed to hearing about break-ins or home invasions, but the presence of pickpockets near restaurants or the vandalism near vacation areas is another way the value stream associated with business and industry is impacted by marginals. In other words, we cannot escape the influence, desired or not, of marginals. As bad, too, is the fact that these examples of a marginal's influence are not restricted to petty crimes. The impact of white-collar crime in business or industry identity, theft or the counterfeiting of goods and services can have far-reaching effects and, perhaps, illustrate a truer picture of the scope and scale associated with the negative economic impact of marginals.

The Impact of Culture and Religion

The influence of marginal organizations isn't restricted to mundane matters associated with the functioning of societies or their economics. Whether meaning to or not, some marginals see it as part of their mission to influence the values, mores, even the very way of life of the organizations, societies or cultures they touch. Pride and self-importance are intoxicating preconditions for a great number of ill-advised actions.

Many religious organizations enter societies and cultures as marginal organizations. They may initiate their entry as part of their religion's organizational vision or mission. In this role, their activities often aim to convert members of a country, other cultures or other organizations to their way of life or to change their view of the "way things should be." In this capacity, these proselytizing organizations are, by definition, consciously seeking to change or alter something about the people, organizations or cultures with which they have contact.

Efforts to "save" or "enlighten" the members of these other countries are more than just another example of a marginalized organization emerging within the larger context of a mainstream and affecting aspects of a society or culture. Often these marginals and their effects are positioned as interventions, whether right or wrong, noble or not, into the way people think, act or, simply, the way things are done. In short, they are intrusions into the mainstream's status quo. These interventions can result in stress, conflict and sometimes the deaths of those involved. Equally important to note is that as outcomes materialize, it's not uncommon for the range of effects spawned by these ventures to ripple through the mainstream touching even stakeholders not originally defined as a primary target or objective. Change stimulated at this scale, especially when one organization seeks to change or tamper with the fundamental core or nature of another group or organization, transcends evident physical effects and can touch emotional and sometimes even ethical levels of the dynamic social systems involved.

Not all negative effects are triggered by marginals outside the mainstream. Sometimes a change experienced by mainstream organizations is triggered by the emergence of marginals from within the mainstream, either from formerly legally functioning organizations that have gone over to the illegal, marginal side or from marginals actually spawned inside the mainstream. A sect within a mainstream religion may create religious and organizational turmoil when it seeks to change operations or the direction of its parent. Martin Luther and Henry VIII are historic examples of figures who didn't stop at resisting the direction of mainstream organizations; they actually changed these organizations—from within. The division and subsequent conflict among and between Muslims in what is now referred to as the Arab Spring is another example and an illustration of how splits can occur within political and social organizations. Finally, recent divisions in the Catholic and Episcopal churches opened when gays and women became priests and later sought higher offices within the church (Garza, 2008; Scott, 2006; Shaw, 1992). These internal conflicts trigger animosities within the mainstream's family, thus adding new dimensions to the organization's already complex stakeholder networks.

Suffering, Injury and Pain

Clearly there are consequences associated with the interactions between marginals and mainstream organizations. In all of these instances discussed to this point, the marginal organization that emerges within the mainstream has the potential to trigger change, division or conflict, stress and strain for all involved. Matters can become more troublesome when organizations from each sector, marginal and mainstream, compete for the same material, people or economic resources. Now complications occur because in addition to attempting to share or coexist within the same geographic region, the organizations can find themselves competing in terms of such illusive concepts like values, ways of life, patterns of existence—a mix of factors that only serve to amplify and aggravate the differences between these organizations.

Add to this the sheer number of different types of organizations potentially involved in the networks associated with these change efforts, as well as the diverse mix of stakeholders these organizations bring to the systemic relationship, and one sees the scope and scale of problems that can emerge. But the types of consequences or results, while often significant, one can see often, are nominal in comparison to the greater deeper effects the change spawned by the convoluted influences of these competing organizations can produce.

Some of the more insidious effects resulting from the interaction between the two sectors have been touched upon above. But that was only the surface treatment of the potential results that might occur. The model we use (Tafoya, 2010, 2013a,b) strings the results associated with organizations across three distinctive levels, which we describe as the products, outcomes and impacts associated with the results of an organization's efforts or activities. For example, all organizations struggle to be influential, to offer products or services, mission or vision that draws stakeholders to it. When an organization's results produce negative effects, the bottom-line impact strikes directly at the organization's capacity to be influential.

Organizational influence can be a fragile commodity and it is one that needs to be consistently managed and groomed; it's a measure and reflection of the organization's credibility or image. Stakeholders use their impression of an organization's influence as a referent; it's a conception assigned to the organization that becomes a foundation for why they seek or avoid contact with it. If the stakeholders believe they may need the organization or if they feel it meets their needs, then we could say that the organization is "influential" or that its influence transcends its relationship with those who find it as meeting their needs. However, influence is seldom a neatly packaged concept for either the organization or the stakeholder. At issue for the stakeholder wishing to work with or use the services and products offered by the marginal organization is that these organizations may exist in a world often defined by uncertainty: their future, sometimes even their existence, may be at best tolerated, at times even perceived as illegitimate or illegal in the eyes of mainstream stakeholders and organizations. In other words, these may be influential organizations, but there are potential costs associated with the use of their products or services.

As a result, the marginal organization may find that its attempt to expand its influence through the sale or distribution of goods or services brings it to the edge or on the verge of conflict with those in the mainstream whose role it is to curtail or prevent the types of influence-building ventures attempted. And when conflict does emerge, those often at the center of the conflict are the very stakeholders lured to the marginal organization who saw it as meeting their needs: those who work for the organization or who make, buy, use, transport or distribute the organization's products and services. A marginal's adversaries have long known that it is easier to catch and punish stakeholders than the offending organization, if for no other reason that there are more stakeholders and they are widely distributed along a very open and frequently vulnerable value stream.

Stakeholders who believe they are the targets of a marginal's adversaries have the potential to create even more stress and tension around the marginal's interactions. After all, and particularly when the marginal's activities are illegal, tension and risk associated with controversy or an organization's general operations can cause stakeholders to treat their relationship with the marginal with caution and sometimes reevaluate it completely. Stakeholders, after all, have to preserve their own image, credibility or "influence profiles."

An organization trapped in conflict or subject to the suspicions of stakeholders or other organizations can find itself engulfed in a stakeholder swarm—a convoluted network defined by a mix of stakeholders pursuing their own agenda and often at the expense of their target, in this case the marginal organization (Tafoya, 2013b). A positive influence occurs when the organization successfully manages the swarm or its participants. A negative influence has an opposite effect. Conflict and stress can erode the positive "influence profile" for all stakeholders in the marginal's network, and for some this is too great a risk just to meet a simple need.

When injury, harm or cruelty, or events that trigger bacterial infection, disease or horrific working conditions are associated with an organization's influential profile, guilt by association says as much about the organization's stakeholders as it does about the organization. Sweatshops, drug operations that foster addiction or dependency, or behaviors operationalized through intimidation, fear or deceit are a very real part of everyday life for both marginal and mainstream organizations. When suffering, pain or injury is associated with an organization's efforts, activities or results, it sets the stage for a virtual cascade of negative effects.

For example, our approach (Tafoya, 2010, 2013a,b) to the analysis of an organization's influence or, more generally, to the effects of an organization's actions, products or services on its capacity to be influential revealed that three particular features are linked to the results associated with an organization's actions. We label these as the products, outcomes and impacts associated with the results observed. Here PRODUCTS are the *observable results of the organization's efforts.* They are the things done or produced by the organization; they are the ways one behaves when offering a service, the decisions made, the actions taken, the behaviors displayed associated with a task, assignment, job, etc. Products may be as tangible or as intangible as a process (e.g., service or information exchange), a sentiment or effort (delivery of a product).

OUTCOMES Are the Result from Products

In many ways, outcomes materialize along the lines of a classic stimulus/response or causal model. "The organization did 'x,' a product, and 'y' is an outcome." There may be more than one outcome associated with a single product and, like products, outcomes can be good or bad, desirable or not. Outcomes often are defined in terms of verbs: for example, to increase, to fear, to purchase, to follow, to behave. Outcomes indicate a potential to direct or shape stakeholder attitudes, opinions, beliefs and/or behavior, particularly given the organization's mission.

IMPACTS Are the End-Result of the Products and Outcomes

Their presence can be long-lasting and can unfold in other areas (i.e., not originally associated with the products offered or actions taken in the first place). Impacts can be viewed as the *real* or ultimate payoff, either good or bad, of the organization's efforts. A desired impact is one that benefits the organization in a conscious, meaningful way. Attempting to produce a desired impact is the cause, basis, antecedent, motive or rationale for activity, action or effort. Unfortunately, a desired impact is not always realized. Impact may be tangible (e.g., market share, defeat of an opponent or the experience of organizational loss) or intangible or abstract (image enhancement or loss, creation of an emotional state—fear, satisfaction, happiness for others or within one's own organization).

There are several ways to explore the results, products, outcomes and impacts associated with a marginal organization's influence, and in this instance we will do so by examining influence vis-à-vis three important phenomena: (1) the organization's capacity to continue to operate; (2) effects on the organization's influence profile; and (3) changes that emerge to affect the organization's stakeholder network.

Concentrating on the first of these is obvious but there is also a more subtle reason why "continued operation" is one focal point of interest in this instance. For most marginals, the potential for continued operation isn't a given, for their operations frequently are under regular and ongoing threat. Most marginals, after all, are operating on the fringe, if not in the pool of illegality. Consequently, there are many in the mainstream who are committed to punish, penalize or terminate the existence of marginals they've established as their target(s). Being a marginal or operating in the margins of a mainstream society is hardly a comfortable, relaxed existence.

Second, influence is a primary interest here because whether an organization is legal or not, it cannot function if it is not influential. "Influence" is an organization's capacity to push or pull stakeholders in directions it wants. Thus, if an organization's capacity to be influential is damaged, so is its potential to operate and sometimes even to exist. Moreover, failure to recognize the role of influence for an organization, marginal or mainstream, is a missed opportunity for the adversaries of those organizations. Remove an organization's products and they get or make more. Deny them the ability to deliver services and they source other services or outlets. Deny them access to their staff or deny their staff access to the organization and others are found. But destroy the organization's capacity to be influential or to be perceived as influential and the organization fails.

Finally, stakeholders are everything to an organization; they are proof that its influence is vigorous and meaningful. As we'll see in later chapters, stakeholders include the workers making or delivering products, the customers who buy or use the products and the regulators, enforcers and competitors interested in inhibiting or restricting the organization's activities. Understanding what is happening to an organization's stakeholders and the overall stakeholder network says a great deal about the organization's strengths, weaknesses and vulnerabilities—and of course its capacity to be influential.

Promotion or Interference and Influence

Perspective adds an interesting dimension to virtually any discussion of marginals. This is particularly true when examining the role of marginal organizations vis-à-vis their mainstream counterparts. Marginals have their own stakeholders, to be sure, and these individuals and organizations—at least the ones who like or support the marginal—are likely to view the marginal differently than those who don't like or support the organization. That's obvious. But what often makes those in the mainstream most perplexed is that marginals, particularly those engaged in illegal or undesirable behavior, do so despite the harm or hurt caused by their activity—and sometimes even to their own stakeholders.

Drugs, dog-fighting, prostitution, slave trading, terrorism and similar activities are illegal in part because of the harm they cause to animals or people—part of a marginal's stakeholder network. Despite this, marginals engaged in these and similar activities promote their organization's products and services and seek to advance their efforts through creative invention (e.g., new methods or products) and a general advocacy of what they do and of the products and services they offer.

Since influence is a measure of performance (and this is true whether the influence results in positive or negative stakeholder responses), marginals have the capacity to influence large numbers of people and organizations. But what makes influence interesting in this instance is that even among marginals some organizations are more influential, more likely to promote a desired response from stakeholders than others. An organization is successful if it influences people's behavior so that they seek it out as a place or opportunity to fulfill their needs. By contrast, even an organization with a bad reputation has a strong capacity to influence people; only, in this instance, those stimulated or influenced are the organization's adversaries, those who do not share the organization's vision, mission or purpose.

In this book, we explore what a marginal organization's "spectrum of influence" may look like and what it means to the organization. Influence is both a threshold and a springboard marking transitions between where an organization is at a given point in time for a given set of stakeholders to where it wants to be, can be or "ends up." So we seek to answer questions that help understand when influence works for or against the marginal's interests. When does the organization's influence profile stimulate conflict with competitors? Or when does influence trigger the emergence and intervention of special interest groups? When does a marginal organization need the assistance of professional groups to support its influence profile and how does its influence profile contribute to or interfere with its ability to get needed assistance?

Finally, what options exist when an organization's influence profile is negative for other stakeholders? Does this actually motivate the organization to invent other paths or opportunities for itself and stakeholders? If so, how? And, also, what about influence and the marginal's interface with a society's citizenry—that diverse amalgam who are often the drivers behind commercial, social, political and legal actions within the broader mainstream environment? At what point do they intervene or become advocates for change in the lives or operations of the marginal organization?

Influence is an organization's lever. It can be used consciously as a tool to shape the behavior of stakeholders so that their participation in the organization helps it achieve a vision or mission. Influence is an organization's most valuable core attribute. With it the organization opens doors that help it achieve a vision and mission, and without it, it drifts, makes mistakes, takes imprudent risks and can even fade into oblivion. Marginals need to maximize their levels of influence in the fields wherein they operate while they simultaneously dodge, evade or sidestep the influence of competitors and adversaries committed to the marginal's demise or failure.

Conclusion

Our investigation of marginal organizations begins with an outline of their nature, role and operation as self-sufficient, self-organized entities. This discussion provides a glimpse of the structure of the basic marginal as well as a typology that illustrates differences among various types of marginals.

This introduction serves as a backdrop against which comparisons can be made among different types of marginals particularly vis-à-vis the broader mainstream in terms of which they operate. Marginals often are in a precarious situation, seeming only to exist at the convenience of the mainstream or, in some instances, because the mainstream has not been successful in terminating their existence. So, more than a discussion about the facts behind the survival, and sometimes prosperity, of these organizations, this discussion introduces the reader to reasons why these organizations survive through time, sometimes even becoming institutions in their own right or, in other instances, part of the very fabric of the society around which they function.

A key trait of marginals and one that contributes to their success is their capacity to move, to adapt, to get out of the way of other organizations or the mainstream generally. Think of it. People can object to drugs, decry the slave trading of people, cruelty to animals, the violence of gangs, the pornography on the web or the brutality of terrorists, yet these and other marginals not only exist but also often grow, spread and avoid eradication and destruction. Marginals exist in part because they present an "opportunity," a means for stakeholders to have a reason for being or a point of interest. Now sometimes that opportunity translates into stakeholders supporting the marginal or buying its products and services, and at other times it's an opportunity for those whose job it is to track, find and sometimes destroy the marginal. In short, marginals create a lot of opportunities for a variety of people with a lot of very different needs, interests, wants and desires.

But, more than a way of life or a reason for getting up in the morning, an opportunity is a means for stakeholders to create their own opportunities, a way to fulfill a need, to express a sentiment, a way to shape a society as they define it. The stakeholders who affiliate with marginals not only adhere to the organization's mission or purpose, but they also actively participate in changing the environment within which the marginal exists and operates. In many ways, a marginal's stakeholders are more than merely a part of the organization's network; they are an extension of the organization and its vision and mission. To demonstrate these and other themes and ideas, we use data collected through interviews, our research and the research of various agencies and organizations that track, regulate and sometimes even struggle or are in conflict with marginals and their stakeholders. The information collected from these sources contributes to a unique view of these singular organizations. All totaled, this information helps us present a model of these organizations in terms of what may be described, to paraphrase Ghyka (1977), as a geometry of a marginal at life. How, for example, might a marginal's life cycle be described? In what ways does a marginal invent ways to exist and survive in an all too often hostile environment? How might one describe a marginal's ecology and, subsequently, its capacity to survive over time? In short, what is a marginal's legacy and for whom is it created?

CHAPTER 2

Profiling the Marginal Organization: A Framework for Operational Analysis

Organizations don't form by accident. In every instance, organizations are a product of decisions and actions. In their simplest form, organizations are a mix of features and attributes that provide some benefit to the organization's operation and/or stakeholders. In this chapter, we explore the formation and makeup of marginal organizations, concentrating on ways an organization's features contribute to defining its capacity to be influential. Influence is central to this discussion because it is a feature stakeholders associate with an organization's authority, credence and, in some instances, power to manipulate, persuade, direct and/or control.

Influence is a core organizational feature for both those stakeholders who back an organization (e.g., the customers, employees or supporters) and those competitors or opponents who associate with it. An organization's features are the traits, characteristics or attributes a stakeholder finds meaningful or significant. These are the reasons why a stakeholder is attracted to an organization; they are a means a stakeholder uses to determine if an organization's products or services may meet established needs, wants or desires.

An organization's features are useful only if they can be linked to or result in benefits for the stakeholder. Benefits *plus* features complete the equation defining the value of an organization for the stakeholder. Benefits are the gains stakeholders believe they can derive from a relationship with the organization. They are the tangible and intangible paybacks the stakeholder receives or gains from the organization's products or services, whether the stakeholder is a supporter or an adversary of the organization. For example, a person with a drug addiction might associate trust and availability as features that define one pusher as more attractive than another pusher without these features. These features are, apart from those associated with the drugs the pusher sells (e.g., their price or quality), reasons for doing business with this pusher over one down the street. If we analyze why these features are most important to the addict, we might find that they simply boil down to a matter of safety or security. The addict can make a purchase with less risk of discovery and subsequent loss associated with detainment by police. And what makes this relationship between the addict and pusher most interesting, however, is that there's little to say about the actual drug purchased. It's not that there aren't differences among types of heroin or marijuana but that if all the addict needs is a "basic" drug, as a member of the marginal society it's the pusher's features and benefits as an organization that separates him from all others.

So what is it that makes one pusher a "better" organization than another pusher down the street? Ultimately, the nature of the relationship between the stakeholder (the addict) and an organization (the pusher) translates as a match between the stakeholder's needs and the organization's features and benefits. For example, people need cash or at least credit to make most purchases, and sometimes having certain skills and competencies also helps. A thief in need of quick cash has a type of dependent stakeholder relationship with the store he's about to rob. The thief depends on the store to deliver the cash he needs.

Now if the thief, in this instance, is a prudent consumer, he's likely to analyze the process necessary for him to obtain his needed cash. At a minimum, this analysis means he's most likely to succeed if he understands his target's features and benefits in terms of his needs vis-à-vis his personal skills, competencies and resources. So the thief might consider a store's features like its location (Does it afford a quick escape?), its security systems (Is there a safe refuge with a measure of privacy?) and whether the store's owner is armed (a safety feature). The thief's originally stated needs for cash give way to emerging needs associated with the process of obtaining the cash. Benefits in this instance again are not necessarily tied to the "cash received" but rather to the possibility of an escape that is safe, secure and without detection.

The features and benefits associated with an organization play a powerful role in the decision- and choice-making behaviors of both those in the organization and those stakeholders seeking a relationship with it or involved in its stakeholder network. For example, consider the marginal organization that offers a prospective buyer or customer the opportunity to avoid paying sales taxes as a feature of the organization's business transactions. Not charging a customer sales tax can provide the prospective customer with several benefits: transactions are faster since there's no need to stop and figure and to collect that extra 6 or 7 percent and there's the obvious benefit of saving money.

Sabatini and Farnsworth (2006) noted another important feature associated with marginals: the manner in which they employ people as workers. Sabatini and Farnsworth wrote that a marginal organization's informal employment relationship with employees "is a two-way street, with both firms and workers calculating costs and making choices. Firms hire informally or extralegally in order to avoid the costs (financial and administrative) associated with formal, full-time employees. Among these costs, broadly construed, is the risk that regular employees will be more likely to organize or join unions that can later press for higher pay and benefits" (53). Compare these costs against the potential benefits that hiring informally promises—less paperwork, no need for extra personnel handling human resources matters, more efficiency and, add Sabatini and Farnsworth, "not only a cheaper but also a more quiescent labor force" (53). Workers, too, must weigh the features and benefits associated with employment with a marginal. The prospective employee has to weigh the income received and sometimes just the opportunity for a job against the features of an organization that operates within society's margins. "There can be little doubt," write Sabatini and Farnsworth, "that informal-sector employment is generally a suboptimal situation for a worker. Those who toil on the fringes of the formal economy often have limited access even to minimal job security or basic benefits and safety protections" (53–54).

The features associated with an organization or its products and services can be a powerful magnet for the stakeholder seeking to fulfill particular needs, especially when those needs can't be fulfilled in the formal, mainstream of society, for example, the opportunity to make an illegal purchase or to engage in an illegal act. Buying illegal drugs, alcohol or sex can help support an addiction or provide an opportunity for the novice to experiment with something that society has defined as banned or forbidden. These are benefits provided by the marginal organization established to provide them.

Sometimes the feature that draws an individual to a marginal is associated with the marginal's business processes, the ways it does business. Anonymity, for example, is one feature attractive to many stakeholders, particularly when the needs they have are outside the parameters of a mainstream's acceptable norms or mores. A marginal's "don't ask, don't tell" feature assures there will be no annoying questions about a buyer's age, needs or if the buyer has a parent's permission. Anonymity offers a measure of safety to the illegal transaction: anyone can do it, there are no age requirements, no prescriptions needed.

On a grander scale, the emergence of marginals can trigger the formation of a new ecosystem within the society as a whole, one whose primary feature is that it provides the potential for the employment of "unemployables," for example, those without needed documentation, the addition of more money into the overall economy (which benefits the mainstream, too) and an overall opportunity for full or at least increased employment, a chance for everyone in a community to have something to do, a place to work (ILO, 1972; Sassen, 2009; Thomas, 1992, 2001). The presence of marginals in this instance is particularly unique because, for all intents and purposes, they become little more than an extension, or in the service, of the larger mainstream even though the features of these organizations (i.e., they may not adhere to local labor laws or taxes) clearly establish them as part of the marginal sector we're examining. In these instances, the mainstream turns a blind eye to the marginals because the functions they provide (e.g., employment) supply a needed benefit to the mainstream's inability to do the same. An organization's features and benefits define its potential influence over stakeholders, its potential to meet expectations and its potential to perform as the stakeholder needs it to perform. Now intuitively, one might believe that organizations with the most features and benefits have the greatest influence over stakeholders, that these organizations are likely to be the most attractive, have the greatest credibility, be perceived as the most trustworthy, etc. But that conclusion only considers part of the equation defining the phenomenon of "organizational influence." As we've seen, there are two sides to the influence equation: the organization on one side and stakeholders on the other. What complicates this otherwise simple equation is that organizational influence isn't simply defined by stakeholders who support the organization; it's also a function of the type of organization and those stakeholders who do not support the organization—in short, its competitors, adversaries or enemies.

Classifying the Type of Organization

The process of fulfilling a stakeholder's needs, from a stakeholder's perspective, begins by determining the type of organization most likely to have the products and services to meet the stakeholder's needs. Have spiritual needs? Find a religious organization. Need new shoes? Find a retail organization that sells shoes. Looking at organizations systemically helps uncover both an organization's purpose or function as well as how it could or should meet its stakeholder's needs. A systemic examination clarifies links between the organization's vision and the day-to-day performance and activities expected to achieve that vision. Moreover, starting one's examination of an organization by looking at features that provide it direction and control goes a long way toward telling the stakeholder if the organization can even begin to meet existing needs.

We use a unique classification system that categorizes all organizations as one of four types, labeled the "community," "enterprise," "team" and "individual contributor" (Tafoya, 2010). It's a straightforward typology that works for either marginal or mainstream organizations. It's useful because it aids understanding of the general role of organizations, their features and benefits and the role they may have in helping stakeholders meet their needs. Consider this brief introduction of each classification.

The *community* type organization's brand, for example, may be as simple as what the followers believe it is; it is often personal to them. Religions, political organizations and even the schools you attend are organized around a core doctrine or mission. Followers take that doctrine and make it meaningful; they personalize it—it is the organization, the brand for them.

Mainstream community organizations include established religions (e.g., Muslims, Catholics, Jews or Hindus), schools or colleges, hospitals, political parties or even military units like a country's army or navy. Community organizations are defined around a mission, and often a set of core values. They differ most from other organizations in this typology because while community organizations need money to function, the pursuit of money is not the primary reason why they were established. Community organizations typically won't turn money down and like all organizations they need some source of income, it's just not the primary focus for the organization; it's not part of their mission.

Marginal community organizations look like their mainstream counterparts but, as is true in most aspects of life, looks aren't everything. For example, marginal community organizations may share the same features as their mainstream counterparts in that their efforts are tied to a particular mission but that is where most similarities end. Cults or trendy offbeat religions are examples but so are terrorist organizations, paramilitary organizations or special interest organizations such as the Ku Klux Klan. These organizations exist and carry out activities defined in terms of a particular vision or mission and whether they're legal or not is not their concern. Mainstream examples of special interest community organizations include the American Civil Liberties Union (ACLU), the Southern Poverty Law Center or the Society for the Protection of Animals (SPCA).

Any aspects related to the community organization's vision and mission, like rituals, rules and procedures, are an integral part of the organization's brand, credibility, image or influence. So when the leadership of a political party fails to perform as expected, when a religion's member behaves in ways that are contrary to the values espoused by the community, when a labor union fails to successfully negotiate a contract or when a terrorist organization fails to model its mission in its communiqués, posturing and behavior, the organization's credibility can suffer and its potential to be influential can deteriorate. Finally, stakeholders who affiliate with a community organization as members can have a particularly unique relationship with them. For example, their affiliation is at the convenience of the organization and may be terminated at any time. Leadership in these organizations is often reserved for a select few, so most members never rise very high in the organization's hierarchy. In fact, most members accept their roles as tools or apparatus for use by the organization, with or without compensation, as it pursues its mission.

The second type of organization, the *enterprise*, centers activities and performance around an effort to achieve monetary gain. The enterprise achieves its mission by increasing growth (e.g., physical or economic), selling specific products or services designed to meet stakeholder needs and/or by managing risks, costs and other exposures that may put its money-making efforts in jeopardy. The enterprise maximizes the likelihood of achieving performance objectives by emphasizing performance through structure, policies and a concerted effort to improve the products and services it offers.

Enterprise organizations are dependent on having stakeholders who need their products and services. These stakeholders can be involved with every facet of the organization's products and services—from production to purchase. If one enterprise doesn't meet a stakeholder's needs, there usually is another, perhaps a competitor, to seek out. Commercial businesses like car dealerships and restaurants are good examples of mainstream enterprises and so are manufacturing facilities, your local cable company or even the local trash haulers.

Many marginal organizations are enterprises. Criminal organizations are a prime example. They exist to make a profit, like the sweatshop that makes knockoffs of popular brand products or those making pornographic movies. An enterprise's features and benefits, products produced or services delivered shape the organization's image and capacity to draw stakeholders to it, to be influential. As a result, poor product quality, missed due dates or general failure to perform as expected may be significant events for either marginal or mainstream enterprise organizations. A drugstore is an example of a mainstream enterprise and the illegal corollary a drug pusher. A dog breeder is a mainstream enterprise that breeds and sells often pedigree dogs and a puppy mill is its marginal counterpart. The casino in Las Vegas or

Atlantic City is a mainstream gambling enterprise while the syndicate running the numbers racket is the organization operating in the marginal sector. Finally a restaurant is another example of a mainstream enterprise while the person hawking hotdogs on a street corner can be the marginal equivalent of a mainstream organization. A third type of organization, the *team* organization, may be the most multidimensional of organizational types. In the mainstream, team organizations communicate their image through a variety of devices: team names, colors, mascots, logos, sometimes even "fight songs" or anthems. Teams exist to accomplish a mission, whether the mission is to win a game for the sports team, to capture a group of criminals for the swat team, to produce a solution for the problem-solving team or to devise a new product for the "skunk works team." But what makes teams most unique among the four included in our typology is that when there are no more games to win, criminals to capture, problems to be solved or products to develop, the teams can and often do simply "go away." The teams reorganize or, in some instances, completely disband to no longer exist.

A mainstream team's brand is uniquely tied to its performance against the mission. Sports teams, swat teams, fund-raising teams operate in terms of a mission that's always tangible and observable. Failure to achieve the team's mission can precipitate a crisis and directly affect the team's future.

The use of teams in marginal organizations parallels their use in the mainstream. A terrorist organization may use specific teams to recruit and train new members, a drug organization may use teams dedicated to smuggling drugs from one country to another or to "enforce" discipline within a village or to attack a rival organization. Once the assignment or project is complete the team members can go back to their regular job—whatever that may be.

The fourth type of organization, the *individual contributor*, illustrates an organization built around an individual who is, for the most part, also this organization's brand. Some cults, terrorists or political organizations may have a key person, "the boss," who is "their" leader. Without that person, the organization may drift, not fulfill the needs of those depending on it and ultimately cease to function. Sometimes an organization will link or tie a person to a particular role. A terrorist or criminal organization may have a doctor or lawyer to handle special needs as they arise. Even the need for a skilled mechanic, a chemist or someone who is a marksman (a sniper) or anyone skilled at making bombs may translate into an individual contributor role. It depends on the organization and its needs.

Other times, particularly if the organization's exposures or business activities are diverse, its stakeholder network may contain a number of individual contributors. In these instances, the individual contributor's operations may be guided by the directional mechanisms of other organizations or governing bodies. Politicians, people in authority such as judges, police officers or doctors are examples of stakeholders who have only an ancillary affiliation with an organization and yet are among those the organization considers as most important. Each has his/her own brand, image and events to manage, and failure to successfully perform them can result in a crisis for all involved. Prostitutes, undocumented day laborers and counterfeiters are examples of individual contributors in the marginal sector.

The typology and classification scheme we use is also unique because it not only allows for the classification of individual organizations but also helps explain the makeup of every organization. All organizations are a composite of these four dimensions with one more dominant than the other three. Each of the four types combine to define the rationale for the organization's classification. For-profit hospitals are a classic example. The hospital is an enterprise because it exists to make a profit. However, the finance department, admissions and the charitable group that sponsors fund-raising benefits are community organizations within the hospital. The surgical team that handles medical operations or the triage team put together to handle an emergency room are examples of teams in the hospital. They exist for specific situations, for specific operations and at specific times. Their makeup is not fixed. The doctors, nurses and support staff usually change with each new event, each new operation or shift. Finally, the doctors and nurses in the hospital are among the numerous individual contributors one finds in hospitals. The doctors may have their own private practice and the nurses their own specialties or expertise. Sometimes other specialists in the hospital also qualify as individual contributors. For example, the radiologist or anesthesiologist who might consult on particular diseases or injuries, the security officer hired to assess and handle emerging risks or the engineer who oversees the hospital's facilities are among the diverse individual contributors who add to the hospital's capability to meet its stakeholders' needs.

Flexibility is another important feature of this classification system. It allows for the reclassification of an organization as it matures through its life cycle. So if an organization is initially set up as a not-for-profit and is classified as a "community" early in its life span and later evolves into an "enterprise" it will be reclassified when the change occurs. This is an important feature because changing from one type of organization to another signals changes in both performance expectations and the means for achieving those expectations.

Revisiting the Features of a Marginal Organization

An organization's features and benefits highlight the foundation of a stakeholder's personal relationship with the organization. Sometimes convenience is a meaningful feature for a stakeholder; other times the organization might simply be able to fulfill a need the stakeholder can't meet anywhere else. Few people associate with an organization or belong to its stakeholder network just to be part of it; affiliation implies there is a benefit, something to gain by being part of an organization's stakeholder network. So, when a mainstream organization cannot meet a stakeholder's needs, the stakeholder can accept that the desired needs are unfulfilled or can try to fulfill those needs in some other way, for example, by going through a marginal organization.

Marginal organizations also contain examples of all four dimensions in the typology just reviewed. Consider the examples in tables 2.1 and 2.2. In table 2.1, a legal food vendor (a mainstream organization) is compared with an illegal drug manufacturer (a marginal organization). Both organizations are enterprises so those dimensions are in the top row and are marked "PRIMARY." The focus of the primary dimension also is in italics to further separate it from the other dimensions. Notice, too, that the secondary dimensions of these organizations are also the same, despite the fact that the organizations are expected to serve a very different purpose.

The organizations described in table 2.2 present a different picture. In this table, one is a terrorist organization and the other a religious organization. Again, they share the same primary dimension; they're both classified as "community" organizations, but the nature of these organizations shifts when one considers how they are organized and how they need to be structured to successfully function. Both organizations need money to fund their operations and programs, so that is the second dimension for each. However, they differ in the way they organize around people. Terrorists, for example, can use individual contributors in a number of different roles. They might be skilled in bomb making, planning and organizing and, of course, carrying out a terrorist event. If the terrorist organization uses "teams," it's usually for a particular event, like a raid or an attack, after which the team is disbanded.

The religious organization, here a mainstream organization, also is a community that needs funds to operate its programs, schools and services. Here too, the funding dimension comes second. However, this organization structures around the use of teams and groups that are sent out on special projects, missionary activities or perhaps to teach in schools or work in hospitals the organization operates. For structural and operational reasons, these teams are not permanent and people are rotated where they are needed. It's not like a university that has a department made up of "math," "English" or "language" teachers. Teams in this religious organization are likely to be more functional than specialists. Moreover, one thing this religious organization discourages is having "individual contributors." There are usually only a few with this designation in the religious community.

Table 2.1 Two Enterprise-Type Organizations

	A legal food vendor (Mainstream)		*An illegal drug manufacturer (Marginal)*
Enterprise dimension (PRIMARY)	Focus: Growth through meeting stakeholder needs (or sometimes just not alienating them). Policies and procedures guide operations. Evaluate products, services, in order that they may even improve.	Enterprise dimension (PRIMARY)	Focus: Growth through effective distribution and sales. Internal policies and procedures that aim at ensuring security and territories are critical. Estimation of vulnerabilities is prudent.
Individual contributor dimension	Focus: These small operations have the classic "chief cook and bottle washer" role. In many ways the food wagon is a distribution point in contrast to a restaurant that may serve as a destination, meeting place *and* a place to eat. Information and communication are nominal. Locations often are determined by others (e.g., local ordinances).	Individual contributor dimension	Focus: Performance is everything, particularly where security and trust are concerned. Knowledge and competencies are usually restricted to a few as are information and communication roles. People are objects with roles and functions.
Team/small group dimension	Focus: Teams selected to meet special needs are often are sub-contracted. Legal teams to handle licensing requirements or appeals are examples. If the vendor is preparing to work a special event, a team might be put together to handle extra food preparation before the event.	Team/small group dimension	Focus: Limited use of teams, usually around production and distribution processes. Knowledge and competency are functional but important.
Community dimension	Focus: Food quality and customer service to meet the business' needs. Not much beyond that—margins won't allow for much. Relationships with people may only be nominally important; few vendors see the same customers every day.	Community dimension	Focus: Utilitarian community style—Robin Hoods to attain loyalty, cooperation and silence. People and relationships are important if they serve the organization's needs.

Table 2.2 Two Community-Type Organizations

	Terrorists (Marginal)		*An organized religion (Mainstream)*
Community dimension (PRIMARY)	Focus: Achieve the vision via collective action aimed at achieving its mission and thereby meeting the needs of its membership. The mission is achieved by ensuring secrecy, insisting on loyalty, control and direction of the membership. Typically, the community dimension has an internal focus.	Community dimension (PRIMARY)	Focus: The organization's vision and mission, often reflected in key values or beliefs, are the reasons the organization exists—even if these are inextricably linked to a particular person (or family). Control and direction via the vision. People and relationships are important.
Enterprise dimension	Focus: Often of secondary importance and then manifested in meeting the organization's functional needs to cover membership needs (e.g., housing, food, clothing) or to support programs and activities (e.g., for weapons or explosives, travel). Sometimes funds are needed when the organization provides services for other organizations. (Growth by meeting stakeholder needs.)	Enterprise dimension	Focus: For some religions this is a very important dimension. Money needed for growth or to meet the hierarchy's lifestyle needs can be important drivers. Other times, money is needed to support schools, programs or activities sponsored by the religion.
Individual contributor dimension	Focus: There are few truly individual contributors. For them, performance is everything. The individual contributor may be little more than an "object"—a tool or general resource needed to accomplish a task. Knowledge and competencies are not critical. Fidelity, trust and commitment are.	Team/ small group dimension	Focus: Teams are a way for organizing activities. Members rotate through teams—few "own" a particular role on a team. Achieve the mission via collective action. Knowledge and competencies are utilitarian in nature.
Team/ small group dimension	Focus: Teams are purely functional and restricted to special tasks (e.g., training) or missions (e.g., a planned attack on an enemy). Knowledge and competency are important; loyalty and commitment to the project at hand are critical.	Individual contributor dimension	Focus: Usually only the religion's leadership is designated "individual contributor." Often it is a critical position, one which the organization's membership relies on for direction. Knowledge and competency are not as critical as mastering, living the role.

Preparing the Tools Needed to Direct an Organization's Efforts: Defining the Organization's Vision and Mission

All organizations, enterprises, communities, teams or individual contributors operate around a purpose, a mission. The person who wants to paint your house, an individual contributor, may want to do it because of a passion for painting but it's more likely that the opportunity to earn money to pay the rent, to have a summer job as a means for earning money for school or just to have a little extra cash to spend during the weekend are more likely motivators. This person's reason for wanting to paint your house is a manifestation of a future vision, a vision of how the money will be spent, what it can buy, needs it will fulfill. In other words, people don't work for money per se, they work for what they envision the money will buy, what it will do for their life or, sometimes, for their image.

All organizations need money but their pursuit of money has to be viewed in terms of its role as a means toward an end. The effort to attain money is cast in terms of some defined or known but unstated vision. The politician needs money as a means for fulfilling a vision of the politician as an elected official. The drug dealer has a need for money to fulfill a vision, as does the religious organization, the prostitute or the person who operates a puppy mill. Each organization is engaged in the work it does to earn money to achieve some vision and, in turn, its mission.

Mainstream organizations, particularly larger, well-established organizations, have learned to carefully define their vision largely because it is the primary anchor for the organization's efforts. The linkage between an organization's vision and mission and their relationship to organizational performance is straightforward. The vision defines the organization's long-term aim; it becomes the common ideal: "Where we see ourselves in the distant future (e.g., over the next 5–7 years)." The mission, usually defines the organization's efforts for the near future. "What we see ourselves doing on the near term (e.g., over the next 1–2 years) that will help us achieve our vision." Achieving the mission facilitates achievement of the organization's vision, all things considered.

Goals, objectives and activities round out this model and the mission's use as a controlling, planning and organizing device. Goals are benchmarks for key areas. Goals are defined to achieve the organization's mission. Typical goals might be written for quality, security, productivity and people. Objectives and activities translate the vision and mission at the organization's operational level. Objectives are measurable benchmarks defined to achieve each particular goal, and activities are the measurable tasks, the individual performance and/or behavior needed to achieve each objective (Tafoya, 2010).

Use of these types of organizational devices is fairly common among mainstream organizations but they or anything approaching them rarely appears in literature describing marginal organizations. There are several reasons for this conclusion. Our research suggests that most people who operate marginal organizations have little formal knowledge regarding the concepts of vision, mission, goals, objectives vis-à-vis their operations. They have a conventional understanding of an organizational vision but it's not something necessarily thought of as a means for structuring the organization's value stream—the various activities and components that serve to define the organization, its processes and procedures, products and services and, ultimately, its stakeholders.

For many marginals, the essence of a vision is tomorrow or "when bills are due" or the "next big event." This isn't offered as a criticism but rather an observation of the realities facing marginals: few in marginal organizations have the type of training or experience that would have taught the relationship between a vision and mission, how to prepare each and, most importantly, how to convert and manage emerging opportunities into new benefits.

A carefully constructed vision and mission statement provides an organization's management and staff the opportunity to speculate, at least nominally, on what is desired for the organization in its future and how that vision can be achieved. Admittedly projecting out five to seven years may not seem as useful for a small business as for a larger mainstream organization that is tied to the stock market, susceptible to seasonal factors or the characteristics of an aging population. But those familiar with these tools know they can provide, given the right conditions, a sense of the future or can help define or monitor an organization's marketplace or its stakeholders. The range of benefits and merit is extensive.

Consider an interview conducted by Marianne McCune on National Public Radio (NPR, May 22, 2013) with an illegal "marijuana salesman." This excerpt from the interview illustrates the value thinking about one's business vis-à-vis the future can have on even a small, illegal marginal organization:

> Chuck used to sell marijuana in California. But the legalization of medical marijuana in the state meant he was suddenly competing against hundreds of marijuana dispensaries. So he moved to New York, where marijuana is still 100 percent illegal. Since making the move, he says, he's quadrupled his income. (For the record: His name isn't really Chuck.)
>
> He spends pretty much every day dealing what he calls "farm-to-table" marijuana. On a recent afternoon in his dimly lit New York apartment, he was just about to complete a daily ritual: loading about 50 baggies of marijuana, worth a total of about $3,000 into his backpack, before

> heading out to make deliveries. "We're helping keep people stoned on a Friday night in New York City," he said.
>
> Eighteen states and the District of Columbia have now legalized marijuana, either for medical use or for fun. And, it turns out, when one state brings an underground market into the mainstream and another doesn't, there are economic consequences in both places.

Clearly if "Chuck" had been thinking about his business in light of the future or at least emerging trends in California he might have been able to develop an alternative plan that wouldn't have involved moving his business to New York. But this incident illustrates how more than just a few marginal and mainstream organizations can be caught off guard without a vision for the future. McCune also pointed out that "dealers aren't the only ones with an incentive to move marijuana out of California. The legalization of medical marijuana led to a rush of pot farmers with permits to grow marijuana legally. That in turn led to a supply glut—and plummeting wholesale prices. Some growers haven't been able to unload all their crops at the price they want on the local, legal market. So they break the law and send it out of state." This last observation is interesting because it illustrates that even those now "legitimate" marijuana growers have to again add an illegal dimension to their operation to deal with the glut resulting from an oversupply of the product and to get the profit they need to operate.

Most small businesses, marginal and mainstream, often do not have the time, money or opportunity to develop the experience or training needed to utilize planning tools like those discussed, but when faced with a choice between getting training in material that "might" be of use and just getting the work ahead done, most target the latter. These organizations are expected to get their product out, sometimes with few or no staff; so their emphasis is on today, not what "might happen" in the future. However, as the material from this NPR program illustrates, an orientation that focuses only on the present and lacks planning can not only create day-to-day problems for the organization and its operations but also affect other aspects of marginal organizations.

Even a small marginal organization can benefit from long-range planning, yet ask the owner of a marginal organization what thought has been given to the business's future and, again not surprisingly, few can offer any cogent idea let alone a plan for the business over the long term, and few, if any, do advance planning for matters associated with disposal of the business should that be necessary. Even worse, perhaps, few owner/operators have any plan for themselves should they no longer be able to operate their business. Retirement or serious illness again are "out in the future," so out of sight of today.

Table 2.3 provides a more detailed look at the relationship between these structural "organizing tools" and different marginal organizations. Each has

Table 2.3 How Structural Tools Vary across Different Organizations

Element	*Counterfeiter (individual contributor)*	*Terrorist organization (community)*	*Illegal drug manufacturing (enterprise)*	*Team hired for one-time yard clean-up (team)*
Vision	Retire early	Enemy is in disarray	Make lots of money	Income derived from contracts and cheap labor
Mission	Make a quality product	Terrorize our enemy	Delivery without discovery	Deliver lawn care
Goals	• Avoid capture • Excellent product • Maintain secrecy	• Display capability • Gain wide publicity	• Quality product • Total security • High profits	• Complete the job • Good service, quality
Objectives	• High quality product • Complete secrecy • Avoid detection	• Build an organization • Build core fighters • Avoid detection	• Get workers • Build an organization • Maintain secrecy • Control processes	• Get needed helpers • Rent equipment • On time service • Accident-free
Activities	• Get high quality copier • Quality production • Planned distribution • Unobtrusive behavior	• Train teams • Successful missions • Implement security	• Manufacture drugs • Ensure security • Ensure loyalty	• Assign tasks • Do clean up • Pay helpers
Typical Resources	• Technology • Trustworthy personnel • Facilities • Financial resources	• Surprise • Loyalty to vision • Loyalty to culture • Training for all	• Raw materials • Distribution • Production facility • Drug labs	• Tools, equipment • Workers • Timelines

its own profile, defined in part by the organization's vision and mission. These two features, an organization's vision and mission, shape how the organization is structured, highlight processes that are important and point out what resources and activities may be necessary to achieve their vision and mission. So, from an analytical point of view, if you know an organization's vision and mission, it's possible to contemplate, given the type of organization (enterprise, community, team or individual contributor), what the organization will need and do to achieve both.

Definition from Structure: Structure Is/Should Be More Than What You See

An organization's structure is a framework for action. Structure, however, can look very different when comparing mainstream with marginal organizations. Your local drugstore has a "footprint," a floor plan you probably can describe from memory. If you need sunscreen, aspirin or a prescription filled, you probably could tell someone where or how to find those products, even without going into the store. That's because your experience is combined with the drugstore's efforts to use the same model when organizing the store. But this is a mainstream organization.

What's the structure that frames a drug dealer's organization? A street corner? What about a prostitute or a street vendor or a migrant worker? These are also organizations and they rely on or at least can be conceptualized in terms of their structure, but it probably wouldn't look like the structures you're familiar with in mainstream organizations. Regardless, structure is important, so it's very useful to describe organizations you are interested in by using their structure as a format for your analysis. In our case, we rely on five elements to define and describe the structures that shape an organization's performance: stakeholders, processes, culture, ideas/materials and technology. Together, these elements are the foundation used to transform effort into products and services, thus helping the organization achieve its mission.

Two things are unique about these elements: first, all are necessary for the organization's success and, second, while the contribution of each will vary, it's ideal if each performs at an optimal level. So an emphasis on ideas only steeped in theory without the contribution of structure can spin an organization's efforts into a quagmire defined by inaction, talk over action and sometimes even conflict. There are several examples of this condition and clichés to mark the problem. Clichés like "talk is cheap" and "all talk and no action" are examples. Notice, too, that some marketing can help even the marginal organization but one has to consider *how* a structural factor is used by the organization, and this is particularly true for marginals in this instance. Our friendly drug dealer described earlier has to be prudent in planning how he'll market his product. He can't be too over the top or he might put his entire operation at risk.

The "stakeholder" dimension is very important to consider. For example, think about the role of stakeholders in terms of our friendly drug dealer. Is he only marketing his "product" or is he marketing himself as well? He admits in the article that he's from California and new to New York; so how does he market himself so that potential buyers know he can be trusted and that he's not a narcotics agent? Collectively, these five elements still make a different contribution to defining the organization's structure and operation, so it is very important to consider their interrelated relationships when operating or examining the organization.

Here's another example. An emphasis on technology can bring an organization to a standstill if the requirements needed to manage the technology are beyond the capabilities of the people expected to use them or if the technologies are so fragile or otherwise temperamental that operators can't consistently rely on their functionality or operation. This stakeholder/technology interrelationship can make or break an organization. The same is true with processes or the organization's culture. Either can encumber an organization by burying it in bureaucracy, rules or expectations that may be out of place or simply a burden on other organizational elements. In short, all five are needed, but they must be well defined, appropriate and used in ways that complement each other and the organization using them.

Size is an interesting variable to consider when thinking about a marginal organization. How big is big enough or too big? Size refers to both the organization's physical presence or scale and the sheer nature of its resources: the number of people working for the organization, the number and range of products and even the number of stakeholders associated with the organization. Remember, most marginals can't handle too large a size variable. Getting too big affects the organization's speed and flexibility and, importantly, its visibility, which can be important if the organization is trying to avoid an adversary. Getting big makes the organization visible to others and this is a potential liability for the marginal trying to avoid attention. Having too many products also can work against the marginal. Look at the menus of food vendors; it's "hamburger, hamburger, hamburger" to paraphrase an old *Saturday Night Live* skit. Food trucks just aren't that big, so the size of this type of organization contributes to what it can carry and offer its stakeholders.

Key among an organization's resources are its stakeholders. Discussing an organization's features and benefits highlights a stakeholder's very personal role in the organization. Few people belong to an organization just to be part of it; they hope to gain something through their affiliation. Think of an organization in which you are a member. Why might someone want to be part of that organization? What benefits would they derive from membership and, importantly, which feature would be most likely to tell the "outsider" what the organization may have to offer? If pressed, how would you measure the benefits you derive from participating as a stakeholder in the organization with which you have an affiliation?

One thing that's particularly unique about stakeholders in marginal organizations when compared to mainstream organizations is that the marginal's stakeholders typically have a narrower, almost singular focus when interacting with the organization. Chitchat about the weather or one's family typically are not topics of conversation around a drug purchase or the time one spends with a prostitute. In contrast, someone might go into a Best Buy store just to look around, to get out of the rain or for just any other reason. These types of activities usually aren't associated with marginals. In preparation for this book, the author tried to engage owner/operators of different marginals in conversations—to little avail. Think about it. What small talk would you think works best when talking to a drug dealer, a migrant worker, a prostitute or even the person selling products on the street? The transaction is what's important to the marginal; they aren't paid to talk, and "time spent" can draw attention to a transaction no one wants to be associated with beyond the immediate objective.

Finally, it's always a unique experience to consider an organization's operating conditions, its environment, the way it works or functions when trying to understand it, what's important to it or why stakeholders might prefer one organization over another. Some organizations pride themselves on their operating conditions. Military organizations are big on this discernible feature. They have uniforms, music, marches, neat camps, big technologically driven vehicles and sometimes great locations, all of which combine to define their truly multidimensional operating conditions and environment. Marginals, by comparison, don't have the same panache or flamboyance. Our drug dealer friend's operating conditions seem limited to a crummy apartment, baggies and maybe the trunk of a car.

If crime movies are to be believed, it seems the trunk of a car is a key transportation element for organized crime's operating conditions. In other words, the less real estate the better for these organizations. Terrorist organizations practice tactics as a prerequisite for survival. Terrorists are constantly on the move, so hiding "under a big rock" is just as good as anything else for them. The point here isn't that marginals don't have operating conditions like their mainstream counterparts; it is that (1) they don't need much when it comes to operating their organizations and (2) having too much doesn't work well for them. Marginals often don't have the time or the money to spend on grooming the conditions under which they operate. I've often wondered, for example, what the farm worker or guy who mows the lawn goes through when they do their laundry. Think about it. They have to find the time to do laundry, a place to do really grimy laundry and, I would guess, a lot of really grimy laundry. But this is their world, and a by-product of their operating conditions.

Nordstrom Has a Brand, Why Shouldn't Pete, the Vendor Selling Knockoff Sports Memorabilia and Smuggled Cigarettes?

Every organization has a brand, something that distinguishes it from all others. Both the organization and the stakeholder have a role in the construction of an organization's brand or image. In its simplest state, a brand is a connotation associated with the nature or type of organization. Stakeholders associate certain behavior with the police, doctors, schools, terrorists and so on. However, letting a brand evolve from the nature of the organization leaves control of the brand's meaning to whatever one sees in it. If one person sees the police as fanatics who brutalize minorities, as biased and as those who take favors from the rich and powerful, and another sees the police as protection from the evils of society or a resource to call on to get help with personal problems, which one is right? Or, what would the police say is their brand and, if they define it, would those in the public agree? Just letting the meaning associated with a brand drift among people can be a critical error for an organization (Taboya, 2013a).

What makes a brand personal for the stakeholder, however, is interaction with the organization. What, for example, is a drug dealer's brand to the addict? Does the addict care or even recognize the pusher as having a brand? Would the prostitute say his/her brand is his/her body or maybe the jewelry worn, the perfume used or the music played in the background? Marginals seem to work with a brand differently than a mainstream organization. Mainstream organizations learned long ago that it's to their advantage to define what *they* see their brand to be and not leave others to speculate on their brand.

For example, the CEO of Abercrombie & Fitch recently seemed to imply that a person's size (not large) was part of that organization's brand (Guarino, 2013; McCarty, 2013). This type of orientation emerges because an organization's brand, its image, is defined by two states: one in the mind of those in the organization and, of course, the second in the mind of stakeholders. In both cases, the brand is what each believes the organization to be, to represent. From the point of view of those in the organization, the brand emerges from the organization's defined features and benefits. For stakeholders, the brand reflects the relationship between their needs and the capacity of the organization to meet those needs. Those in the organization speak of the brand in terms of standards, in terms of performance, in terms of the image conveyed by the organization's performance against expectations. Stakeholders speak of the brand in terms of values, particularly the brand's value to them. Trouble can ensue if there's a wide gulf between the organization's and its stakeholders' view of the brand.

Our drug dealer's brand may have less to do with the product sold as with the extent he can be trusted or is selling "safe" drugs. A dictator may believe the brand that best conveys his organization's image are flashy cars, big, ostentatious houses or the people who fulfill the dictator's whims and fancies. Other stakeholders, particularly those who suffer under the dictator's rule, may define his brand in terms of ruthlessness or cruelty, the detention centers and prisons used to hold stakeholders or the general selfishness that denies many the same rights and privileges possessed by a few.

Mainstream organizations use their brand to drive their businesses. They shape their product containers a particular way, their stores need a certain "look" or their logo is theirs alone; it can't be touched or owned (infringed on) by another, or else! Marginals seldom make that level of commitment to a brand. The people brewing illegal booze out in the woods don't use Ball jars because "they're funky" but rather because they are easy to stack and their wide mouth makes them easy to fill and, of course, to drink from. Add to this the fact that if you ask most marginal owner/operators what their brand is, they're likely to just stare at you—having a brand means having a level of visibility and most marginals don't seek visibility. No, what you need to do to get the owner of a marginal to respond to you is not to acknowledge them as a brand but rather to do what's important to them—buy something.

But it makes sense to understand what a brand is and means even for a marginal because a brand separates one organization from another. Since most marginals deal in a society's shadows, trust, safe products or services and sometimes even some measure of quality are the features most of their customers expect from them. These features reflect values that are attached to the organizations for very important and valid reasons. If you were to ask a drug addict to name the top three people to buy drugs from, there would be important reasons why the top dealer is named the most preferred, why number two is in the middle and so on. To the addict, the "top" or preferred dealer, this individual contributor, this marginal organization is or can be the difference between feeling good and not and, sometimes, living or dying. That's brand definition on the streets of the marginal economy.

Opportunity Stems from Events, and Events Are Transactions Defined by a Setting

Events are the focal point of every activity in an organization. Stores focus on the sales event, doctors the surgical event or patient meeting, educators on a lecture (teaching event), politicians for campaign events and even subversive groups on acts of terror, threatening, intimidating events. Events are opportunities for the organization to achieve its mission. Marginal organizations live the relationship between events and mission achievement every day.

The marginal organization measures various aspects of the transaction as micro-events. Marginal events are little more than a nest within which transactions are constructed given a particular setting. The route to appreciating the role of events in marginal organizations begins with understanding two features of their events: first, how events emerge for the marginal organization and, second, the manner in which transactions are constructed given the event at hand.

Regarding the first point, it's important to point out that both marginal and mainstream organizations experience, generally speaking, the same range of events. To illustrate this, consider what Tafoya (2010, 2013a) has called the "Spectrum of Events." The Spectrum of Events illustrates the types of events that can affect organizations regardless of their type. Perhaps, the most important feature of the Spectrum is the realization that even with the best intentions and/or framework it's impossible to anticipate and successfully manage every event that might emerge. As a result, those faced with an event for which they haven't been trained must know how to transfer the skills and competencies they have to manage the unanticipated or unfamiliar event or simply do what they can to "get out of the way" of the event.

The reason the Spectrum of Events is so important is because it illustrates that marginal organizations, largely due to their status in society, must operate within the parameters of two different conditions: the first are events defined by the nature of the work to be done or generic to any organization and the second are events that emerge because of the marginal's status as an illegal or less-than-desirable organization. In other words, some events happen to marginals because they are marginal organizations.

Consider the spectrum's category of "Routine" events. These are the most planned-for events in an organization. They are events that regularly unfold within the framework of the organization's general activity. Routine events are designed to shape an organization's efforts to meet its fundamental goals and objectives. The teller at the bank, the "order taker" at the fast-food restaurant perform routine events that can define more than 60 percent of an organization's activity (Tafoya, 2013a,b). They are routine, but because they represent so much of the interaction between the organization and its primary operations and/or stakeholders, failure to handle them correctly can result in real problems for the organization.

At the other end of the spectrum are "extraordinary events." These are events that are beyond the scope of the organization to control. (For a more complete breakdown of these events, see www.Compcite.com.) We expect these events to be problematic; they are hard to anticipate and, as a result, often are not planned for by the organization's management. As a result, since these can't be planned for or controlled unlike routine events, emphasis is on managing effects of the events and any recovery process that's needed. Natural disasters like hurricanes or the unethical behavior of professionals like lawyers, doctors or the police aren't expected: they aren't the norm for most people or organizations. These stakeholders are professionals, people we trust. The same is true when an informant, someone thought to be a friend or who could be trusted, turns in undocumented workers to the government. There's no way to plan for these occurrences and yet all organizations, marginal or mainstream, have to handle them as they arise.

And Then the Setting Gets Sticky…

Organizations exist to perform but they perform in a universe also defined by other organizations. Sometimes these other organizations just happen to be there, sometimes serving a functional purpose (e.g., regulators) and sometimes as adversaries. Adversarial relationships don't just exist between opponents, however; sometimes they emerge among partnering organizations when tensions develop because of competing visions and missions or processes or practices.

Consider the relationship between airlines and the organizations hired to increase airport security. Here are two enterprise organizations that have a common opponent, the community-type organization, the terrorists, and should operate as "partners" but they can find themselves working at cross-purposes—not as partners but rather as opponents (Tafoya, 2010). The airline wants to move passengers quickly, to keep them happy and hassle-free and to ensure on-time departures and landings. Airport security needs to be deliberate, take the time needed to ensure that there are no threats and stop passenger movement if a problem is observed. Obviously there's the potential for emerging tensions…and sometimes complete breakdown between these partners.

When an adversarial relationship emerges between organizations, behavior typically shifts in three ways. First, the organizations engage in activities to manage the emergence of hostile acts or events. This makes sense.

If there's a fire, put it out! Second, the organizations engage in activities devoted to support their own aggressive plans. Here's what we have to do to win, to beat them. Finally, resources must be redirected to address a growing bureaucracy. Think of it. A crisis has occurred, the organizations involved have responded with appropriate offensive and defensive strategies, and they both have to do the regular things needed to pay the bills, to keep the doors open. Only activities that aim to keep the doors open are routine, expected events. The rest are an extra expense, overhead and bureaucracy designed in response to the crisis. Except for the crisis, they add no value to the organization and its pursuit of its mission. These typically aren't budgeted activities and, moreover, they are part of a growing bureaucracy: increased secrecy, extra vigilance or additional people to handle any needed defensive (whatever that is) and offensive (whatever that is) strategies and tactics.

The offensive and defensive activities aim at preventing the destabilization of the organization. Conflicts only amplify the reality that an organization's vulnerability and/or subsequent destabilization may come from *internal* as well as *external* causes, a theme we'll address in greater detail in chapter 3. There we'll demonstrate another key difference between marginal and mainstream organizations: marginal organizations, again because of the nature of their position in society, generally have more adversaries than mainstream organizations, and that means more opportunities to waste critical resources on extraordinary offensive and defensive activities. But for now, back to the fundamentals.

Order from Key Practices

We conclude this chapter by examining one more component of a marginal organization's profile: the key practices that can or should underlie its operations. Marginal organizations are not usually as sophisticated as mainstream organizations. They typically don't have the people, monetary or material resources that mainstream organizations have, nor do they have the time and experience to devote toward building what those in most mainstream organizations would assume are the minimum practices needed for operation: the policies, procedures and practices that define day-to-day activities.

For example, in table 2.4, seven operational practices that we associate with effective organizations are outlined (Tafoya, 2010, 2013a). The list probably wouldn't come as a surprise to those familiar with organizational theory, but what makes it most useful for this discussion are three things. First, the objective for each practice does more than label a reason for the practice it summarizes and what one should expect when the practice is in place. For example, "Communication management practices" assumes that

Table 2.4 Strategies for Managing Events: Key Practices That Drive and Maximize the Use of Organizational Components

Critical practices and strategies	*Description*	*Broad representative indicators*	*Challenges, risks and threats*
Communication management practices and strategy Objective: Get our message out	Methods, practices and techniques used to transfer, exchange or generally deliver information between or among individuals, groups and organizations.	Language skills Good leadership skills Good coaching Mentoring skills Public relations Listening skills	One-way communication Closed-door policy Bias Miscommunications Incomplete information Poor language skills
Evaluations practices and strategies Objective: Continuous improvement	Processes, procedures and practices used to evaluate, assess or appraise performance for individuals, groups, or organizations as needed.	Reliable processes Valid processes and tools Consistency Skilled evaluators Systematic use	Bias in administration Poor procedures Inconsistent procedures Poor evaluation skills Failure to conduct evaluations
Knowledge practices and strategies Objective: Maximize core competencies	Strategies, practices or procedures used to acquire, build, develop, maintain knowledge and/or skills and competencies.	Training and development strategies Problem-solving skills Decision-making skills Needs assessments	Competing priorities Restrictive environment Limited resources Limited leadership vision
Relationship practices and strategies Objective: A strong stakeholder network	Strategies, practices or procedures used to acquire, build, develop, maintain relationships between or among individuals, groups and organizations.	Selection and hiring strategies Negotiation and bargaining skills Team work is supported Customer service goals	Few "people" values Careless hiring processes Careless job definition Orientation to individuals Lack of cohesiveness Self-centered over team

Performance practices and strategies Objective: Goals attained	Routines, processes and/or methods used to introduce, propel and/or guide operations and ensure that performance meets goals, objectives and standards.	Planning, goal setting Strategy and tactics No surprises Quality skills used Disciplinary processes Product quality expected	Inattention to detail Lack of follow-up Poor coaching skills Sloppy investigations “React” rather than “think” Trial and error
Direction and control practices and strategies Objective: Maximize organizational alignment	Strategies and practices identify and define the vision, mission, goals and objectives. Primary point for interaction with organizations, stakeholders, regulators; protect their interests.	Planning, goal setting Vision and mission Skills in negotiation, bargaining, mediation Evaluations Operations management	Poor information Angry regulators Poor internal communication Weak management Meaningless evaluations Poor planning Anarchy
Information and confirmation practices and strategies Objective: Strength through information	Strategies, practices, tactics for collecting, storing and distributing information. Track sentiments of key stakeholders. Share information with each other.	Database searching Research is encouraged Information is shared Solid research skills Needs assessments used Program evaluations used and quality, service measured	Unpredictable accessibility Accuracy of information Poor research skills Poor quality research Bias Consistency of application Poor security

"communication management" takes place, as addressed in the organization. The same is true for "evaluation practices," where evaluations should occur, for "performance practices," performance and not "just doing things" and so forth.

Second, the indicators listed are important, measurable benchmarks for those building and managing an organization. These are not "nice-to-have" practices; these are (or some facsimile of them) "musts" for an organization to function to its highest potential. In fact, one thing notable about marginals compared to mainstream organizations regarding the use of these practices is that many marginal organizations really do focus on having or developing these practices. In other words, it's not uncommon for many of these otherwise unsophisticated organizations to not only have in place but also regularly use a number of the practices listed in table 2.4. Moreover, and what's most interesting about this observation isn't that marginals use the practices, but that they do so without instruction or direction and also not because they are interested in "doing things right" or "by the book" but more often because the marginals that use these operational practices have learned that they work; their use is a means for surviving in an otherwise unfriendly and sometimes hostile environment defined by the mainstream.

Many marginals are always under the "gun" (sometimes literally) because they operate outside the law; so, many have learned they need practices like those listed in table 2.4 just to survive. Like the drug czar who demands accurate, timely and complete communication in order to ensure that shipments leave and arrive as scheduled or the drug pusher who evaluates the security of a street corner or parking lot before entering to open up shop. Both recognize that use of communication, evaluation or control practices like those listed is both strategic and smart if the organization expects to survive.

Use of these practices also is a way for gauging an organization's overall strengths and vulnerabilities in the management of key events or as it matures through its life cycle. The fact that many marginals are forced to be mobile and not tied down has been noted, but the value of mobility to survival can't be utilized if the organization's leadership doesn't receive information about an unfolding threat with sufficient time to move. After all, the capacity to "cut and run" is as important a competency for some organizations as are the competencies needed to prepare a successful business plan, a marketing and sales program or the logistics and inventory system for a large shipping and warehouse operation in a mainstream organization. Different organizations have different needs and the use of these practices can benefit a variety of organizations, whether in the margins or the mainstream. A quick simulation illustrates this point. Take two organizations, opponents in a conflict situation, and eliminate every other practice from one of the organizations. Then, resist the temptation to predict a winner because that's not as important or as interesting as writing a script about why and how the delimited organization will falter and stumble through this conflict. It's an instructive process.

Finally, the list of practices in table 2.4 can be read and used in different ways. Used one way, the list is a guide or prescription for building an organization and another way for evaluating the organization or its leadership. The Smithsonian® channel's documentary "The Hunt for Bin Laden" illustrates these points. In the documentary, some of those interviewed point out ways the Federal Bureau of Investigation (FBI) and Central Intelligence Agency (CIA) were not able/allowed to share key information before the 9/11 attack on the World Trade Center and the ramifications this had on the event, al-Qaeda's overall operations and, subsequently, the United States as a whole. Using the material in table 2.4 as a checklist against material presented in the Smithsonian® documentary, we get an idea of the ways the absence of communication, evaluation, knowledge, information and relationship management practices between and among critical organizations can facilitate the emergence and unfolding of a tragic event. Events emerge to be managed, and the organization that has in place and uses these key operational practices will be more likely to successfully manage the event than an organization without these practices or experience in using them.

The key strategies and practices listed in table 2.4 address fundamental areas associated with all organizations. They are most effective when clearly defined and are used consistently and appropriately. When examined systemically, the key practices reveal how they can be used alone or in conjunction with other practices for the benefit of an organization or its leadership. Referring back to the capture of Bin Laden, a subsequent examination of materials collected during the raid on his hideout revealed the scope and scale of his use and reliance on practices like those given in table 2.4, with respect to the administration of his stakeholders, resources and overall operation of his organization. Bin Laden was an able administrator and leader.

Moreover, the most successful organizations are those where these operational practices aren't reserved for use by a few but are made available to many throughout the organization. But having these practices in place is only of marginal benefit if people aren't trained in their use, so another way to approach the material in table 2.4 is as a guide that outlines what people in key positions need to know and do to maximize their successful management of events. It's a neat package. Key practices, defined, used and integrated with and in conjunction with the other organizational components discussed above, increase the likelihood of successful management of a range of events.

Finally, the practices should be regularly evaluated and revised as needed. Most important, however, the practices must be used to be effective. Again, the information in table 2.4 is familiar to most and, as most would agree, valuable to any organization. Unfortunately, they're also frequently misused, underused or not used at all. Want proof? Use the information in table 2.4 as a checklist and compare its contents with operations in your organization. See any gaps between what should be and what is?

Conclusion

Explaining why marginal organizations fail is not the primary focus of this book, but touching on reasons why that happens can't be avoided and, at times, raising the question helps illustrate key points or themes being discussed. There are several reasons why marginal organizations fail and while we've already touched on a number of possible reasons, there's room for a quick summary.

Four factors immediately stand out. First, marginals have little room for error; the littlest mistake can bring disaster. The use of organizational practices can offer a safeguard to alert the organization's membership of potential problems or vulnerabilities. For example, it's not uncommon for illegal organizations to have large and sometimes very sophisticated communication and information networks as part of their operational profile. These networks can screen potential candidates, serve as a lookout for unwanted visitors or provide ongoing feedback regarding the status of a target or business objective. In addition, they are relatively easy to set up and modern technologies make them relatively inexpensive and easy to operate.

Second, since many marginals focus on today, dated information can create significant risk for the organization. When an organization's central focus is on the immediate future there may not be much need for a "succession plan," but that doesn't mean that personnel evaluations or training and development should be shortsighted. Most organizations need some depth so that when vacancies occur they can be quickly filled by those known to be trustworthy—perhaps those already working for the organization and with a proven track record.

Third, marginals are risky ventures for many reasons and one ramification of this condition is that opportunities for growth/advancement are often limited or nonexistent. Having a good set of operational practices in place can communicate an image of an organization working to control its destiny by reducing risk and being on guard for emerging risk and threats.

Maintaining materials and documenting processes and procedures may add just enough credibility to the organization's profile so that it looks like a better risk to those stakeholders in a position to support the organization. Moreover, since a marginal's niche often is limited or focused, this trait can be used to concentrate improvement efforts around what the organization knows best, rather than attempting to expand operations into unfamiliar ventures. Developing a core set of operational practices helps those in the organization think about it from different perspectives while maintaining its focus on what it knows and does best. Even if just one or two key practices are targeted, the organization can be in a good position to benefit from improved knowledge and information.

Finally, going through the exercise of evaluating the presence or absence, use or nonuse, of a marginal organization's key practices is also a good opportunity to see how the organization stacks up against competitors, adversaries or important stakeholders. An audit in this instance doesn't have to be very detailed to be informative. For example, conducting an audit of the organization and then a competitor may be just the catalyst needed to motivate the organization's staff to identify and address deficiencies or weaknesses.

CHAPTER 3

The Emergence of Marginal Organizations in a Mainstream Society: Translating Influence into Strategy in an Effort to Drive the Marginal Organization's Success

What Is a Marginal Organization and How Does It Fit into Society and Relationships with Others?

On paper, marginal organizations can look a lot like mainstream organizations. They have structure and stakeholders, they engage in activities designed to produce results, again to maximize the organization's chances of achieving its mission. Organizations from the two segments of society look alike but they are different. Very, very different.

Once formed, three things define the difference between marginal and mainstream organizations: the nature of the missions they pursue, the means by which they seek to achieve their missions and the products, outcomes and impacts associated with the results they are seeking or trying to achieve. It's romantic to view the marginal organization as the spirit of entrepreneurial behavior but the extent to which the marginal pursues its mission by avoiding society's rules and regulations or at the expense of others can make the marginal organization the antithesis of what a society needs, wants or desires. In this chapter, we delve into the nature of the marginal organization to explore the thinking, the logic behind its operation.

An ever-present clue that marginals operate outside the mainstream is evident in how they avoid exposure. For example, consider the nature of the organization as an entity. It has value, is visible to stakeholders and is approachable, at least to those stakeholders it values or who value it. These features generate a variety of potential benefits for all involved.

The organization has the potential to fill its stakeholders' needs and, in turn, the organization's. But to meet these needs, the marginal must expend a significant amount of energy and other resources on nonproductive tasks and activities—particularly those that limit its exposure and visibility to non- or undesirable stakeholders. To do this, the marginal may restrict contact or admittance to stakeholders it doesn't value or those it perceives as a threat. It also has to build processes founded on secrecy, security and privacy.

A marginal's stakeholders are unique, too. In the first place, these stakeholders are not likely to pledge any special allegiance to the marginal organization. As long as it fulfills their needs, they will support it, for example, through the purchase of its goods and service. You won't see the marginal offering a special "shopper's club card" or, for that matter, its stakeholders looking for such a perk. Names and lists are to be avoided. Often, the marginal's stakeholders are in a dependence relationship with the organization. They are captives, held by addiction or heavy reliance on the organization's products or services. These are stakeholders who don't have the luxury to "shop around" for the products and services the organization offers. In all likelihood, the organization may not even offer a range of products or services. Moreover, while a product may be what a customer needs, you usually won't find a wide variety of products or a range of services. What you see is what you can get. This "one size fits all" approach is efficient and makes for expediency; it defines a predictable set of conditions for both the marginal and its stakeholders.

Transactions between marginals and their stakeholders can end quickly; often time is measured by an exchange and not by deliberation. This isn't relationship-building behavior. Building a relationship toward the future isn't an objective, and bartering is not advised. Rather, the fact the stakeholder maintains a relationship with the marginal illustrates something about the stakeholder—what economists might call the stakeholder's revealed preference or revealed dependence. Quality and service are not the chief issues or foremost among the stakeholder's goals: satiating a need is.

Can One Marginal Organization See Itself as Better Than the Next Marginal Organization? Where's the Difference?

Marginal organizations are unique in many ways but when looking at their relationship with other organizations from a stakeholder's viewpoint, two features stand out. First, marginals typically don't compete with mainstream organizations. The pusher selling drugs on the street corner isn't in direct competition with someone in a similar position in a mainstream organization. Even with the legalization of the sale of marijuana in some parts of the United States, there still are a variety of illegal drugs to be sold by marginals without fear of a mainstream competitor.

Second, marginals typically don't compete with other marginals. Large marginals, like those in the illegal drug or alcohol business, usually divide up a territory with one organization serving one region and another or others servicing other regions. This strategy usually emerges because war among marginals often results in a lose/lose game. Not only do warring organizations run the risk of hurting each other as the cost of the conflict takes its toll in lives and money, but also wars drive customers away and, as importantly, draw unwanted attention to the combatants from their natural adversaries: local, state and national law enforcement, politicians and regulatory agencies among others.

Smaller marginals also don't usually get into conflicts with other organizations. Not only can these organizations suffer from conflicts like the larger organizations but they also typically don't have the resources or "position in the community" to go head-to-head in competition with a mainstream organization. Food vendors, for example, simply don't have the leverage to go up against a mainstream, "sit-down" restaurant, and they are not likely to have friends in the community willing to operate on their behalf. They are often viewed and treated as "outsiders," and that's always a weaker position from which to fight.

Rather, marginals of all sizes and types focus on certain key skills and competencies. Like efficiency. Efficiency is a way the marginal can maximize resources by concentrating on four attributes: direction, speed, size and results. For example, marginals most often define a straight and narrow path for their organization to run. It has visible, measurable targets but little more. It's a "stop and go, not stop and shop" operation. Customers are encouraged to see what they want, to make a purchase and to leave. It's goal-directed behavior; there are no receipts if at all possible (they can be traced), no place to linger or sit around and very often a limited product selection (it helps in the decision-making process). This environmental approach also maximizes the speed of a transaction. Convenience and expediency coupled with a matter-of-fact, no-nonsense approach to interactions makes for short transaction times and quick turnover or sell-through.

Third, most marginals are, from the customer's point of view, small shops or organizations. Transactions are usually handled "standing up" with only a couple of logical exceptions. Sales volume is measured in terms of what's available or can be afforded. Portions are measured for a quick turnaround; it's a "hit and run" transaction. Anything more may mean discovery or increased exposure and that's a risk.

Finally, results are predictable and meant to maximize benefit to all stakeholders involved. A marginal's products or services offered can be measured in terms of their immediacy: there are observable, tangible outcomes and a discernible, real payoff. Moreover, if the transactions are illegal, risk is shared between the organization and the stakeholders involved. And, while the ideal is a simple exchange between the marginal and a stakeholder there usually is no need for third parties to get involved except in instances where the marginal is engaged in actions like the theft of property. In these instances, the help of a third party may be needed as a "fence" for the stolen goods, as a "money launderer" or as a "reseller." These conditions add an expense for the marginal that must be covered for the transaction to be deemed complete and add to the marginal's potential vulnerabilities as more people, over whom the marginal may have little control, become part of its value stream.

Mainstream organizations like to "stand behind" their products and services and often are especially proud to offer a wide variety of products for consumers to "meet their every need." Most marginals don't have the capital to cover that type of orientation nor do most have the physical capacity to warehouse, show or sell a large variety of products and services. Moreover, an approach or orientation that includes browsing, questions, possible web and inventory searches to the transaction time can add features most marginals may not be prepared to handle and, of course, additional exposures. So, it is "what you see is what you 'can' get."

Does It Make Sense to Even Talk about a Marginal Organization as Being Influential? And What Makes a Marginal Influential Anyway?

This description of marginals as little more than a little storefront or street corner transaction point makes one wonder if more robust concepts typically associated with organizations, concepts like "influence" and "strategy," can be used when talking about marginals as organizations. Is there a proactive dimension to their operation or are they merely, and sometimes exclusively, reactive in nature? In fact, there are influential and strategic elements to a marginal organization's behavioral profile, but like so much that a marginal does to function or even exist, influence and strategy must be managed and implemented in a marginal's way and not necessarily in ways that parallel how the two materialize in the mainstream economy or organization.

On average, two factors contribute to an organization's capacity to draw desired stakeholders to the organization and its products and services: the organization's capacity to be influential and the strategy it uses to manage its operations vis-à-vis environmental conditions, for example, stakeholder needs and other organizations. Influence is a particularly unique phenomenon and one intimately linked to the organization involved. Influence speaks to an organization's ability to pull or push stakeholders, usually customers or potential members, to the organization and/or its products and services. All effective organizations are influential but the influence they command is a personal and specific construct explicitly defined in terms of a particular organization and stakeholder.

What Is Influence and How Does It Emerge?

There's a bright and a dark side to organizational influence. On the dark side, the organization seems to push the individual or other organizations to behave in a particular way. The organization may be in a power position and that power extends over the individual or organizations that fall under its power. The organization able to use a "push style" of influence can exert pressures to get the desired movement. Sometimes this comes from a position of authority or control that it has developed or been granted, at other times it may be associated with circumstances like the organization's capacity to exert pain or punishment on its target.

Another view sees an organization as influential because it has the capacity to pull stakeholders to it. Frequently, organizations capable of drawing or pulling others to it seem to do so because they persuade stakeholders to join it, use its goods or services or, generally, not to be an opponent or adversary. Most often, the organization is seeking ways to use influence as a means to convince others that it is the organization with which to interact. In either case, influence is directly linked with a perception of the organization's credibility, a perception that links the organization, its claims and the stakeholder in some personal and meaningful way.

Consider the relationship between the push and pull nature of influence. The "pull" side of influence implies that the stakeholder is drawn to the organization. At the "entry" level, the organization is perceived as having a product or service the stakeholder wants or needs. It's a simple analysis: "I want it, I need it, I'm persuaded."

At this level, "pull" reflects the stakeholder decisions that are based on assessments of the organization as an institution. These decisions entail concluding that the organization is safe and that "I'm convinced it's a good place to do business." The stakeholder's decision-making process concludes with a simple comparison: a final step that involves the stakeholder making a decision regarding the organization, but in this instance as a comparison between this organization and any other offering the same product and services. For example, can I get a better price somewhere else, or more for my money, etc.? An organization's influential pull is highest when the stakeholder concludes that "this is the best organization." For example, it's totally reliable and has great credibility. The "push" side of influence is different. The stakeholder again agrees to choose a particular organization or its products and services but the decision to do so isn't arrived at as when one is "pulled" toward the organization.

The push side begins with the stakeholder realizing that the organization is "pressuring me to act"! Transaction statements like "this is the last one we have" or "someone else just called about this product and wants to see it" are meant to prod the stakeholder to act; they are typical pressure statements. The next level of the push side also involves the stakeholder coming to a conclusion regarding the organization, in this instance, recognizing that "the organization has the 'authority' to get me to act." For example, the organization has "push leverage" when it is the only game in town or when other options are out of reach for the stakeholder, perhaps because they are too far away. Other times, "authority" is confirmed in terms of the organization's position in society. When the police officer tells you to "move your car," you do so because the officer has a position of authority you don't have.

The final feature of push-sided influence is defined by another conclusion the stakeholder arrives at, that the organization "has the power to get me to act." This last step clearly is the culmination of the relationship among influence, credibility and action. Returning to the example of the police officer used above, it's one thing to say that the police officer gets you to act because he has the authority to make you do something and it's something very different when you recognize that the officer also has the power (e.g., a gun) to get you to act. In that case you are "totally pushed"!

A study of the relationship between push and pull influence draws one to several observations regarding an organization and its capacity to be influential. First, influence has certain costs associated with it. Push strategies can require an organization to maintain its position through the use of force, and so some marginals literally operate their own army or paramilitary units to motivate (to "push") stakeholders to do as they want. These are channels for physical force to drive the organization's influential profile. Fear of punishment or loss motivates in these instances.

Second, being influential requires that the organization, through its staff, design and operations, possess a certain level of competency, capability, skill or ability. This appears to be true whether the organization is using a push or pull approach to influence. Managing an army, for example, requires the competencies associated with leadership, planning, organizing or directing others. Drawing customers to your organization necessitates offering products and services with the features and benefits that stakeholders need and, as importantly, having the means to deliver on marketing or promotional claims.

Clearly, some of the things an organization does contributes to the influence it has over stakeholders and, other times, the organization's sphere of influence appears more related to the type of organization or the products and services it offers: it's the stakeholders who define the organization as influential, as important to them and as one meeting their needs. This is more than anything the organization does by design. But influence is a critical component and ingredient necessary for an organization to grow and flourish, so the focus of this chapter explores the nature and development of organizational influence for the marginal organization.

Influence as a Function of the Nature of the Organization

When looking at any phenomenon in terms of organizations, it's important to examine the organizations in terms of their primary classification, like those outlined in chapter 2. In that chapter, a typology was introduced to illustrate inherent differences among four types of organizations—the enterprise, community, group/team and individual contributor. That discussion summarized features and benefits of each classification and concluded by pointing out that a given organization is actually a composite of all four elements with one being primary to the others. So an enterprise is primarily driven by a need to make a profit from the products and services it offers, but at the same time it has, to a lesser degree, some combination of the elements of the community, team/group and individual contributor organizations as part of its makeup.

To illustrate how influence and strategy differ across the four types of organizations and why, parenthetically, it is important to consider the type of organization when looking at how an organization uses influence to its benefit, we will examine each type of organization in turn, focusing on ways influence emerges and is used in the marginal organization. It's an important discussion for several reasons not the least of which is that influence functions very differently in marginal organizations than in mainstream organizations.

Organizations in both sectors need to establish their capacity to be influential, but influence in the marginal sector is often crafted in terms of the use and juxtaposition of the four components that define the organization, that is, in terms of the enterprise, community, group/team and individual contributor. Mainstream organizations rely on their component parts, too, but not out of a particular need created by the fact that one organization is in the mainstream and the other operates in a society's margins. This becomes particularly clear when looking at the group/team and individual contributor organizations.

Influence and the Marginal Enterprise Organization: Direction and the Enterprise Organization's Influence

The enterprise organization's mission is embedded in efforts to gain money and wealth and the results of those pursuits, for example, status and power. These are features and benefits of influence whether the organization is in the mainstream or in the margins of society. So the vendor on the street hawking bootlegged or contraband goods, while small by comparison to other "retail operations," is an example of a marginal organization we'd classify as an enterprise organization.

So, too, are marginal organizations that deal in human trafficking like sex for hire or the smuggling of migrants across the US border. These organizations don't exist for humanitarian reasons; they are looking to make a profit at the expense of other human beings. Illegal growers, producers, manufacturers and sellers of illegal drugs also are enterprises in the marginal sector. Because money is a prime ingredient in the operations of these organizations, extra efforts to ensure the security of the organization and their operations are often needed. Efforts in this instance can translate into seemingly unorthodox strategies and tactics for both the organization's operations and ongoing activities. For example, marginals often operate as streamlined machines with little bureaucracy, particularly when compared to mainstream enterprise organizations. Marginals adopt this posture largely because they often rely on mobility and the ability to move operations should that be necessary. The top of the organization, its leadership team, is usually small—most employment opportunities exist at lower levels. This is a by-product of the organization's focus on business activities and also a way to keep aspects of the business private.

Influence for the marginal enterprise engaged in illegal activity is often linked to two streams: shared risk and the power of money and force. For example, the marginal enterprise's need for operational practices built around secrecy and privacy stems from the fact that its operations, products and services are capable of putting both the organization and its feeders, supporters and customers at risk because of their activities. This is a theme explored in greater detail below.

A second source of influence for the marginal enterprise is linked to the power it derives from money and/or the intimidation of workers, customers or competitor stakeholders. Money allows the marginal enterprise the opportunity to "buy" influence among key stakeholders in its existing or potential network. For example, instances of police, members of the legal community or other professional organizations working with criminal enterprises is not uncommon. Bribes, kickbacks and other inducements are often used to secure the protection the illegal marginal needs by making these professionals stakeholders in the organization's operations. This, in turn, gives the marginal freedom to operate, thus extending its image and position within a community or society at large. It's a form of metaphorical mobility. Having those who would pursue or chase you among your intimate stakeholders reduces the need to have to physically be on the run. The vulnerability is addressed and the threat managed.

Enforcement and intimidation are other strategies for gaining influence. In these instances, stakeholders and sometimes whole stakeholder groups are targeted in an effort to communicate the organization's power or authority. Enforcement and intimidation activities define performance expectations for the targeted stakeholders. Interestingly, too, intimidation doesn't always have to be in the form of force. Sometimes pseudo-bullying associated with a denial of service can be just as effective. For example, the vendor whose pitch is "take it or leave it" or "buy it as is" sends a powerful message to the addict who needs the product just as the smuggler who threatens—"that's the pay, you work or you're out"—illegal aliens hoping to find a job in the United States doesn't need to use force as well. The threat of being without is often sufficient.

Stakeholders and the Enterprise Organization's Influence

Discussing the role of a marginal's stakeholders is one of many recurring themes in this book. Stakeholders can reflect both those who support the organization as well as those who are among the organization's adversaries, detractors or opponents. Stakeholders will be discussed in greater detail in chapter 5 but they are introduced here because they play a major role in shaping different facets of an organization's influence profile.

Tafoya (2013a) described the stakeholder network associated with an organization as comprising five primary segments. At the network's center is the organization. It's the place where the organization's mission is presented and managed for the network and stakeholders. "Feeders" are primary stakeholder suppliers for the organization. Feeders contribute to the organization's resources. They may be the organization's source for supplies or raw materials, financial assistance, external guidance and sometimes those who source or find other stakeholders (e.g., customers) for the organization.

Feeders have a strong, positive relationship with the organization; without them the organization would have a difficult, sometimes even impossible time achieving its mission. The marginal enterprise has a mix of feeders. A sweatshop has backers, suppliers and buyers of material needed to make products for manufacture. Growers associated with marginal agricultural enterprises need backers and producers of seeds or starter plants.

"Supporters" also have a positive effect on the organization but their role and contribution are not as dramatic as those of a "provider." Sometimes it is helpful to think of supporters as more tactical and "feeders" as more strategic. Supporter stakeholders are a generic collection of individuals and groups. An organization's supporters may be invisible to outsiders. Their importance, however, stems from their role as contributors to the marginal enterprise's overall effort. A marginal's "customers" are obvious supporters. Like the drug addict, the customer who agrees to pay the merchant untraceable cash to avoid paying sales tax or the person who buys illegal cigarettes, pornography or sex for hire. These people are all supporters of illegal marginal activities. They are the everyday supporters of a marginal organization. At a more strategic level, however, the cop who looks "the other way," the judge on the take or the municipal inspectors who take bribes or kickbacks are also supporters of the illegal marginal enterprise. In some industries, particularly those involved in government or municipal activities, supporters can be key enablers for the marginal enterprise's success.

Two other network components, "demanders" and "reliers," draw on the organization's resources and, in some instances, its overall capacity to perform. "Reliers" are stakeholders the organization needs to function. For example, the marginal enterprise organization producing illicit liquor by setting up an illegal distillery or a meth laboratory may need to subcontract work to plumbers and electricians in order to get their operations running. This can be a risk for marginal organizations. If the organization doesn't have internal staff able to provide these types of support services, hiring subcontractors may be both an unanticipated expense and an avenue for potential exposure. Lawyers are often an invaluable "relier-member" of the marginal enterprise's network.

"Demanders" are the fourth segment of the marginal enterprise's stakeholder network. Like the other three segments, demanders are part of every stakeholder network, whether the organization is in the marginal or mainstream of a society. Their societal role is most often associated with regulations, laws and policies and procedures; they are the tax collectors, law enforcement, local, state and federal agents and the myriad groups of

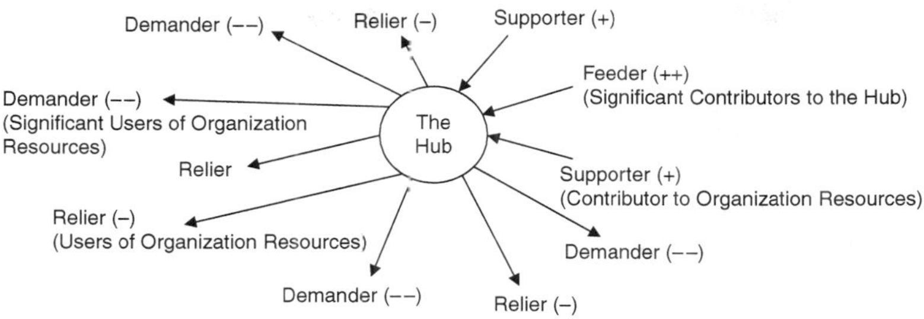

Figure 3.1 Shifting Equilibrium as a Stakeholder Swarm Engulfs the Initial Stakeholder Network. (Arrows reflect if resources are supplemented or drained.)

inspectors and bureaucrats associated with the general operation of organizations in society. Add to this the local, state and national legislators, special interest groups and the media, and the full scope and scale of the demander segment becomes immediately apparent and so does an indication of how and why demanders can play such a dominant role for the marginal enterprise.

Demanders are the border patrol agents tracking the moves of the marginal enterprise that hopes to smuggle aliens into the United States; they are the special interest groups monitoring organizations so as to ensure their operations protect the people and animals they serve or handle (Hauser, 2012); they are the health inspectors ensuring that food producers process foods or use pesticides or food additives in accordance with state and national regulations (Charles, 2012; FSIS, 2012); and they are the police officers working the weigh stations on national highways looking for contraband or smuggled goods, such as cigarettes, passing from one state to another in attempts to avoid paying sales taxes (Elfrink, 2009; Povich, 2013). Figure 3.1 outlines the relationship among the four stakeholders. Each segment plays a role in the marginal enterprise's operations but demanders are one segment that cannot be ignored. The illegal marginal must then find a way to avoid this segment or, if possible, work with them.

Threats and Vulnerabilities to the Marginal Enterprise Organization's Capacity to be Influential

Because marginals tend to operate outside the rules and regulations of the mainstream, they are constantly at risk from those in law enforcement, people with a grudge, well-meaning citizen organizations or the informer and whistle-blower working for a competitor or law enforcement organization. There are ways to manage the marginal enterprise's risks, threats and vulnerabilities by cloaking the organization in secrecy, taking care in hiring and working with only a trusted few and, of course, by attempting to "buy" security or protection for its operations.

These tactics are useful but cannot be used alone or relied upon as the singular strategy to protect the organization. Accurate vision and regularly updated information about changes in the marketplace or threats from adversaries and opponents must be incorporated in the marginal enterprise's efforts, particularly if the risk of exposure and threat can result in police or legal action. As a result, some marginal enterprises protect their own capacity to be influential by buying security, protection and sometimes even the influence of others. For example, instances of police, members of the legal community or other professional organizations working with criminal enterprises are not uncommon. The bribes, kickbacks and other inducements described above are often used to secure the protection the illegal marginal needs to operate.

Finally, because the marginal organization operating as an enterprise is involved in the production and distribution of products and services, it must also manage risks, threats and vulnerabilities associated with the very processes that allow it to operate. The key operational practices discussed in chapter 2 can serve as a checklist for the marginal enterprise to use as it assesses its operations or as, importantly, in terms of the different stakeholder segments (i.e., demanders, reliers, etc.) discussed above.

Influence and the Marginal Community Organization: Direction and the Marginal Community Organization's Influence

Influence is manifested differently in the marginal community organization. Recall that the organization classified as a community focuses on achieving a particular mission, only in this instance, the mission is one grounded in values, morals or a particular way of thinking or behaving. Community organizations are very special organizations and this is particularly true when they operate in the margins of a society's mainstream.

Terrorist organizations, cults, gangs and political extremists are typical of the marginals in this segment. Their culture can be defined by rituals, a narrow, specific focus and rules and procedures that seek to limit membership to those who follow or profess allegiance to the organization's mission and values. Discussion regarding the range of influence these organizations exert is often limited to their influence on the organization's membership but that's only part of the scope of their influence.

Their capacity to influence a society at large is a central part of the way in which they demonstrate their mission. As a result, terrorist acts, acts of violence, bullying, harassment, discrimination and other radical and fanatic acts can trigger unprecedented responses by those affected. Marginal organizations such as paramilitary organizations, the Ku Klux Klan, al-Qaeda or street gangs trigger increased police activity, influence the ways other organizations are forced to behave or challenge the sense of security the average citizen may feel about a particular town or situation.

In all of these instances, it's the vision and mission of the "community marginal organization" that defines the expectations the organization has toward internal and external stakeholders. In other words, unlike the enterprise organization that seeks to influence stakeholder behavior in response to products and services designed, built and distributed, the marginal community organization uses its vision and mission to pull or push stakeholders in the direction it wants. In many ways, the marginal community organization's vision and mission influences others to view it as a threat or menace, or as an ideal or panacea for society's ills.

Stakeholders and the Marginal Community Organization's Influence

More than most other organizational types, marginal community organizations extend the scope and scale of their influence through the stakeholders making up their social network—and this is true for both, those who favor and those who oppose the organization. For example, feeders not only follow the community's vision and mission but they also extend it through their own proselytizing and actions. Indeed, what makes community organizations particularly interesting is that in contrast to each of the other three classifications (enterprise, group, individual contributor), each member of the community is both an extension of the organization and, in many ways, a microcosm of the parent organization. This is one reason why "demanders" find community organizations so difficult to contain or control: even if the physical organization is destroyed, the ideals, values and the organization's mission and potential influence live on through its members.

"Supporters" of the community organization often operate behind the scenes or, in some instances, under cover. Supporters may be willing to fund a marginal community's activities but they prefer to do so anonymously. Political Action Committees (PACs) are an excellent example. PAC members can make contributions to extremist positions without disclosing who they are. They have a positive effect on the organization and when their efforts and roles are combined with those of the "feeders," the extent of their contributions can be truly dramatic.

Again, it is helpful to think of supporters as more tactical and feeders as more strategic. Supporter stakeholders are a generic collection of individuals and groups who may be invisible to outsiders, and in the case of radical or extremist groups they like to keep it that way. Their importance, however, stems from their role as contributors to the marginal community organization's overall activities.

Threats and Vulnerabilities to the Marginal Community Organization's Capacity to Be Influential

Often one of the biggest threats to a community organization is the loss of its leader or a key figure. To get around this, some marginal community organizations breed the spirit of the organization into each member making the membership its symbolic leadership. It is a powerful idea but this runs the risk of another challenge and that is the desire of some members to be their own stars or to become members of the organization's tacit leadership function. Unchecked egos and ambitions in these instances can lead to division and subsequent loss of the organization's capacity to be influential. Diluted influence is never as robust as focused, centralized influence.

Other times, a marginal community organization's capacity to influence can be challenged when its programs and activities lose their effectiveness. For example, imagine how powerful and influential a terrorist organization like al-Qaeda would be if it had no weapons or explosives. Threats buried in words and ideas aren't nearly as influential as the power to back words and threats with fear of injury, pain, death or destruction.

Demanders are a constant challenge for marginal community organizations. Demanders like the police, military or special interest groups can brand the marginal community as an "undesirable element," a threat to society, a danger to a "way of life" or, generally, as a burden whose need for constant monitoring or management strains society's resources. Use of re-branding efforts by society or even the marginal itself can go a long way to undermine efforts to associate a negative image with a marginal community organization's sphere of influence.

Influence and the Marginal Group/Team Organization: Direction and the Marginal Group Organization's Influence

One of the interesting anomalies of the marginal sector is that one doesn't see many illustrations of the organizations labeled as teams/groups. This is partially a result of the fact that this organizational type often emerges as a spin off of an existing organization (e.g., when a project team is associated with an enterprise or when a fund-raising group is associated with a community organization). These groups/teams have a specific task, exist until the task is completed or against a defined time line and perform against identified objectives or goals.

They do exist among marginals, however, and, like their use in the mainstream, they are often extensions of an existing organization. The terrorist's "strike teams" used to launch specific attacks are examples and so are groups used to raid businesses or to "enforce" a marginal organization's influence in a particular neighborhood or a section of a city. At other times, specific teams often are formed for product distribution, for example, teams to move goods from their point of manufacture to a distribution point, as when drugs are transported or the recent attempts to smuggle goods like cigarettes from states with a low sales tax for resale in states with a higher sales tax (Povich, 2013).

Because these teams and groups have been selected for particular assignments, they carry with them a level of influence that adds to their credibility given the mission at hand. In some instances, they can be viewed as "specialists" like those operating submarines used to smuggle drugs from South America to the United States (Anonymous, 2008, 2010). These individuals are responsible for both the transportation systems they use as well as the product they are moving; it's a significant amount of responsibility.

Stakeholders and the Marginal Group Organization's Influence

When the marginal teams/groups function as just described, they occupy a unique position in the social network associated with marginal organizations. On the one hand, they are at the point, often the extended point, of the marginal organization's distribution stream. In this capacity, they are responsible for moving product from manufacturing to a sales setting. If these teams are successful, the marginal gets the effects (money, fear, cooperation) it needs to meet its mission. On the other hand, demanders in the network see these teams/groups as one of their primary targets in efforts to prevent the marginal organization from being successful. Stop these groups or teams from achieving their mission and the parent organization can suffer a loss of revenue, image and, of course, its influential profile.

Threats and Vulnerabilities to the Marginal Group Organization's Capacity to Be Influential

The role of groups/teams among marginal organizations cannot be dismissed. If the parent marginal organization cannot distribute its products or services, whether goods, like drugs, pornography, or people, or ideas, like fear or threats, it cannot be successful. This illustrates one of the most distinctive parallels between marginal and mainstream organizations: both are completely dependent on the development, maintenance and successful management of a supply stream—part of its overall value stream. These streams not only exist as tangible extensions of the parent organization, but also are populated with an array of different mini-networks, each comprising their own stakeholder groups.

Clearly, then, there are two broad areas where threats and vulnerabilities enter into the use of marginal group/team organizations. The first is that if the marginal teams fail, or if they fail to successfully carry out their mission or if individual members fail to function in ways that make the marginal team successful, this directly impacts the organization. As a result, it is important for those studying marginal organizations to identify these players in the parent marginal organization and then describe their contributions and performance. The second significant threat sequence that can emerge is associated with the team's function vis-à-vis the supply stream of which it is part. Breakdowns in key practices associated with this stream can directly impact the team and/or its ability to carry out its mission. In this instance, the team's performance not only impacts the parent organization but failure to perform as needed can also damage the entire stream, including the stakeholders who are part of it. This is widespread systemic damage. In the first instance, only the parent organization was affected; but in the second, negative effects can ripple throughout the stakeholder network. This last point illustrates an important strategy for those seeking to hamstring a marginal's performance: if it's not possible to destroy the marginal, destroying its supply and value streams would be the next best move. The "end" may not be as immediate, but a process of protracted pain and suffering will eventually have its effects.

Demanders, then, can focus their attacks on individual team members who are central to the team's effectiveness; they can focus on the team as a whole or they can attack the stream in which the team operates. Once marginal teams/groups are used as part of the parent marginal organization's distribution efforts, the multiple dependencies that are inherent in teams/groups can make them one large point of exposure and vulnerability—as long as the demanders know what they should be looking for in a marginal team/group.

Influence and the Marginal Individual Contributor Organization: Direction and the Organization's Influence

As described in chapter 2, we view individuals as self-sustaining organizations on par with the enterprise, community and team/group organizations.

In this instance, however, the individual contributor has a focus built around his or her skills, competencies or personal mission. The jobber who takes in "work for hire" is an example, as are the individuals who offer child care, the prostitute, the person who robs the local convenience store or hijacks a passing car. They are organizations in their own right, pursuing a mission, accomplishing goals and objectives and operating in terms of specific tasks or activities. They appear in both the marginal and mainstreams of society.

Focusing on the relationship among competency, influence and individual performance makes sense when talking about individual contributors like doctors, lawyers, plumbers or mechanics in the mainstream. We associate skills and competencies with these professionals and we rely on them to operate in ways that contribute to our health or general well-being. Mainstream individual contributors are well known to us.

But even though the nature of the work to be done in the marginal sector may not be like that done in the mainstream it still has value, can create problems if not successfully completed and makes a contribution to a marginal organization's mission. The potential influence among individual contributors in the marginal sector is also linked to their competencies given the task at hand. The skilled plumber needed to make an illegal distillery or meth lab operational is more influential than the unskilled worker. When the marginal organization wants to send a message defining its authority or power in a region, it may rely on the proficient assassin over the cheap thug, and a trustworthy individual is more likely to be used as a drug runner than one with no history or whose trustworthiness is not established. In other words, influence for the individual contributor marginal sector is also tied directly to the individual's competencies for the given task to be completed.

Stakeholders and the Individual Contributor Group Organization's Influence

But examining influence vis-à-vis an individual contributor draws our attention to another unique feature of influence within the marginal organization—that influence is something others designate or assign to the individual contributor, enterprise, community or team/group organization; it is not something the organization can simply claim to have and then assume that others will agree. In other words, it is the stakeholders in the organization's social network that designate an organization as influential or not, define the level of influence the organization may have and under what conditions the organization is influential or not. If the stakeholders don't see an organization as "influential," then it's not!

What's more, all members of the stakeholder network have a say in defining the scope and scale of influence for them. Influence is a very personal matter, so if the feeders and supporters don't see the organization as influential to them then the organization may not receive the funds or materials it needs to operate or to build its products or services. This is true whether the organization is operating in the mainstream or in the marginal sector. Every organization needs stakeholders in its network to see it as influential, and in some instances more influential than its competitors or adversaries. Otherwise, why put yourself at risk through association with a weak, non-influential partner?

Threats to and Vulnerabilities of the Individual Contributor Group Organization's Capacity to Be Influential

Organizations in the marginal sector are usually not in a position to offer "second chances" when problems or screw-ups occur. Marginal organizations operate on too fine a line between success and failure, and coupled with the poor esteem with which others typically view marginal organizations and the ongoing harassment of these organizations by demanders in their networks, it is easy to see that marginal organizations always need competent, reliable performance from everyone all of the time. The smallest error can mean the difference between profit and loss, exposure or unmanageable risk. This is the "way of life" for marginals; it is how things are every day.

Moreover, because marginals are usually small organizations with only a few members, it is easy to see how one person's poor performance can cause major problems. So the individual contributor operating in the marginal sector is at the greatest risk and vulnerability when poor performance leads stakeholders to challenge or question the individual's credibility or competence. Lose one or the other and you're in trouble. Lose both, particularly in the marginal sector, and things can get very bad, very fast.

In addition, since people competing for work in the marginal sector typically outnumber the jobs available, there's often a lot of competition for a job when there's an opening. In this sometimes rough and tumble economic sector, competition can be brutal and sometimes even physically brutal. So if someone believes he or she can do a better job than a particular individual contributor, a challenge may be on the horizon. Leaders of marginal organizations have work that needs to be done; they usually don't have time or the luxury of having favorites within the organization. This isn't the mainstream where nepotism, favoritism, bias or preferential treatment are used as managerial perks. The work has to come first in a marginal organization.

Other factors, too, are potential threats to the individual contributor in the marginal sector. Age, for instance, is an insidious threat to anyone's career in the marginal organization. Work in the marginal sector can be very demanding. Long hours doing hard, sometimes dangerous, work can take its toll and, in time, may be too great a burden for an older worker. Couple this with the fact that few organizations in the marginal sector offer anything like a retirement program and it's quickly clear that aging works against the individual contributor in a marginal organization.

Finally, illness and disability are real challenges to the individual contributor in the marginal sector. Marginal organizations typically don't offer health benefits, and even if they could most wouldn't because they can't afford the risks associated with the exposure that comes with offering a health plan or program through the legitimate mainstream. People in marginal organizations get paid for the work they do. If someone is disabled or too sick to work, their source of income can vanish, sometimes only aggravating an already bad situation.

Strategy and the Marginal Organization

Influence is important but it's not a stand-alone feature for the marginal organization. Influence, as we've pointed out, ultimately rests with an organization's stakeholders (or potential stakeholders) to attribute to the organization. If the organization doesn't have the capacity to fulfill a stakeholder's needs, it's not likely to have a positive influence on the stakeholder. On par with influence is the way the organization strategically negotiates the challenges, events and threats it faces. But before we shift our attention to issues related to the use of strategy in marginal organizations, there are three other features that need to be addressed.

First, while the marginal organization may manage a large, sophisticated supply stream and run manufacturing centers that turn raw product into street-grade pornography, drugs, illegal cigarettes, alcohol or even "protection," changing laws, ease of access or production have seriously cut into the product mix of large, dynamic, organized marginal organizations. Indeed, changing conditions that affect the availability of once illegal products combined with the marginal's efforts to maintain anonymity can erase all association it may have with some products or services consumers desire. Influence? Who is there to be influential when the need for a product becomes generic, commonplace or readily available?

Second, government interventions that sponsor ancillary programs also can impact the marginal organization. Needle exchanges, anti-smoking campaigns, safe sex and the legalization of marijuana and, in some instances, prostitution, have gone a long way to remove the core consumer from the end point of the marginal's value stream. Of course, there will always be room for the pervert or weak-kneed cocaine user to get a porn or drug fix but these numbers are containable and don't provide the economy of scale large organizations or syndicates need to survive. Here, again, influence rests not with the marginal organization producing the product or service but in this case with the supply stream associated with the product. So influence is attributed to the supply stream—the party where the local marijuana is served or the Internet where the porn is sourced becomes the influential point, rather than any particular organization. Like the grocery store that offers a "store brand" for 30 percent less than the national brand, influence shifts from the cereal manufacturer to the grocery store where the purchase is made and that can be a big shift for some organizations.

While the parent organization may be the manufacturer, supplier or distributor of the products and services that stakeholders value, it's not the organization the stakeholder interacts with but rather some individual often far down the supply stream. As a result, stakeholders are more likely to value those they deal with, the guy selling the drugs, the prostitute or the gang threatening them, than the marginal organization that fronts these people. How many people who buy their drugs from a pusher have any idea where the drugs originated or who runs the marginal drug company, and how many people who seek the services of a prostitute have any idea who the prostitute's pimp is or even care? In other words, influence often is only captured at the end of the value stream, where the deal actually goes down, and in these instances it is often the group/team or individual contributor element that's the influential element. This can be a real problem for the marginal should members of the team/group or individual contributors break off from the parent organization to compete against it.

So marginal organizations often find themselves in an interesting but potential quandary that most mainstream organizations don't have to worry about. The marginal engaged in illegal activities must do what it can to avoid attention and so, in some respects, it is vulnerable to the needs, interests and behavior of those who work for it. How do those organizations capitalize on the need to promote their products and services when phenomena like influence and credibility, so important to marginal and mainstream organizations, are so easily manipulated or compromised by those who work for the marginal organization? The answer lies in the creative use of strategy, including the plans, tactics and lines of attack the organization uses to establish its influence and, in turn, move its products and services.

Strategy through the Commoditization of Influence

One of the first strategic acts a marginal can implement is the commoditization of influence. This can be a complicated move but it can solve a number of different problems for the marginal organization. Commoditization deemphasizes the role of the organization as a whole and/or its management and concentrates on the transaction point. Now it's what the organization does vis-à-vis its target stakeholders that is emphasized. Everything else is secondary and behind the scenes. This move has the potential for simultaneously reducing the organization's risk exposure by making those further down the supply stream handle the illegal goods while focusing attention on the transaction point, the place where the stakeholder's needs are met. It's both a practical and smart move. The marginal can afford this strategy because image isn't as powerful a motivator for stakeholders using the marginal's products or services as money received from the sale of its products or services. In many respects, the drug addicts and individuals looking for pornography, illegal cigarettes, a job as an undocumented alien or favors from a prostitute don't care who or what makes up the parent organization; they just want their needs satisfied.

By focusing on the transaction point, the marginal organization is taking a "back-seat" approach to image management. The organization's capacity to deliver products and services is the focal point and any use of influence is captured in doing what is necessary to *get things done*. Moreover, placing emphasis on the transaction point lets those at that point in the supply stream do what they do best: exchange the product or service for money and this alone keeps the marginal parent organization one step away from what may be a criminal transaction point.

Marginals are an excellent example of organizations and stakeholders self-organizing (Tafoya, 2010) to deliver the performance needed to achieve a mission. Beyond this, however, a laissez-faire approach to influence management provides a unique means for seeing the role and capacity of influence as a product of wit, fluidity, ingenuity and adaptation. Allowing individuals in the supply stream to self-organize their approach to stakeholders can stimulate innovation. It allows those who do the work to speculate on ways the work can be done better, faster and with more efficiency. Then, all the organization needs to do is to ensure that those doing the work do it so that the organization gets the money it deserves and the protection or anonymity it wants.

Self-organization also opens the organization to potentially new and different ways to do what it needs to do to achieve its mission. Opening the system hasn't changed the organization's membership requirements; those rules remain fixed. Rather the organization moves to a relaxed attitude toward change and new ideas. This orientation can uncover process and production problems as "ownership" is expanded to include those throughout the organization's value stream. This can lead to cost-savings, improved problem-solving and new ways to generally improve efficiencies in the organization and its operations.

Finally, shifting emphasis to the transaction point stimulates initiative and growth and creates new opportunities to assess capabilities of staff involved. All organizations need reliable, competent and trustworthy staff and one of the best ways to gauge the extent to which they perform against these standards is by letting them do the work that needs to be done. This may be especially advantageous when what's being done is related to routine or noncritical matters. If you can't rely on your staff to handle routine matters, it's doubtful they'll be able to manage a critical situation or a crisis (Tafoya, 2010, 2013a,b).

Clearly shifting emphasis to the transaction and increasing responsibilities of line staff has its risks but potential paybacks may offset them, particularly if the process is well managed. It is prudent risk taking when involving employees in this manner relies on established patterns and norms that can serve as boundaries for performance and action. Such prudent risk taking can reduce or help prevent tensions or divisions from developing among the organization's staff. Taking a careful, thoughtful approach to organizational change in these instances reduces the likelihood that some may feel left out or that others are favorites and they are not. In reality, there's nothing wrong if these types of sentiments develop or are expressed if the organization's management is prepared and capable of managing them.

Finally, while experimenting with change may look like a good idea from inside the organization, it's important to remember that the entire stakeholder network also includes some outside the organization, and too much change may make them uncomfortable particularly if it comes as a surprise. Any hint of trouble or an impression that things are very different from what they've come to expect can make these stakeholders nervous, and as Tafoya (2013a,b) has pointed out, in a crisis "supporters" and "feeders" in the organization's social network are among the first to flee or abandon the organization. Because marginals so often operate in the dark side of a society, they cannot risk confusing stakeholders they rely on about who's in charge, the organization's mission or direction or what to expect next time. Shifting responsibilities to those not skilled or prepared to handle them can put people or the organization in danger and thus expose them to more problems and extra expenses. If the use of unskilled or unprepared people in key areas of the supply stream results in delays and process breakdowns, the resulting stress and tensions may not only affect the organization and its stakeholders but they can also undermine the organization's leadership as concerned stakeholders question the decisions being made and back away from participating in an already risky enterprise.

Strategy by Focusing on the Basics

Once the transaction point is isolated as the position where influence becomes a commodity, the strategies that enhance the nature of the transaction point for stakeholders become the objective—with a few twists. A few twists because as we've already seen marginal organizations are not like the standard, run-of-the-mill kind of mainstream organizations. They can't be, if for no other reason than most are obligated to maintain a low profile and, in many cases, remain as invisible as possible. Marginals are different, then, and that difference becomes most clear when examining how strategy is used by marginals, again particularly in contrast to mainstream organizations.

Michael Porter, in his keystone book, *Competitive Strategy* (1980), offers an excellent compilation of the "Dimensions of Competitive Strategy" (127–128). That discussion merits attention here because it's a delineation of what strategy can look like for a mainstream organization and hence it is also a good place to examine strategy for the marginal organization.

The 13 strategic dimensions Porter discusses are well worth the read but for our purposes we only need to cover a few of the dimensions to illustrate how strategy can differ between marginal and mainstream organizations. For example, Porter sees the typical mainstream organization as focusing its strategy around concepts we've already referred to: product specialization, brand identification, push versus pull efforts to promote the brand, channel selection for product distribution, product quality, technological leadership, vertical integration through its distribution system, cost position, service, price policy, the organization's financial and operational leverage, its relationship with a parent organization and its relationship with its home and host governments. Reading through the list with mainstream organizations in mind is like reviewing a performance checklist one might use in the design and/or evaluation of an organization; the list is a commentary on the blending of both theoretical and practical considerations one can use when examining a mainstream organization's strategic posture.

But the list is useful also when speculating about strategy vis-à-vis a marginal organization. For example, if one wanted, it would be possible to "make a case" for each of these strategic dimensions for a given marginal organization but, to our mind, that would be little more than an interesting classroom exercise. The marginal organization's reality makes most of the items that Porter presents nonissues or nice-to-have but otherwise not meaningful. Take product specialization as an example. Among the people I talked to during the research for this book was a "buyer" of illegally made moonshine and he told me about ways some moonshiners have tried to keep pace with customer preferences by flavoring the product. They add fruit in the production process so they can offer different flavors for customers wanting something other than just high proof alcohol. Given Porter's discussion, it would be a stretch to think of someone adding peaches to a jar full of moonshine as representative of Porter's product specialization strategy but, for a marginal, it might be considered a start.

Prostitutes are known to service different "types" of clients. Some target high-end executives as "escorts" and others, well, others. This is another version of specialization but again, it's not quite like Porter's definition of specialization as "the degree to which [the company] focuses its efforts in terms of the width of its line, the target customer segments, and the geographic markets served" (127). Clearly, these "items" are part of the transaction and service chain the prostitute is working with but the prostitute's specialization often is more by default than by strategic plan.

Porter's "brand identification" strategy offers another illustration. Brand identification reflects "the degree to which [the company] seeks brand identification rather than competition based mainly on price or other variables" (127). Here again, something like brand identification for a marginal is either a misnomer or a point for potential risk exposure. In the first instance, many marginal organizations are so far removed from the transaction point that they are invisible to the buyer, and in the second, attempts to link the organization to a particular product can add a traceable path back to the organization and that's also too great a risk. True, looking down a line of food trucks that specialize in Greek, Chinese or another type of food may look like "brand marketing" but to call that "brand identification" as Porter outlines, is a stretch for the marginal organization.

In fact, most marginals cannot use or think about strategy the way mainstream organizations do. The channel used to distribute their product is some combination of what's available given their line of work or, again, what's safe. "Product quality" isn't as much a strategic concern for the marginal as it is a safety or health concern. Again, most marginals want a low profile and few things draw the attention of "demander" stakeholders than unsafe products or people getting sick or injured because of tainted drugs or contaminated food.

So the prudent marginal organization might take this or a similar list of strategic dimensions into consideration, but each has to be managed in ways that are particular to marginal organizations. Porter's last dimension, "relationship to home and host government" (128–129), is another good example: many marginals see their best "relationship to home and host government" as one that is invisible at a minimum and ideally nonexistent. So Porter's and other lists such as his work well in the mainstream but are only useful for marginals after careful reinterpretation and with certain specific caveats.

What Does Strategy Look Like for the Marginal?

It would be a mistake, however, to assume that just because a marginal doesn't fit the profile of a mainstream organization it doesn't have an operational strategy. After all, the owners or managers of these organizations aren't fools. Many not only have pride in their business but also are intelligent and, like our bootleggers, know that sometimes there is value in modifying product and services to appeal to customer needs, interests and preferences. They realize that they have competitors, some of whom are in the same line of work and others who are simply adversaries who desire to prevent the marginal from operating. A good operational strategy will address if not account for the fact that distributed among the organization's social network are stakeholders who don't have the marginal's best interests in mind.

As a result, marginals do develop their own strategies and often around three general themes. First, they develop an operational strategy that reflects both the organization's internal and external needs and opportunities. This might be called "strategy by limitations." Second, marginals can define their strategic approaches in terms of their particular type of organization: an enterprise, community, team/group and individual contributor. This might be referred to as "strategy by organizational category." Finally, marginals often construct a strategy around the nature and type of operation they manage, possibly called a "strategy by business interest."

Marginal Strategies Given Internal and External Operations and Inherent Limitations

Particular strategies associated with a marginal's internal and external operations are a recurring theme in this book and will continue to be so. This is a required discussion point because of the marginal's often illegal activities or general membership in the informal economy. Organizations that don't pay taxes, don't adhere to labor laws and regulations or that engage in illegal operations need to consistently oversee internal and external operations and activities.

As a result many marginal organizations operate as closed systems, restricting interactions or membership only to a few trusted individuals. So, in some instances when many workers are needed and trust is difficult to guarantee, threats, intimidation, coercion or pressure are used to keep performance aligned along desired dimensions. Similar concern for external operations and exposures results in other strategies and tactics. Consider the merchant who avoids paying state sales taxes. In this instance, the merchant may make a "deal" with the consumer that if the consumer pays for a product, say a large piece of equipment with cash, the merchant will not attach sales tax to the bill. Each seems to benefit from this. The merchant gets untraceable cash and the customer can save sometimes hundreds of dollars in taxes that otherwise would be added to the cost of the equipment.

Strategy That Reflects the Type of Organization

Strategies that address a marginal's inherent internal and external exposures are fairly straightforward and apply to any marginal. There is more strategic variability among marginals, however, when one takes the type of organization into consideration. A cash-driven enterprise that uses tax avoidance schemes like the one just described illustrates how enterprise organizations can reframe what they do to create a strategic advantage for the organization. But enterprises can also cut costs by using slave labor or by buying illegal or substandard goods for use in their production processes. They can also be careful in the ways in which they manage the revenues they do receive. Money laundering is both a practice and a strategy used to privately handle the vast sums of money some marginals collect.

Community organizations like terrorists, cults, extremists and paramilitary organizations use a variety of strategies to promote and/or protect their organizations. Threats, intimidation, coercion or pressure are often relied-on strategies and tactics for these organizations as they engage in illegal activities. Marginals fitting the community classification pursue a mission based on values, ideals or unique principles and the strategies they devise often reflect their mission-based needs. These organizations need a cohort of members or followers who believe in the organization's mission; so strategies aimed at recruiting like-minded individuals are particularly important to the community organization. These new recruits and followers must adhere to the organization's mission, values and vision; so many community marginals strategize about things they must do to ensure members think and behave as they should. This often translates into tactics that address the type of training the recruit will receive, the best ways to ensure the needed indoctrination occurs and, if necessary, when and how punishment will be used to ensure that members mature and perform in ways that best represent and support the organization's efforts.

Community organizations also think strategically about their mission and how to promote it given the broader mainstream society. This involves important considerations that seek to protect the organization from what may be perceived as unfair or biased rules and regulations that aim at restricting organizational performance or behavior or, in some cases, prevent it from operating at all. So, if the community organization engages in militaristic activities to establish itself as a dominant organization, its strategic planning should reflect this orientation.

Team/group marginal organizations devise their strategies around two fundamental needs: recruiting those best able to function in the team and ensuring those recruited also have the skills, capabilities and competencies needed for the team/group to achieve its mission. The first is relatively straightforward. The team should comprise people who possess and use good communication, planning, organizing and other functional operational skills. The team members don't have to like each other, they just need to be able to successfully work with each other.

The second need is more dynamic and particular to the purpose for which the team was developed. So a team developed to design a new product or to attack a military outpost will have skills that reflect those objectives while the team launched to raise money to fund organizational projects or activities will have a completely different orientation and, consequently, a different set of competencies.

The drug dealer, an individual contributor, needs strategies and tactics that contribute to efforts aimed at establishing a fitting image for this line of work. The strategies required here should communicate trust, and the transactions should be conducted in a place that's safe for both the dealer and the clients. Think about it. If you were selling drugs what tactics would you use to communicate these two conditions?

Safety and health strategies also are important for the prostitute, the smuggler transporting undocumented aliens into the United States and the food vendor selling homemade sandwiches at the street fair. Each of these are individual contributors who have to go to some lengths to communicate or at least give the impression that they and/or their products/services are safe. Here again, the individual contributor's strategies are tied to key features of this organizational classification. In this instance, credibility and reliability are features the marginal tries to communicate through the tactics used when pushing or pulling a customer to the products available. They are strategies and tactics designed to protect the marginal while advancing its operations and safeguarding the stakeholders involved.

Marginal Strategy as a Function of the Type of Operation, Defined in Terms of Its Business Interests

A final consideration for the marginal seeking to develop strategies to accomplish its mission while protecting its internal and external operations focuses on the organization's functional makeup. Generally speaking, our four types of organizations—the enterprise, community, team/group and individual contributor—design and build operations around three types of operations: manufacturing, service delivery or a harvesting effort.

Make versus buy decisions

When an organization decides it is going to launch a manufacturing-based strategy, it is important to recognize that the organization has based this decision on at least one other important decision: the organization has decided that, for whatever reason, it has more to gain from making the product itself than from buying it from some other producer. This is not an insignificant decision.

Manufacturing, as you will see, requires a considerable amount of money to buy raw material, to get the equipment needed to process raw goods, for packaging and, of course, for the people to do all of the work required. Manufacturing can be very complicated and requires particular skills and competencies for the production processes or just to keep equipment up and running. Finally, all manufacturing involves waste and the organization has to be able to absorb the cost of that waste in both money and time needed to complete the product. This is an important point because, with production, processes for waste equal lost revenue and there's waste associated with the purchase of raw goods, spoilage, the warehousing of goods and materials, the production process and, of course, the ever-present potential for theft.

If a marginal has decided to take on the job of manufacturing its own products, it is prudent for the analysts to wonder or ask why that decision was made. For example, some products are fairly easy to make. Growing, drying and packing marijuana has few production risks (you need water, sun, etc.) so it's a fairly easy and inexpensive production process. There's more involved in making illegal moonshine, but with the right mechanical skills, building a distillery is a fairly straightforward process.

Other processes are more complicated and some require very special skills and competencies. So, apart from the process itself, some marginals go into manufacturing as a way to maintain a low profile within the product line they are operating. They may believe that having fewer "outsiders" involved in the production process reduces the risk of exposures along the value stream.

Some go into manufacturing in order to control the entire value stream associated with a product or service. The drug cartel that grows, processes, distributes and sells its product is a vertical monopoly. They own the process from start to finish and so, apart from paying the people who work for the organization, it is not necessary to share profits with other organizations or stakeholders.

Still others, particularly if they are skilled in the manufacturing process, go into it to make the product and then send it to others to package, distribute or sell the final goods. This model keeps the organization as far as possible from the exposed transportation and transaction points, so it allows for a source of income but trades off total possible revenues for overall reduced risk.

So a manufacturing strategy begins with the decision to manufacture or not, to make or buy the product. But deciding on a strategy is not the same as the plan needed to implement the strategy, the plan that turns an idea into a tangible product or service. If the organization decides it is going to manufacture its product, then the planning needed to turn a manufacturing strategy into finished products begins by determining the type of manufacturing process that is best given the organization's needs and the product to be made.

Manufacturing can be approached in four different ways: as a project, job shop, batch flow or continuous flow format. Projects cover activities with a designed end result, like the pornographer's movie. Project planning focuses on developing teams with particular skills and competencies related to the project at hand. Quality is often dependent on the skills and competencies available, so it is important that the project team's membership is closely aligned with the project's objective. Project teams don't need people who are friends, they need people who can do the job.

A job shop is a manufacturing center that concentrates on having the skills needed to handle a variety of different projects. The skills related are usually similar across jobs especially at the core competency level. Counterfeit operations that make different types of illegal products (e.g., passport, currency for different countries or illegal identification cards) or car garages that can service different types of vehicles and make a variety of repairs and modifications are some examples. A job shop does not necessarily do only one type of work or produce a single type of product, but rather has the capacity to handle the requests of various customers. Planning for a job shop has to take these factors into consideration as well as the fact that some products can have associated time-sensitive features (i.e., they are needed immediately or for special events) and often must meet special design requirements. Job shops are information dependent; they need the right information at the right time regarding the product's due dates, specifications and any special features or characteristics associated with the final product.

Batch flow operations offer a steady production process around a central product type. Meth labs or "sandwich labs" that produce bulk supplies of ready-to-use drugs or ready-to-eat sandwiches are examples. In these production centers, a product moves from area to area in production batches. Raw material may move from a receiving room to a processing room, then to an assembly area and finally to a packing area for distribution.

Continuous flow processes are the last type of manufacturing to be discussed. Marginal organizations that operate through a street vendor or from a sandwich truck are examples of continuous flow processes. The most significant feature of this production process is how the product flows through the production process to the consumer. There can be a real level of immediacy associated with a marginal's use of a continuous flow process. After all, the customer may be standing in front of the food wagon simply waiting for the order to be completed. This means that planning for most continuous flow processes is very dependent on ensuring the right materials are available for production on time and as needed.

Preparation and planning for the production processes described begins with matching the right production process for the task or products the marginal wants to produce and/or sell. Which process to choose can be affected by several factors. For example, the number of people needed, the nature of the equipment needed, the type of flow given the product and equipment to be used, the complexities and competencies required to operate the needed equipment, the cost and ease with which the equipment is obtained and space and operational requirements, including the need for special resources such as water, heat and fuel.

There also are a number of ancillary matters to consider. Some goods or materials used may be perishable or expensive to acquire, so the cost of loss has to be factored into any decision while choosing the production process. Inventory processes also need to be considered. Where will the products be stored before and after production? Are there special storage necessities such as temperature control or security that need to be considered? Remember, too, that some marginals handle more than just dry goods like marijuana, cocaine or smuggled cigarettes. Some marginals deal with people, illegal aliens, kidnapped people for a slave trade or captives used to produce the organization's products or to smuggle them across borders. In these instances, these humans (and sometimes animals) are part of the inventory that needs to be handled, cared for or just kept alive.

Importantly, then, addressing logistical matters such as these can increase the organization's visibility and profile, so care must be taken to ensure the safety and security of materials, staff and the work site itself. These last concerns can be especially important if the organization has to hire subcontractors or turn part of the production cycle over to others or other organizations. Finally, everything about distribution increases the marginal's profile or exposure.

Service, but Not Necessarily with a Smile

Service delivery is a second strategy marginals often rely on to achieve their mission. Service delivery can range from providing accommodations through hotels or safe houses, food services, education, health (illegal abortion clinics) to retail trade, financial services (underwriting costs for an illegal operation), recreation (prostitution), distribution, computer or software services (e.g., code breaking, spamming, malware and hacking).

A service-based strategy can spawn a number of different issues for the marginal. For example, should the service be delivered on the spot like drug sales, be tied to an extended production process like prostitution or, in some instances, gambling? Should the service offer a level of anonymity like online pornography where the consumer cannot touch the service?

Some services require significant process considerations. Sex trafficking and drug sales that remove the service from the production center to a separate transaction point require attention to processes at both points. Other service-delivery strategies can be built around a service factory model where the service is customized to meet a customer's needs, wants and desires. Prostitution, repair facilities that service the vehicles for other marginals and trucking and distribution centers are examples of a service factory model.

Some marginals engage in mass service strategies like money laundering, drug delivery and distribution, online pornography or the operation of terrorist training centers. These centers provide other marginals the benefits of the service so they don't have to invest in equipment, learn technical processes or get close to the actual transaction point. The strategy ensures that needed competencies are in place without the customer having to build or develop them. Relying on organizations that provide these services can add a nominal amount to the organization's overhead but the price may be a value given that those offering mass service strategies are assuming the costs and risks associated with the operation. As importantly, in special instances, services can be tailored to meet special needs or can incorporate highly professional, state-of-the-art features the stakeholder might not be able to otherwise afford or secure. The hired hit man, escort service, illegal abortion clinics and medical services are examples.

To Harvest Is to Eat

Harvesting is a particularly unique production process and one that is often layered with skills and competencies not usually associated with the other processes discussed. Harvesting ranges from simple and mundane scrounging, scavenging or rummaging efforts at the low end of the harvesting spectrum to more sophisticated foraging or hunting efforts at the spectrum's other end. The pickpocket, the "hit-and-run" thief, the racketeer and the prostitute are seekers looking for the right target, mark or client to "harvest." Sometimes the scavenging or foraging tactic used is defined by the skills or resources possessed and at other times by the opportunity. Periodically, it's even possible to overlap different tactics as when the prostitute gets paid for services rendered and then picks the client's pocket on departure.

Like the other production processes, harvesting aims at contributing to the organization's health and well-being. At the low end, harvesting is little more than scrounging, but higher up the chain the harvester can be a trained professional who operates on the street and face-to-face with the resource or stakeholder involved. It's a front door level risk. Whatever the circumstance, the marginal involved has one significant consideration in the equation that defines the harvesting process: what resources (time, money, personal risk) are needed to collect the payoff needed to justify the risk, continue operations or, in some instances, simply survive?

Concluding Comments Regarding the Emergence of Marginals in a Mainstream Society

Looking back over the two dominant themes discussed in this chapter, one may begin to understand that unlike a mainstream organization, a marginal often doesn't operate from a standing storefront, a fixed location, promoted by marketing and sales plans that foster the development and management of an organizational brand. Rather, marginals are often fluid entities fashioned around equally dynamic caricatures of influence and strategy. Mainstream organizations embed influence and strategy into the very fabric of their organizations. Marginals can't think of and work with influence or strategy as mainstream organizations do. Marginals certainly are organizations in both the traditional sense and in terms of the model used in this book, which characterizes them as enterprises, communities, team/groups or individual contribution by nature. But what marginals must do is construct and use influence and strategy in ways that make them part of the actual transaction between the marginal's agent and the stakeholders involved.

By necessity, marginal organizations target a specific customer. Marginals are always open to receiving new stakeholders but they don't necessarily canvas for them or, once secured, conduct elaborate needs assessments or focus groups to cement a match between the marginal's products and services and the stakeholder. Rather, it's a "Here's what we have. Do you want it?"

Next, marginals know they typically only have one version of a product, and it's usually not that elaborate, and sometimes only a brief opportunity to deliver the product or service. As a result, product delivery is a key component of a marginal's operation. There may or may not be a lot of variability among different types of marijuana but the customer does know whether it is available or not. Distribution is important for all organizations, mainstream or marginal, but it's critical for the marginal. For example, if you want something for your headache, you can go to a drugstore, a grocery store or sometimes even to a convenience store to find what you need. Mainstream sources for mainstream products are virtually everywhere. Marginals don't have that advantage. Often, what you want from a marginal can be purchased only at designated places. That's why distribution is critically important for marginals.

Promotionals, like promotional pricing, offering specials or discounts to draw customers are frequently used in the mainstream but they're not an option for the marginal; they're a risk. Marginals have to be careful; they don't want to draw attention to themselves by having mainstreamers see them as adversaries or a potential threat in the same business. Mainstream organizations like restaurants and lawn care companies don't relish competition in the first place and certainly not from marginals. Anything that draws attention to the marginal is usually avoided.

Marginals must manage information while managing its exposure. Exposure, even for a very visible organization like the local street food wagon, isn't something to be desired. With visibility comes the likelihood that someone who doesn't like you or what you stand for will see you and take action against you. It's a theme touched on in this chapter and it's the major focus of the next.

CHAPTER 4

The Emergence of Marginals in the Active Context of Mainstream Society

Although the focus of this book is on marginal organizations in the United States, from an analyst's point of view the material can be applied to any marginal organization anywhere in the world. That's important because outside the United States marginal organizations can be the major source of employment for many citizens in regions within Africa, Asia and Latin America, among others. Moreover, as a major source of employment, marginals outside the United States are often allowed to flourish; they are a needed component for economies that cannot support formal, mainstream organizations.

Matters affecting marginals in the United States can be quite different from those elsewhere. Marginals in the United States have a number of different, sometimes even natural adversaries. Some of these are regulatory agencies, some are linked to law enforcement and still others are the numerous mainstream organizations that may offer services and products similar to those offered by marginals, particularly when mainstream organizations view marginals as competitors or a threat to their organization or way of life.

Of most interest to us in the chapter are those moments when marginals meet mainstream organizations and, in particular, their adversaries. To address this situation, this chapter is divided into two parts. In the first part, operational fundamentals that can contribute to marginals' and mainstream organizations' meeting and coming face-to-face with each other are outlined. This is an important discussion because it reveals how vulnerable a marginal can be as it tries to achieve its mission. The chapter introduces the reader to two important features of a marginal: its operational processes and the very important value stream that defines the significant course the organization follows as it engages in activities to achieve its mission. The treatment here of a marginal's processes and value stream differs from most in that it illustrates how even the most insular, secretive marginal organization must emerge within the mainstream society it may try so hard to avoid and when it does surface, it becomes most vulnerable to threats and attacks.

The first section ends with a discussion of how processes and operations define performance expectations and patterns for the marginal organization. This section illustrates the challenges a marginal faces that stem from its fundamental structural makeup, features of its processes, procedures and overall value stream. So even before a marginal organization is positioned to perform vis-à-vis other organizations or, simply, as part of a wider society's environment, it must deal with and overcome an inherent array of threats and vulnerabilities.

The significance of an organization's threats and vulnerabilities is magnified when the organization begins operation that brings it into contact with mainstream stakeholders. Material in the chapter's second section illustrates how contact between the marginal organization and mainstream stakeholders can trigger a crisis. This analysis offers an opportunity to explore the nature and roots of dissonance and conflict that may emerge for the marginal. It's an important section because the stress, conflict and general discord the marginal experiences often pose significant threats to the organization's operation and well-being. These threats compromise the organization's operations and may result in significant damage to the point of its complete failure.

Part I: When the Pursuit of a Mission Triggers Clashes, Quarrels and Conflicts: The Marginal in Contact with the Mainstream

Organizations exist to perform and they perform in a universe defined by other organizations. To negotiate this universe, the organization relies on routines, processes and procedures that define and shape its operations and interactions; they are among the tools used to achieve the organization's mission. Sometimes they emerge as a natural part of the organizational experience, but most often they are constructed, designed and developed by the organization's staff to facilitate internal and external operations. Every organization constructs its own. They are part of an organization's operational profile and they define ways the organization will interact with stakeholders throughout its network, ways it will navigate routine events and how it will respond to the crises and emergencies it experiences.

Consider this example of an attempt by organization "a" to sell products in an area where organization "b" already operates. Now, unless "a" goes directly to "b" and announces its intentions to sell product in "b's" territory, the two organizations may never intentionally come into direct contact with each other, even though their activities and behaviors affect each other. For example, "a" may only interact with members of "b's" social network, in this case, "b's" customers and "b" may not know anything that is going on until the customer leaves and buys "a's" products. This is a frequent scenario and one of particular interest when thinking about the role and management of marginal organizations as they operate in society.

For example, suppose a marginal, a drug dealer, wants to sell product to kids who attend a school nearby. The interesting point about this situation is that while the marginal's target is "kids in a school," the organizations the marginal is about to engage are not limited to the school and its staff. Rather, the drug dealer may potentially encounter the local police, a neighborhood watch, citizens from the local town and so on. Each organization involved has missions, different organizational profiles, different ways of managing routine events and its own ways of responding to extreme, non-routine events. In other words, interaction between and among organizations is seldom neat, clean or easily summarized. In fact, the interaction may be defined by so many ancillary events and relationships that actual contact between the marginal and its primary target never really occurs and yet, when the competing organizations do meet they affect each other and the networks of which they are part. The focus of this section concentrates on ways a marginal's operational formats are affected by and shape the products, outcomes and impact of those interactions.

Mission versus Mission

Tensions between organizations often begin when the actions or the paths they choose to achieve their missions collide. Consider the potential for conflict between a mainstream business enterprise and a police department. They may have a common adversary, say a criminal organization, so one would expect the two should operate as "partners" but in many instances, they don't. In fact, they may become trapped in a contentious rather than a cooperative relationship. This can happen in different ways. For example, both the business and police organizations engage in activities they believe are suitable for managing the emergence of criminal acts or events. The police may want to use surveillance techniques, perhaps have officers patrol specific areas or streets and sometimes even use aggressive techniques such as "stop and frisk" programs.

Stress can emerge when the activities each organization promotes are challenged by the other organization, often even before a criminal enters the picture. The local business may see the law enforcement organization's programs or activities as intrusive, as potentially scaring good customers away by creating an image that the area is not safe or may simply feel the police actions are "over the top" and abusive, even restricting the business's freedom to operate as it wants.

When a collision like this occurs, the emerging conflict amplifies the fact that despite a common interest, two organizations that should be cooperating can find themselves at odds. Each believes in a common goal but they cannot agree on a means for achieving the goal: one organization succeeds by being creative, innovative and open to anything that can bring customers into its operations while the other may practice or promote more restrictive, conservative strategies while all the while the true adversary, the criminal organization waits in the shadows.

Now consider the relationship between two true adversaries. Terrorist organizations or gangs, for example, often pursue nonmonetary missions and strategies. We classified these as "community" organizations with missions that are often grounded in values, ideals or principles. Organizations charged with dealing with these marginals must, at a minimum, develop strategies and plans that reflect their unique orientations to their targets. However, it's also important to remember that attempts to contain or manage any organization can involve and be mediated by a mix of different stakeholders (e.g., social workers, policy makers, politicians, the military or academicians, to name a few) with their own particular and possibly different missions and each believing his/her "path to success" is the best. The potential for disaster is evident.

For example, if you have seen the movie *Zero Dark 30*, you saw, depending on your perspective (1) an account of the capture and assassination of terrorist leader Bin Laden or (2) a movie documenting the confusion, breakdowns, conflicts and challenges to decision making and action among different stakeholder groups: from various government agencies such as the CIA, to the needs and interests of politicians or the behavior and functioning of a military unit. In other words, in addition to the obvious pursuit of a common mission, the movie accounts for ways the mission and processes of partnering stakeholder groups can clash, sometimes resulting in the "partners" losing sight of the mission while they fight with each other as they try to protect their own ideas, plans, strategies and tactics. And this among organizations that are "partners"! In the end, what creates potential conflict between partners sharing the same mission but lost in the particulars regarding how best to achieve that mission is that the target of their mission, the opposing organization, continues to function and may even avoid their efforts.

A Successful Mission Is One That Targets the Right Reality

From our point of view, one that looks at a leader like Bin Laden as the head of an organization, efforts to destroy Bin Laden are only part of what it would take to weaken or destroy an organization like al-Qaeda. The organization's mission still exists and, as importantly, the various operational processes and procedures that help the organization function as an organization also exist—with or without its leadership. These processes, procedures, practices combine with the organization's value stream to define a series of steps that enables the organization to function and, as importantly, prepare it to interact with other organizations. Now, standard organizational theory maintains that if these processes, procedures and value streams are well defined and functioning, the organization stands a good chance of being prepared for its interaction with other organizations. There's at least one significant caveat to this assumption, however: since the other organization(s) possess their own processes, procedures, value streams and the like, there must be some level of agreement or sync between the interacting organizations for an effective transaction to take place. At least, that's what contemporary organizational theory would lead one to conclude. However, marginal organizations don't function like mainstream organizations and this can be an advantage for them in some instances.

Consider the criminal organization foraging for customers or, having found its target, about to prey on it. The marginal in this instance wants its processes, procedures and value streams in sync and operating but not necessarily those of its target. In fact, a "surprise attack" is little more than the predator organization seeking an advantage by attacking its opponent at a time when the opponent's cycle is out of sync with it and is disrupted by the surprise attack, particularly if the attack coincides with a weak or vulnerable point in the target organization's process chain at that moment.

This makes sense when you consider the makeup of the processes, procedures and value streams organizations use to manage their efforts. For example, all organizations have vulnerabilities and frequently the most significant vulnerabilities occur only in an organization's value stream—particularly if it is a long, protracted stream. In these instances, the greater the complexity, the greater the likelihood the value stream can be disrupted, particularly if the organization attacking it happens to hit it at one of its vulnerable points. In organizations with significant vulnerabilities, the probability or chance of failure or loss becomes a consequence of a match between a vulnerability and a targeted attack.

Most organizations plan for routine operations and events. In fact, their operational procedures, processes and practices are often defined in terms of the routine event; it's their baseline performance level. Trouble ensues when the planning for the routine is flawed and/or the organization doesn't have a grand plan or transferable skills and competencies to manage nonroutine events, and particularly when those nonroutine events are spawned by adversarial stakeholders with their own missions and plans in place.

Process Operations, Organizational Complexity and Subsequent Strengths or Vulnerabilities

Organizations seek to manage risk by containing it, avoiding risky situations, reducing it when it occurs and sometimes transferring it to others. A vision and a mission are one means for both giving the organization direction and, in turn, reducing some risk. However, pursuing a vision or mission without the benefits of a sound structure can create other risk exposures. As a result, organizations also structure their operations around six process points, each of which can translate into organizational strengths or, if poorly prepared and managed, opportunities for weakness, vulnerability, exposure and subsequent stress or dissonance.

These operational areas cover the organization's physical features related to the materials and equipment used, operational processes, people and, of course, exposures associated with the organization's culture and management. Each of these will be treated in turn, paying particular attention to how breakdowns in any of them can expose the organization to unwanted risks or vulnerabilities. Before beginning this discussion, however, some points must be made regarding strengths and vulnerabilities associated with the organization's overall value stream—the activities, processes and actions that can contribute to an organization's overall well-being and the accomplishment of its mission.

The value stream is multidimensional. It stretches from the organization's uppermost leadership levels throughout the organization; it encompasses entry points where ideas, people, even the raw materials used in the production process enter the organization on their way to becoming ways of thinking, plans or products and services. The value stream is the organization in action. The stream's scope and scale are both a strength and potential liability for the organization. Its strength comes from the potential to push and pull information throughout the organization.

The stream is populated with internal and external stakeholders, contact points for stakeholders to engage in activities associated with the organization's mission to get and/or exchange information or to measure progress and performance, particularly against established goals or benchmarks. However, with so many contact points the stream is also subject to a number of potential exposures. For example, the length of the stream is an important consideration because each process point that marks the stream is a potential failure point. The more steps or links in the stream, the more people involved, the greater the probability for a potential vulnerability. In addition, many links in the process or operational chain means there's a greater complexity from point A to point B. Extra complexity may be associated with greater distance as well as more process time from the conception of a product or service to its delivery, again adding opportunity for error. Finally, a long value stream can also mean there are points where special requirements or expectations are built into the process. Special requirements can be associated with the product or service being developed such as permits and permissions from government offices/officials. Each, in turn, can become another opportunity for delay or system breakdowns. Finally, a long stream also means there may be the need for holdover warehousing or storage points as well as the need for different transfer points, sometimes even national borders to negotiate—a very special consideration. To understand how a stream may be susceptible to failure, five of the most prominent stream features are highlighted below. A review of these reveals that exposures for an effective organization often surface when critical stream performance centers fail to perform as expected.

Process Centers

Process exposures are directly related to the number of links in the value stream or operational processes. Simply stated, processes are "the way things are done" in the organization's value stream. Processes are especially interesting because they create bridges that link concepts like quality, service, secrecy and security to the manufacturing and service activities associated with the organization's mission. These bridges can be especially important to an organization and a critical vulnerability if they are disrupted or missing. Accidents are an example. An accident can impact a given process but because processes often overlap other processes, what could be a containable exposure can broaden and spread throughout the organization or even to stakeholders in its social network.

People Centers

The number of people involved in an organization can be a real opportunity for exposure. Competencies (poor or missing), disgruntled employees, loss of key personnel or criminal activity are representative of people-related failure points in organizations and their operational processes. The role of personnel can become especially troublesome when subcontractors are involved because they are not formal members of the organization and as a result are not usually invested in the organization's mission the way a regular member can be. Moreover, use of contractors creates end points where goods and services are to be transferred or passed off to others, the contractors, for handling. If they are not prepared, are not trustworthy or have performance standards that don't match the organization's, then troubles might ensue. People are where the organization's processes and value stream translate into action, and this makes people the critical elements throughout the organization's value stream.

Materials/Equipment Centers

Materials and equipment are an organization's physical enablers. They are the means for turning raw material into finished products, so can be critical to the organization's efforts to achieve its mission. Materials and equipment can also introduce a variety of exposures to the marginal organization and its network, however. Raw materials may require special processing and in some instances the material may be inherently harmful to those who work with them, the environment or both. Moreover, some materials require that those working with them have particular competencies that are hard to develop.

Sometimes the materials used by the marginal require special standards or levels of quality without which the marginal's risk exposure or vulnerability can increase dramatically. Counterfeiting money from plates requires that these materials and the paper used be flawless, particularly with new detection methods. As a result, some thieves resort to using high speed, high quality photocopiers as an alternative.

It's also possible for the materials used by the marginal to be dangerous. Materials such as acids or explosives require special handling and skills and can be difficult to acquire because they are regulated by government agencies, so even obtaining these materials can add a level of exposure for the marginal. Other times, if materials are contaminated or damaged they may not function as designed.

Finally, old technologies, inadequate equipment or dangers associated with the use of equipment can create special problems for the marginal. If a marginal's employee is injured in the process of doing something illegal, the marginal may not be able to find a health care facility to use that won't bring undesirable exposure. There are few good options in these situations—for the organization or the employee.

Organization Culture Center

One important but often overlooked source for risk, threats or vulnerabilities to emerge in the marginal is that associated with the organization's culture. An organization's culture sets the tone for virtually everything the organization does internally as well as its interactions with other stakeholders. Trust levels, paranoia or even xenophobia can be traced back to an organization's culture. Admittedly, for most marginals some level of reserve is prudent because of the nature of the organization's mission and operations, but any walls or barriers the organization puts up affect anyone interested in interacting with the organization: friend or foe.

Some organizational cultures materialize in hostile environments, which in turn can create internal threats and, perhaps worse, internal enemies. All organizations have a cultural component, and culture is an important mechanism for increasing the likelihood that the organization will display a consistent front while maintaining defined standards of performance for those inside the organization. However, while a culture defined by rules, punishment and inflexibility can effectively shape behavior, it risks alienating those it needs most—those who produce the organization's products and services, those who make up the organization.

An austere culture, dominated by rules and procedures that extend beyond what's necessary to get the job done, may be needed for the marginal trying to protect itself, but this culture can also restrict or limit an employee's innovation, creativity and capacity to invent solutions for new or emerging problems. These traits are often very valuable to the organization that regularly needs to adapt or deal with changing situations or challenges. Marginals sometimes have to walk a thin line defined on one side by efforts aimed at protecting the organization and, on the other, by efforts that seek to grow the organization, promote its products and services or help it dodge tricky or dangerous situations. The risk an organization takes when building impregnable cultural walls it needs to protect itself is that there's also the possibility that it is also building a resistance to change or an inability to manage disparities, diversities or differences that may be useful in certain problem-solving situations. Perhaps worse, the leadership that's building this abrasive culture under the guise of "what's best for the organization" may simultaneously bury the organization in useless bureaucracy, nepotism, bias, discrimination and atrocity. Cultural hypocrisy is an unstable poison.

Management Centers

The last element common to all organizations that can work for it as a means of reducing risk and vulnerability or against it by increasing the same is the organization's management. All organizations have a management component, and two factors challenge the overall effectiveness of management: erratic or unpredictable style and poor competency. Both are unique because they transcend every aspect of an organization's management and, in turn, the organization itself. For example, a poor or inadequate vision and mission promoted by unskilled or otherwise ill-prepared management teams undermines organizational reliability. Even management deficiencies in the definition, communication and management of such illusive concepts as values, attitudes, opinions and beliefs can be traced back to questions of reliability and competence.

The leadership/management problem for marginals can be aggravated by the fact that those who lead or manage these organizations often do so from a power position; the rule is, whoever is the strongest rules. Working through this mentality can be fraught with danger and in the end a pointless effort. After all, Bin Laden wasn't "elected" to lead al-Qaeda.

Finally, when power and authority are centralized in one or a few people, losing them can create massive problems for the organization. These problems erupt for two primary reasons: First, self-preservation is a driving theme behind a marginal's behavior, so even when part of a collective, marginals assess situations and events in terms of their needs, their well-being. "Loyalty among thieves" may exist on the street but even here there are limits. Second, if those at the top of a marginal's network are lost or incapable of acting, those left in the network don't wait for some others to assume a leadership role. Power may shift to whoever is strongest but even in a world where "the strongest rules" it's obvious there are no guarantees. For example, how many marginals have the vision or interest to create the skills to develop or the capacity to manage an organizational succession plan? Very few. So, if it's a family-owned business, give it to one of the kids. Of course, the assumption is that the kid wants the job and, more importantly, has strong leadership and management skills to run the operation. If there is no convenient solution like those in closely held organizations, then the organization's future, at least from a management point of view, is uncertain.

Definition of the Value Stream, Its Means for Introducing the Marginal to the Mainstream and Subsequent Vulnerability

An organization's supply chain structure creates opportunities for the organization to build and use performance routines. Briefly, an organization's supply chain represents the string of activities, from the ideas or raw materials that enter the organization, to the production of its products and/or the rendering of its services. Feeding the supply chain can bring the organization into contact with stakeholders on the outside, but its overall focus is internal; get the stuff needed to get the job done. In contrast, the value stream encompasses all operational processes and is the mechanism that formally brings the organization into contact with the mainstream. There are internally and externally oriented streams. Our treatment emphasizes the relationship between them and the stakeholders in their networks.

Both internally and externally oriented streams must link to the organization's vision and mission. This must occur in order to achieve both the organization's *and* the stakeholders' needs. They are central in deciding how the organization will get the materials it needs, how it will turn raw material into products and services that meet stakeholder needs and how anything (and ideally) or everything that is done adds value to the organization. The steps in the streams integrate the organization's production and process operations discussed above. So people, material, equipment and operational processes meld into the steps outlined in figure 4.1.

Several features make the value stream distinctive. For one, it's always defined in terms of the overall stakeholder network. This, then, includes the organization, those involved in the production/development effort and the recipients at the stream's end. What and who's not pictured are also important. For example, once the products or services are delivered, all those associated with stakeholders receiving the products and services make up that network. There are also networks associated with any subcontractors used as well as those who "emerge" in response to the product or service being delivered. Regulators, border guards, medical staff, media and law enforcement who are linked to a drug stream often emerge further down the value stream. Finally, once the delivery is made, the organizations or stakeholders involved expect something in return. An enterprise may expect money,

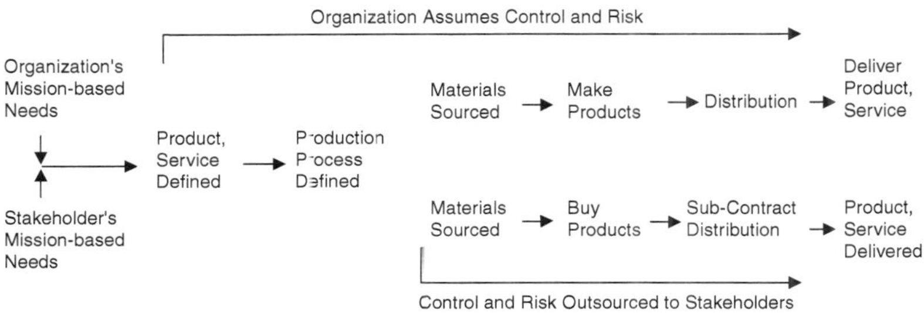

Figure 4.1 A Value Stream for an Enterprise.

a community organization new members, a terrorist organization media coverage or fear, an individual contributor money or new contracts and a team the answers to problems researched or the achievement of a goal.

Figure 4.1 also illustrates how the organization can seek to maintain all value from the stream (and subsequent risk) or can share the stream's value with subcontractors who, in this example, handle the production, distribution and delivery or sale of the product/service. This also is a way to see how other organizations, such as stakeholders, are integrated into the value stream. If a terrorist organization needs to have someone assassinated, it may subcontract the work to a professional assassin just as an enterprise might subcontract manufacturing of a product to an organization with a manufacturing facility. Many organizations and people regularly "subcontract" the education of their membership to training centers, schools, colleges and universities to provide needed training.

The value stream is also a useful way to see how key operational processes and practices like those aimed at directing or controlling the network, information and knowledge management or evaluation management can merge into design, development and distribution processes. These practices were discussed in chapter 2 and now it's possible to see how virtually all of the key operational practices surface at various times throughout the value stream and, moreover, why it's important that organizations are proficient in *all* of the practices discussed in that chapter.

The stream's end varies from organization to organization. An enterprise could define the delivery of goods and services as a sale while a community organization could define a stream's end as the delivery of a message, goodwill or a bomb depending on the organization and its mission. If the value stream functions well, then the organization will be closer to achieving its vision and mission. If not, threats and vulnerabilities can ensue.

Value Stream Threats and Vulnerabilities

Marginal organizations are always under pressure from natural competitors, and an array of stakeholders in the marginal's network can be traced back to the mainstream. Some from the mainstream are competitors, some are regulators or in law enforcement and others are those special interests opposed to the existence or operation of the marginal. These are sources of external pressure for the marginal.

Beyond the pressures exerted on the marginals by external members of its stakeholder network, faults emerging from a poorly designed, poorly managed, incomplete or an inadequate value stream create pressures from within the marginal organization. In addition, disgruntled members, partners and subcontractors, cliques and power struggles are among the internal pressures stemming from internal stakeholders.

Systemically, the value stream, the organization's strategic practices and the key process components discussed are also sources from which threats and vulnerabilities can emerge. The value stream is central to an organization. So any threats or vulnerabilities creeping in or emerging in conjunction with the stream can result in significant loss to the organization. Cost, loss of stakeholders and attacks are among the range of threats to an organization that has lost the capacity to function properly. Finally, as if to compound matters, there are also opportunities for adversity to materialize at the very top of the organization, with its management.

Tafoya (2013a) has touched on seven areas where threats and vulnerabilities can emerge given management negligence or error. The first of these is obvious: the mismanagement of negative events. Marginals, as we discussed, are plagued by the potential for negative events; it's almost inherent in the nature of organizations that operate outside the law to be a suspect and, generally speaking, under regular surveillance. Because of the thin line between operational freedom and attack or allegations, a marginal's management must be prepared and able to handle or transfer the risk associated with negative events as soon as the risk is evident.

Tafoya's (2013a) "crisis spectrum" is a useful guide when planning a response to different negative events. The crisis spectrum illustrates the level of risk associated with a negative event and a "potential damage rating." The spectrum has four levels. *Level I—A predicament* represents less of a problem and more of an incident. Those in the organization might describe it as a jam, a pickle or a simple mishap. Still it can be disconcerting. At a minimum, a Level I crisis is a mess that may cause confusion, chaos and general disorder or disarray within the organization and certainly among those directly affected by the crisis. The scope of a Level I crisis is typically within the capacity of the organization to address. Damage may occur but will likely be local and containable.

A Level II crisis presents a dilemma for the organization and its membership. A Level II crisis can create an impasse, problem, quandary for those involved and may be described as a misfortune, adversity or hardship for those affected and sometimes for the organization as a whole. Damage is possible from a Level II crisis, so the crisis is addressed within the organization in conjunction with some external assistance.

At Level III, the organization is facing a disaster. For some, the crisis is a tragedy, a cataclysm. This level of crisis can be a real blow for the organization and its membership. Danger, adversity and wreckage are labels often associated with a Level III crisis. Moreover, the crisis is sufficiently severe so that external assistance will be needed and, in all likelihood, it will take a lead role in managing the crisis. Damage and loss are probable and possibly extensive in a Level III crisis.

A Level IV crisis is a true catastrophe. Tafoya uses a ten-point scale to rate each level and a Level IV receives the highest "Potential Damage Rating" of 9–10: devastation and destruction are outcomes associated with a Level IV crisis using his scale. For those involved, the crisis presents a calamity, ruin, an upheaval or a tragedy. Because of the crisis' scope and scale, external assistance is required and, subsequently, it leads the crisis management effort. Moreover, since damage and loss are inevitable and likely to be extensive, immediate action is required to manage the effects and recovery. Post-crisis plans typically take into account the fact that the organization will be a very different place in the future.

As a tool, the Crisis Spectrum© is a valuable asset for those involved in managing a crisis because it offers a guide so that all involved in the crisis event management have a common basis for describing the problem at hand and possible steps to manage the problem facing the organization. This is important because the types of events that may threaten a marginal organization can be very different from those that threaten a mainstream organization.

For example, most mainstream organizations aren't exposed to prejudice, discrimination, profiling, targeting, tracking, harassment or aggression on the same scale as marginals. Moreover, if they do experience these types of events, they can appeal for help from local authorities. Marginals often can't appeal to authorities for help since that would mean the marginal would have to disclose its activities or the entire organization. That said, unless the marginal "buys" assistance, for example, in the form of "protection," the only real resources for the marginal to use in managing negative events or risk are those it possesses and in particular the marginal's leadership/management.

Indifference to the risk is a second source from which threats or vulnerabilities can arise. Failure to recognize the role of risk for the organization is a significant mistake. What's more, the potential for risk exposure only increases if the organization has an extended value stream, a stream that subcontracts activities to those outside the organization or a stream that borders or sometimes enters the mainstream. Each of these conditions merits special attention, but in the end, there may be no small or insignificant risks for the marginal organization since any risk may result in exposure.

An extended value stream contributes to another possible area for risk to emerge: a loss of focus, attention or synergy. Members of a marginal organization must be fully engaged in the organization's operations in order to ensure focus is maintained and that activities, products and service are in alignment throughout the organization. This certainly is part of every member's job or position, but because marginal organizations are so often under the scrutiny of competitors, regulators, special interest groups or the like, it is incumbent upon each member of the organization to look beyond personal responsibilities to the organization as a whole. After all, if the organization fails, their job, and sometimes even their freedom, is at risk.

Using and keeping key operational practices up-to-date is one way to maintain and maximize alignment where necessary. Direction/control, information and knowledge management and evaluation practices are among the most important to have in place when defining and managing an organization's focus. And also, every member of the organization has a responsibility to keep up his or her own skills and competencies.

Another threat to an organization's alignment is what Tafoya (2013b) calls mission drift. Mission drift is the failure to manage and keep the organization's mission updated. It seems like this should be a non-issue for most organizations, particularly if they define their mission as "to make money" but few missions or mission statements are that simple. For example, even if an organization states that its mission is simply "to make money" that doesn't necessarily mean it will make enough money to be profitable. Or is a mission statement such as "to profit through the sale of safe, high quality drugs" more appropriate? Management must keep in mind that while a simplistic mission may be easy to remember, that doesn't mean it will accurately represent the organization's vision to which the mission is directly linked. Recall, too, that an organization's mission statement is the primary link to its goals and objectives and these must be clearly defined and, ideally, measurable as well.

Carelessness or inattention to detail or overall operations can result in pure madness, particularly for an organization laden with threats, risk and vulnerabilities. One way to think about an organization is as an island inhabited by dangerous animals and vipers and surrounded by a sea filled with sharks and other hidden dangers. Everyone on that island would probably agree that carelessness or inattention would be a threat to one's safety or life, and yet, given the marginal's role and place in society, that metaphor isn't too extreme a description of what existence is like for the marginal vis-à-vis the mainstream. Marginals cannot afford mistakes, particularly mistakes that lead to exposure.

Another valuable use for the strategic practices described earlier is as a tool to monitor the market or environment given the organization's vision, mission and capacity to perform. In this instance, use of strategic practices helps avoid the threat of market displacement, a phenomenon that results in the marginal being out of phase or alignment with the market in which it operates. Clearly, this, like the other threats, can put an organization in jeopardy. A community-type organization, like a terrorist organization or cult, may misread the changing sentiments of the populations they target for funds, membership or support. A criticism of al-Qaeda, for example, is that its violent tactics drive people away, making it, rather than a Western nation, the local population's perceived enemy.

Religions are notorious for being displaced by a changing marketplace. Shifts in society can take a population in directions the religions don't understand or recognize and this mistake can lead to painful consequences. Sometimes, too, the marketplace no longer needs the products or services offered by the marginal. The legalization of marijuana in some states and countries eliminates the need of users to buy from criminal organizations, thus adding extra pressure on marginals engaged in this type of activity ("Drug legalization," 2013, p. 31).

Finally, internal or external conflict always presents a threat to the marginal organization, particularly if the conflict results in police or legal action. Sometimes the potential for conflict may seem like an ever-present part of a marginal's way of life. And, while some might dispute this claim generally, for a marginal, no conflict is too small not to be a problem. When internal conflicts cause division, they force people to take sides and since there's always a loser in a conflict, hard feelings or resentment are by-products.

When conflict comes from external sources, the potential for exposure is a real problem, particularly if the conflict is widespread. The battles among drug cartels in Mexico are an illustration. At first glance one would assume that Mexico and the towns and villages around the drug-related activities would find the manufacture and sale of drugs the biggest issue with which to contend. Ultimately, however, the scope and scale of conflict among competing marginal organizations became a greater problem during the production and movement of drugs in Mexico or across the border. As a report in *The Economist* explained, the arrest of Miguel Angel Trevino Morales, the head of a notorious drug, kidnapping and extortion gang "was more a victory in the war on violence than in the war on drugs" ("Zeta zeroed," 2013, p. 35).

Part 2: A View from the Top—Understanding Why the Marginal Organization Has the Image It Does

Introduction: Sometimes a Poor Image Is... Earned.

Conflict can result in loss of life, property and, of course, the organization's overall mission. As a result, conflict management is a must for those in an organization, and particularly a marginal organization, since virtually any conflict puts the entire organization immediately at risk of exposure. When conflict within or between marginals spills over into the mainstream, it's no longer just a problem among a segment of society, it becomes a management matter for the society as a whole. The fact that conflict can bring the marginal into direct contact with the mainstream, however, is only one way the two economic and social segments overlap.

We conclude this chapter by examining the many ways conflict, aggression, stress or any of a number of negative results come about when the activities of the marginal and mainstream organizations overlap. Indeed, an overlap of these two segments is often almost predictable; the nature of their missions can make it almost impossible to prevent them from coming into contact with each other. Figure 4.2 illustrates this situation. In the figure, the value streams of a marginal and a mainstream organization are presented. In the figure, these streams, somewhat metaphorically, are presented as running contrary to each other as a way to symbolize the contrasting nature of their missions and operations. After all, one might expect that since the two have different missions, needs, interests and values, those differences will surface in the ways they interface with other organizations or society in general.

The organizations come in contact where the streams overlap. For example, a drug pusher (a marginal) selling drugs in a schoolyard (the mainstream), a food truck (a marginal) selling lunch outside a sit-down restaurant (the mainstream), a radical cult (a marginal) trying to recruit members from a local church (the mainstream), a police unit (the mainstream) breaking up a gang's (a marginal) street activity. Now what makes the conditions described in figure 4.2 important to this discussion is that when contact is made between the two organizations, the value streams of the organizations involved may be at different points, so some immediate

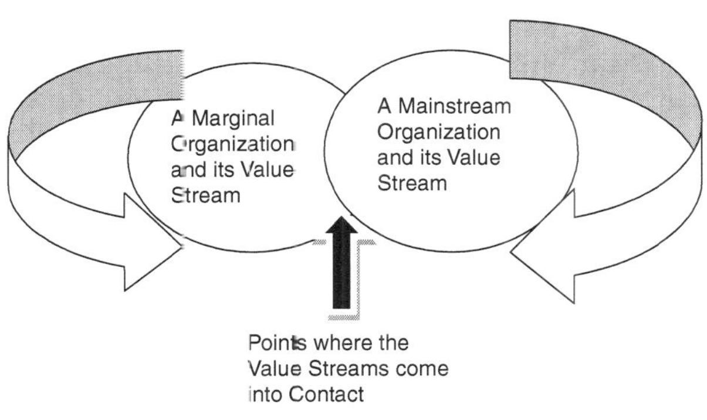

Figure 4.2 When a Marginal Organization Comes into Contact with the Mainstream.

adjustments have to occur on the part of both organizations in order to successfully manage the event.

The ingredients for stress or potential conflict are present when streams overlap. The context, organization and makeup of their respective value streams define the profiles and agendas of organizations in pursuit of different, sometimes competing, missions. At least that's what seems immediately apparent. We can also see that the differences between these two organizations are more than simply saying "one pays taxes and the other doesn't" or that "one's engaged in legal affairs and the other in illegal matters." In fact, the context is defined by a rich mixture including who's involved, what they are doing, how they are acting and where all of this is occurring.

Consider the first element, who is involved. People from the mainstream regularly drift over to the marginal sector to obtain the services of prostitutes, to buy marijuana or, as we'll see in a later chapter, to buy dogs from puppy mills. Others will hire undocumented aliens or buy goods that may have been stolen or are clearly "knock-offs" of licensed products. For the "mainstreamers" who support these marginals, these are just unfortunate people trying to earn a living. Call it rationalization, but it's one way to justify what's going on, and it can be especially hard for the mainstream or society to prevent.

Others, however, might object. "It's not who they are, it's what they are doing, that's the problem." The doctor performing the illegal abortion, the prostitute and the drug pusher may be nice people, but some in society just object to what they do, more than who's doing it. Those who object may be the special interests who want to see these people put an end to what they are doing and sometimes even put out of business. Those objecting to the marginals may be the politician needing votes, a competitor fearing a loss of market share or a laborer fearing a loss of work or income. "I don't have anything against them, it's just..."

Still others have "process objections." These objections are based on how those associated with the marginal act, how they look (they're dirty or wear "wild" clothes) or how they behave. In these instances, people object to the scroungers, foragers for food or money or the beggars and the homeless sleeping in parks or on the sidewalks. The mainstream may object to these people because they see marginals, like the foragers, as targeting the weak or vulnerable. These marginals are viewed as predators that prey on our people, our children or women. The marginals are predators, and the mainstream only offers the prey. They are dirty, they are uncouth, they are not like us.

An article in *The Economist* reflects this point of view. In the magazine's obituary of Mr. Lo Hsing Han, he is described as one who didn't care about people or the lives that are lost because of his drug empire.

"It was Mr. Lo," said the obituary, "who, in the 1960s and 1970s, shipped to Vietnam the heroin that ravaged 10% of America's forces. Not that he turned a hair. There was a saying among the ethnic Chinese in Shan state, like him: commerce was commerce" ("Lo Hsing Han," 2013, p. 78). In sum, the mainstream's view of the marginal is that they are different from us. They don't speak our language, practice our religion, vote as we do. We're not like them.

Finally, there are those in the mainstream who boil everything down to that real-estate mantra: location, location, location. It's not who they are or what they do; it's where the marginal operates. This ethnocentric view is as much based on geography as anything else. Sometimes, this physical orientation translates into a question of property rights. "This is our town, our state, our country, our land. We worked for this. We died for this." But even geography can be manipulated and used in multiple ways. Another view might conclude that as long as the marginals don't come into contact with us, everything is fine. It's another way of saying "out of sight, out of mind." For these mainstreamers, "we don't care if it doesn't touch us."

Points of Contact. Points of Contention. Preconceived Notions

Reactions to marginals from those in the mainstream can't be completely explained by a simple review of what the marginals do, how they behave or where they carry out their acts. One other factor must be considered in order to complete an analysis of why the interface between marginal and mainstream organizations has the effects typically observed, and that factor can be described simply as "preconceived notions."

Tafoya (2010) defined preconceived notions as "starting points. They are ways for adding fast order to what may be a new, disorganized or unknown process" (155). They are, for Tafoya, "pre-engagement assessments" people use prior to participating in an event (155). When it comes to marginals, the foundation for preconceived notions seems to boil down to three conclusions. Conclusions that help those who object to marginals explain or construct a view of marginals as an "impending menace."

Two of the three elements that lead one to view a marginal as an impending menace are trauma related. Trauma in these instances is a multidimensional construct that refers to the physical pain and suffering one can or might experience in this case because of the marginals. Trauma is unique in this instance for in addition to a physical dimension it also encompasses emotional and cognitive distress or shock triggered by the trauma. So, one view sees marginals as contributing to physical trauma and the second, to cognitive or emotional trauma for the mainstream or its membership.

In the first instance, physical trauma includes conclusions regarding the potential for harmful effects to mainstreamers or their property. This level of trauma is direct, sometimes surprising the involved victim or group. Physical sources for trauma are tangible to the extent that the mainstreamer fears a measurable loss or quantifiable damage associated with the marginal's actions or behavior. Marginals in this instance are viewed as a source of physical trouble. They are why conflicts emerge or are what makes fears real. Moreover, the overlapping value streams noted above are points where the actions or behavior of marginals cost the mainstream money, either directly through a loss or indirectly through the need to pay for police or other support services, for example, by raising taxes.

The effects of physical trauma to people or property can be significant. A knife wound carries pain and physical damage but these effects often pale in comparison to the sometimes long-term effects associated with cognitive or emotional trauma. Not all scarring associated with injury is physical. The nature of trauma in these instances may be real or even imaginary. Victims, or potential victims, associate marginals with real or imaginary dangers; it's a fear of contamination or corruption linked largely to notions such as "they attack you through what you care about, through what's important to you." In this instance, the mainstreamer's images of possible mental and emotional disturbances, suffering, pain, strain or distress are a form of "conceptual trauma." The potential trauma is a cognitive referent the mainstreamer uses to prepare for, shape or evaluate potentially damaging interactions with marginals.

Trauma's role in the interaction between marginals and the mainstream has both theoretical and practical importance. For example, the emergence of trauma signals mainstreamers that the marginal is capable of triggering a condition that has real negative value or salience for the mainstreamer. Mainstreamers can use trauma or the threat of it as a tool for use when constructing a response to marginals or their existence. Second, the nature of a response to trauma or its potential tells us something about the mainstreamer's makeup and needs, about what the mainstream sees as important or of value. If it's not important, why waste time, money or physical or emotional energy with it? Third, strategies to manage or address the resulting trauma also tell us something about the perceived strengths and vulnerabilities of both the marginals and mainstreamers. A cogent, planned response is a clue to the well-being of the mainstream, just as a violent, "shoot-from-the-hip" response can convey the opposite impression. Finally, tracking the traumatic profile over time provides an indication of the potential costs of the trauma on those stakeholders affected. Physical and cognitive or emotional traumas require different types of treatment plans, with their own timelines for recovery. In addition to traumas triggered by or associated with the mere presence of marginals, there is one other level of trauma that also merits mentioning and that is the trauma associated with prescribed change, plans or efforts.

Change-related trauma affects marginals when the mainstream seeks ways to, for example, incorporate marginals or their products and services into the mainstream to legitimize these organizations or their products and services. Consider the controversies associated with women as priests, the legalization of marijuana, legalized gambling, same-sex marriages or the legalization of abortion. What's common to each of these is that prior to being "legitimized," they all were restricted to the reality of the marginal sectors of society. Changing their status, that is, bringing them into the mainstream, produces a level of trauma that is comparable to other historic periods and events, including giving women and African Americans the opportunity to vote or, more broadly, equal rights for all regardless of their race, sex or religion. Looking at the controversies associated with marginals in this way suggests that perhaps the scope and scale of the trauma experienced wouldn't be as great if some of the underlying causes of the trauma were eliminated. Causes like prejudice, for example.

Trauma versus Prejudice

What makes these trauma-related reactions to marginals different from a third factor is that the trauma produced by the two discussed are triggered in response to the marginals while the third factor, prejudice, surfaces in response to the real or anticipated presence of the marginals; its source is independent of anything the marginal does; its source is a self-organized response of one individual to another.

Although this description of prejudice is straightforward and clear, prejudice is, in fact, a rather messy concept. Allport's (1958) landmark treatment of prejudice summarized it as "natural and common capacities of the human mind" (17). According to Allport, overcategorization, the tendency to form judgments about people, places or things on the basis of "scant, even non-existent, probabilities," is perhaps the "commonest trick of the human mind" (9). "There's a natural basis for this tendency," he wrote. "Life is so short, and the demands upon us for practical adjustments so great, that we cannot let our ignorance detain us in our daily transactions. We have to decide whether objects are good or bad by classes. We cannot weigh each object in the world by itself. Rough and ready rubrics, however coarse and broad, have to suffice" (9).

In the relationships between marginals and mainstreamers, prejudice plays out in a number of different ways. Prejudice isn't only "they're not like us" but rather expands to broader and more complex fears. For example, fear that one's business will suffer, of increased competition or even the likelihood that the need to manage marginals will contribute to increased bureaucracy in the society as a whole are sufficient to stimulate prejudice against marginals for the individual. Marginals after all have produced undesirable outcomes in the mainstream. Mainstreamers have experienced financial loss; there often are increased expenses for those expected to manage the marginals or for societies generally that have to accommodate the presence of marginals. Other times, responses to marginals result in the diversion of resources from routine (and primary) tasks to nonroutine or extraordinary tasks that wouldn't (it is believed) be necessary if marginals weren't involved.

Finally, perceptions that the costs associated with marginals are not restricted to what the mainstreamer sees today also can contribute to the prejudice or bias they feel toward marginals. In this instance, fears may not be based on any real experience or confirmed events, just the notion or belief that there's a likelihood the marginals will "haunt" the mainstream over time, at some point in the future. So, to safeguard what they have, mainstreamers in this instance act first, before it's too late. Admittedly, it's not a provable fear but, if realized, it can be significant, so why take a chance it won't happen. Better safe than sorry.

Conclusions: Why Marginal/Mainstream Conflicts Emerge? What Makes the Fears Real? Overlapping Value Streams

Because marginals and mainstream organizations do not exist in isolation or deal exclusively with "their own kind," they will, by definition, come in contact with each other—and that's when the dynamics of their mixing becomes evident. Trauma, for example, can be a real outcome of the interaction of marginal and mainstream organizations. Trauma elevates real and potential damages associated with the interactions of marginals and marginals in the mainstream to a higher level. The evening news and the Internet confirm this everyday.

At this point, the trauma experienced makes the events and crises that occur personal; it doesn't mean responses to the actions of marginals have to be rational but they must be real, they must send a message. Trauma affects stakeholders, their organizations and their society now and in the future. Because of the potential for the mixing of marginals and mainstreams to have negative effects, there is a stimulated need to respond to the marginals; their presence or behavior triggers a sense of urgency on the mainstream's part.

Sometimes, this sense of urgency results in legislation restricting the range of activity or movement of marginals, programs that aim to control or eliminate marginals and, in some instances, incorporate the marginals into the mainstream. But one point is evident. When this type of rationalization is guiding mainstream behavior, an unchecked marginal does not benefit the host country, particularly when the marginal is engaged in criminal or otherwise illegal acts. Moreover, any deleterious effects resulting from the marginal's behavior are not restricted to a few but rather any organization in the mainstream can be at risk, from local, state and national communities to the society as a whole.

Chapter 5 continues to explore the nature of marginals vis-à-vis the mainstream by focusing on marginals and what life is like for marginals existing in and around the mainstream. In that chapter, one begins to see the impact of an orientation that views marginals as an "impending menace." In some instances, that orientation triggers a measure of defensiveness in the marginal driving their organizations underground or at least out of sight. Other times marginals adapt and launch their own unique competitive strategies. When this happens, the notion that the marginal is the mainstream's target or prey gives way to the marginal countering or reversing that theme and becoming a predator with the mainstream as prey. Recall that both mainstream and marginal organizations are part of each other's stakeholder network—they're just not necessarily valued members of those nets. This means that, at a minimum, both have an impression of the other and, in this regard, a sense, however accurate, of the other's potential to cause harm or injury. Viewing marginals as an impending menace is the type of preconceived notion that sets potential interaction between marginals and the mainstream on edge even before it occurs.

Mainstreamers often approach a marginal's acts as always having an effect that's usually negative and that if left unchecked may spread beyond those immediately involved. Whole networks can be destroyed, other organizations may join the fray and society's governing bodies may be expected to respond, sometimes by enacting new legislation, other times by creating or launching organizations designed to specifically control, monitor or destroy the marginals.

One reason why many in the mainstream avoid or, when they have contact with marginals, react with aggressive actions toward them is because a marginal's acts are often expected to unfold in a linear fashion and most often to produce negative, harmful effects. This is not a well-reasoned, passive or unbiased orientation. Rather an orientation toward marginals that sees any interaction with them as flawed and likely to trigger problematic events or a crisis can result in a mentality governed by extremes. Orientations to marginals is "black or white" and responses to them are "fight or flight." Reasoning in these instances can give way to bureaucracy, as the mainstream seems to layer itself with rules, regulations and institutions to safeguard what it has and/or to limit what it believes it doesn't want.

But what's perhaps worse is that the conditions just outlined actually can give way to a more dangerous condition, one defined by fears and actions guided by self-fulfilling beliefs, interpretations and views that marginals are a threat to the mainstream society. This is an emerging theme when a marginal is involved in some criminal or hostile activity but while marginals may be classified as belonging to a segment of society, not all marginals are alike or are likely to cast the same effects on the mainstream. The casual street vendor, farm worker or food truck often suffers "guilt by association" because of the actions of more devious, dangerous organizations. Concluding that all marginals are alike may be an injustice on the one hand but, on the other, it's a stimulus that can breed defensiveness, wariness or fear for whole groups of people simply trying to earn a living or to provide for their friends and family.

The synopsis presented above seems extreme and perhaps even irrational but when bias, prejudice, narrow-mindedness and intolerance are ingredients behind the impressions organizations have of each other, what seems extreme for the outsider can be the norm for those who believe they are facing trouble or danger. For marginals, potential vulnerability and uncertainty regarding their future trigger a need for immediacy and this is sometimes evident in how the organization's purpose and structural processes are defined. Some marginals, for example, become masters in the art of "risk pooling" where they draw the sources for risk together so that any exposures are restricted or at least limited. This risk orientation can result in strategies that seek only brief or shallow encounters with the mainstream.

Other times, the marginal can shift the ways it presents products and services to mainstreamers. Some efforts to promote its products and services might be referred to as "marginalized marketing," promotions that target the transaction center rather than within or across the mainstream's ecocenter. This enables the marginal organization to use targeted urgency as the stimulus behind foraging, group or swarming activities. Marginalized marketing also translates the organization's value stream management strategy into efforts designed to unobtrusively push and pull stakeholders to meet its needs. In this way, a marginal's operations become the personification of change management—change management that aims to embrace, discern, adapt, incorporate, invent and innovate in order to avoid predation while seeking ways to grow the marginal's organization or, simply, prolong its survival.

For the mainstream, the marginal's acts, actions or events are not the crisis; it's the marginal's presence that gets the mainstreamer's attention. The emergency for the mainstream is the marginal's existence and thus potential for future negative impact on mainstream organizations, their stakeholders or society at large. One might describe the mainstream's orientation to the marginal's presence as "progressive distress." The immediate effects of a marginal's behavior surface in the emotions and/or psychological or physical pain or loss that the mainstream anticipates or believes can or will occur, and this, then, serves to compromise the mainstream's systems and ways of operation.

What's worse from the mainstream's perspective, however, is the evolutionary nature of the marginal's effects. Toxic conditions emerge and uncertainties regarding ways to stop or deal with the marginals and their effects mount. Moreover, as the marginals grow in number, strength, scope and scale, mainstreamers can find themselves without the fundamentals needed to cope with or, worse when in actual competition for the systemic access points or control centers that have always been theirs, to vanquish their real or imaginary adversary. Who owns the border, the city center and the transportation hubs? These fears only increase as the number of marginal stakeholders involved increases and the likelihood for risk-taking thresholds appears.

Finally, as treatment plans fail, damages mount, competencies are strained and the effects of the marginal's activities are perceived as reaching catastrophic or uncontrollable potential, the mainstream begins to see what are believed to be the real threats: its organizations are compromised, at risk and forced to change and act in ways they were not designed for. If history is any guide, these are the moments when fear, ignorance and confusion guide the decisions and actions of those who aim to prevent the unwanted from occurring and, thus, shape the lives of organizations in the margins of society's mainstream.

CHAPTER 5

Analyzing the Marginal's Persona: Existence as a Marginal Organization and the Marginal's Impact on the Mainstream

Broadly speaking, a society's physical, organizational makeup is divided into two broad segments—mainstream organizations and organizations at the periphery of the mainstream, an area populated by organizations we call marginals. When viewed systemically, organizations in both segments combine to form a patchwork environment defined by various social and behavioral interactions. Some of these interactions are defined by economic transactions; others may be aggressive, supportive, destructive or any number of other behavioral interchanges. It's a dynamic environment driven by the decisions and choices people make.

To this point in the book, we've generally focused on one or the other of these two segments. In chapter 4, we began to look at what can happen when the activities of the marginal and mainstream overlap. Contact between these two segments is most often built around a mainstreamer seeking either to get something from the marginal, its products or services or, in a different context, to "get" the marginal. Marginals, after all, typically aren't a favored group for those in the mainstream. Survival of the fittest isn't an option for the marginal; it's a requirement.

When contact is established, virtually everything about the interacting organizations is affected, either at the transaction point or, over time, somewhere else in their systems. This may sound like a trite, somewhat simplistic generalization but what is occurring is anything but trite and certainly not simplistic. To illustrate, we'll focus our discussion on four features: First, the nature of the marginal/mainstream relationship within the broader society. We explored the foundation for that relationship in chapter 4, with a particular emphasis on the negative features or effects of those interactions. This time we'll look at the effects their past experiences with the mainstream and its agents has on marginals. Second, we review ways the relationships between the marginals and mainstream materialize among a collected network of stakeholders. Every organization has its own network of stakeholders, but it's always important to keep in mind that each of those stakeholders is part of their own network with their own stakeholders who in turn have their own networks and so on. The multifarious nature of these comingled networks adds a level of complexity to the interactions of marginals with the mainstream.

Third, we'll examine the results and consequences associated with transactions between mainstream and marginal organizations. There are always costs and benefits associated with marginal and mainstream interactions but where and how the costs and benefits arise have a lot to do with one's perspective. If the transaction is hostile, the costs rest with both and, theoretically, the greatest costs belong to the loser. But even in nonhostile interactions, the relationship between costs and benefits exists in a complicated manner. An addict buys drugs at a cost for the short-term benefit of feeling good, but over the long term the addict has to pay the protracted cost of being an addict.

Finally, we'll end the chapter by examining how the interactions between mainstream and marginal organizations can change and sometimes even redefine and/or reposition the organizations and the communities of which they are a part. This has significant implications for both the ways these organizations operate and for their future interactions, to say nothing about the ways the communities and society of which they are part are affected. Complacency is not an option for the marginal organization. Only the foolhardy or naïve marginal will let down its guard when operating within the shadows of the mainstream.

Part I. Marginals and Their Relationship with the Mainstream

Mainstream and marginal organizations have very different relationships with the greater society of which they are members. Mainstream organizations are linked to the broader society. For example, on one level, mainstream organizations are tied to society's values, its mores and social codes. So a mainstream organization's labor and employment practices reflect a society's standards for worker rights, safety and health. The mainstreamer's links with society also reflect other features of the parent society. Mainstream organizations may operate on a for-profit or non-profit basis or in service to the broader society as police, fire or military units. In short, mainstreamers are both members of their society and an intimate part or extension of the same.

Being a member of the mainstream society is not a free ride, however. There are prerequisites for affiliation with "the" society. Mainstream organizations sustain their bond through their behavior and by adhering to society's requirements and demands, its rules and regulations. Organizations, for example, are expected to pay taxes, adhere to rules, regulations, and procedures and operate within the performance expectations defined by society. Failure to do so can make an organization or its membership subject to prescribed penalties or punishment or make it an outcast to the marginal sector.

In return, mainstream organizations also have expectations for the parent society. Societies are expected to turn revenue from taxes and fees into different services aimed at maintaining, nurturing or protecting its stakeholders, in this case the mainstream organizations. The mainstream organization derives benefits and rewards from this arrangement: the mainstreamers reap the benefits derived from taxes and fees paid and, of course, there's the general stimulus provided by a strong or stable economic and social environment. The latter because mainstreamers also require that society play a role in creating a safe, nurturing environment for organizations and a willingness to step in and offer protection for those organizations should they be attacked or subjected to unfair treatment. It's a linked give-and-take relationship. Its objective is to be at least reasonable and complementary and ideally balanced or in equilibrium. And, when protection is needed, mainstreamers often believe protection from marginals is most important.

Marginal organizations don't have the type of relationship with society the mainstreamers share. In fact, the relationship between society and marginal organizations can be purely adversarial and sometimes hostile, especially when society's agents are acting on behalf of mainstream organizations. The relationship marginals have with the mainstream society is not an accidental one. As we've said throughout this book, marginals, by nature, often try to avoid paying taxes, dodge policies and procedures meant to protect stakeholders and, sometimes, are even at odds with society's laws, rules and regulations. These organizations avoid being tied or linked to society and seem to float in and around society and its agents. All too often, society for marginals is only a source for their gain or benefit or, on the downside, a source of harassment, aggression or punishment.

This seemingly one-way street may seem to be the ideal. Marginals earn revenue and/or position in a society so that they can achieve their mission, like the drug pusher, prostitute or terrorist, all the time without having to pay taxes or adhere to rules and regulations. It seems like an enviable position but, as we'll see in this chapter and in chapter 6, there are "costs" associated with the decision to operate as a marginal. Marginals operating illegally, for example, have to avoid being caught or, at a minimum, have to avoid detection. As a result, they often can't call on protection from law enforcement if they are being harassed or threatened by others.

Mainstream organizations benefit from operating in the open, often in close proximity to other mainstreamers, like at a strip mall or shopping center. In these instances, mainstreamers benefit from grouping; it's a residual or a spillover benefit. A consumer may come to the mall to visit a particular store and soon find the mall is also an opportunity to visit any number of other mainstream stores in the same shopping center. It's the classic "one-stop" shopping model but it's not a benefit marginals can enjoy.

Drug pushers or prostitutes or terrorists may "target" certain populated areas because the odds are greater that they may have more opportunities to sell their products or to achieve a particular goal, but they have to invent this benefit of association; it's not one naturally, or reliably occurring. The marginals move into and around society's mainstream because the nature of their operation can't let them be a fixed part of the visible, mainstream world. If a marginal experiences any aspect of "grounding," it's grounding through movement—from one grounded site to another.

Separate and Unequal Environment

Ecologists use an interesting approach to describe and discuss systems composed of marginal and mainstream organizations. They approach these natural systems as an assortment of small subsystems called patches. The concept is of use to us because patches can be examined in their own right, as a particular segment of a larger district or neighborhood or as a community or an entire population. The concept also allows for discussions regarding movement of people or agents between or among patches, of a patch's life cycle or simply in terms of a particular patch's general well-being or conditions.

Our use of the concept is particularly unique because using it allows us to talk about, for example, an environment made up of "patches" of marginal and/or mainstream organizations or, at different times, only collections of patches. In these instances, the patches we are interested in might just comprise a particular type of marginal organization, as when a large event, say a fair or carnival, draws agents from different and discrete marginals, like pickpockets, to the same event. The focus of a large sporting event, for example, may result in the emergence of a large population of spectators interested in seeing the event but may also produce a wide variety of marginal and mainstream organizations, mobile patches, which seek to prey on or protect those in the crowd. In other words, the concept of patches provides a convenient way to approach the conditions that bring marginals and mainstream organizations together as well as the effects of those interactions.

Relationships as Patches and Networks, Marginal Organizations and Their Stakeholders

The formation of mobile patches comprising mainstream and marginal organizations forming in response to the temporary colonization of a particular location is an example of spontaneous network optimization. Those marginal and mainstream organizations drawn to a particular event or occasion, like thieves and prostitutes and corresponding police and security personnel, shift elements of their organizations from some "home base" to set up "mobile patches" in and around a temporary location.

The marginal and mainstream organizations involved are, for all intents and purposes, functionally the same at any given time; only when engaged in activity in support of their missions, they reshape their social network (its stakeholders, use of resources such as time and money and objectives) to meet the needs of a new and particular setting. It's also interesting to note that when agents of marginal or mainstream organizations are sent to "work" a particular event or occasion, they may be only a fraction of an organization's parent population. So the functional patches formed in response to an event can be represented as hybrids of the larger patch. They're like the parent organization, but they reflect only aspects of the parent and, sometimes, may have the latitude to make decisions or generally act using their own best judgment, without direct guidance of the parent organization.

In this chapter, we'll concentrate on describing and analyzing the nature of marginal organizations vis-à-vis the environments in which they "live" and those they create when operating in terms of a particular task or to accomplish their mission. We'll concentrate first on the formation of the marginal's primary environment, a place it might call "home." We'll explore what makes a particular habitat desirable by focusing on the types of features and benefits it might offer for the marginal. This gives us an opportunity to sketch a marginal's "near-stakeholder network," to identify key operational processes, practices and procedures and, of course, to map into the analysis organizations that may have a competing or adversarial relationship with the marginal.

Next, we'll explore the marginal in action, from planning to the execution of activities designed to achieve its mission. This analysis will focus on ways a marginal's organizational and operational complexity changes with time and events. Beyond a simple discussion of an organization's physical makeup, this analysis will also examine the particular ways in which the organization's members and stakeholders generally are affected or expected to be affected by the organization over time.

Finally, we'll end the chapter with an examination of how a marginal's interface with mainstream organizations affects the organization, its environment and, of course, the elements of that environment. This discussion is one of the most important to the book for it maps the movement of a marginal from an environment that is closed, known and at least "safer" to interactions in the open, potentially threatening environment defined by mainstream organizations. The discussion is important in its own right for many reasons but one of particular import is that it challenges a conventional notion that "process determines patterns," that is, an organization's evolution culminates in the establishment of particular processes that determine how the organization will perform. When marginal organizations leave the safety and security of their own environment to engage mainstream organizations, the axiom is probably best reversed to: "patterns (that emerge) determine process." Finally, this last section of the chapter is both a way to bring closure to the chapter's treatment of the emergence of marginal organizations and is a way to introduce chapter 6, which explores how marginals are affected by their interactions in and with the mainstream.

Home Base: For Many Marginals, Home Is Where You Find Yourself

Location, location, location. It's a banner for those in the real-estate sales industry and, in most instances, mainstream organizations. Location for the mainstream organization is an anchor; it's something to establish, to protect and to use as a referent, for example, when attempting to let stakeholders, like customers, know where you are located. Want to find the nearest Best Buy® store or movie theater showing the film you want to see, just look them up using Google Maps® or similar technology. Finding a mainstream organization is relatively easy; its location often boils down to a decision designed to meet the needs of as many elements of its stakeholder network as possible. That's not a strategy a marginal organization can use when locating its operations.

Most mainstream organizations want to be identified with their location; indeed, some, like theme parks, even incorporate location as part of their organization's brand. Moreover, a mainstream organization's store "footprint" can reflect the brand, the products it carries and even its approach to service. Some mainstreamers have learned that their customers like to shop at stores that follow the same pattern or layout so they try to make every store look and feel like every other store the organization may operate. Moreover, some mainstreamers even go so far as to make their production centers available or at least visible to stakeholders. These organizations may want stakeholders to see how products are produced or how services are provided, how quality is "built into" the product, how products and services reflect the organization's "core values," etc. For these organizations, visibility is part of the stakeholder bonding processes.

Most marginals don't and sometimes can't use location to link with stakeholders the way mainstreamers do. In fact, if you try to do a search for the nearest and best deals in marijuana sales, a local prostitute or other marginals, you're not likely to turn up any useful information. In fact, the only organization you're likely to find after doing your search are those members of the mainstream Justice Department who might track those types of searches and would be interested in finding you because of your interests.

Marginals are, by nature, mobile organizations. They typically can't value a particular home base as a mainstreamer might, even though they often can afford to do so. Having a "permanent" home means you can be found, watched and sometimes attacked. So most marginals don't want any type of permanence associated with their location, with two exceptions: those marginals who need some type of production center for the manufacture of their products and services and those who define their business center in terms of a particular location. In the first instance, "home" may be that place where the illegal bootlegging still occurs, cocaine is produced or marijuana is processed for sale. These are secret, often hidden, centers woven into the overall fabric of a local setting or geography. It defines the marginal's parent environment while hiding it from the view of adversarial stakeholders.

What may be most important in this instance are the ways an organization's environment shapes and is shaped by the nature of the organization—in this case, whether it is marginal or mainstream. For example, consider two key constructs presented earlier. The first regards the way an organization centers or grounds itself in a particular vision or mission. Table 2.3 in chapter 2 compared four marginal organizations to illustrate how fundamentals can vary among different organizations. Stressed in that discussion was one particular point: that while organizations may be part of many different networks they simultaneously pursue their own, often different missions, even when those missions may be at odds with any or all other organizations involved. As we read through the table, we're not surprised that the organizations ultimately produce environments that reflect their missions. What is of greater interest are the ways these environments are linked with the organization's vision and mission and that these environments can be a source of tension for the organizations involved in the broader social network. We expect the terrorist organization to be at odds with the others but, at the same time, we also know that it's possible for a measure of harmony to emerge between or among some involved with the terrorist; that's not necessarily a foregone conclusion, but it is possible. A terrorist, a drug manufacturer and a counterfeiter might form alliances of mutual benefit with other organizations, perhaps linked around money or the disruption of targeted mainstream societies. Their missions may be different but these three can benefit from a temporary relationship while sharing the same status vis-à-vis the mainstream society: they are all on the outside and often held in contempt.

Closer analysis of the table illustrates that differences among organizations often are linked to a single or a few elements and can be easily explained. Differences among these organizations' operational processes or particular missions may make "negotiations on how to proceed" difficult, often protracted and sometimes never fully satisfying, but the differences can be managed. Interestingly, too, it seems easy to envision the terrorist in this instance seeing particular value in, if not relishing, the tension and divisions a partnership among the three might contribute to its mission vis-à-vis the mainstream. For the terrorist in a leadership role, any action by the other organizations becomes a way for the terrorists to extend or "make points" in their games with the mainstream. If these marginals are even somewhat successful then counterfeit money or drugs flood the mainstream, thus making the terrorist's stakeholders see their success as reinforcing the organization's efforts, vision and mission. It's an outlandish scenario but not an unreasonable one given what we've learned about the methods, motives and madness of organizations like al-Qaeda.

The Role of the Environment in a Marginal Organization's Use and Interpretation of Territory and Operational Practices

Any of the structural elements discussed contributes to an organization's form and the function of key operating policies, procedures and practices. For example, we're used to seeing key direction and control factors like the organization's vision and mission used to define operational practices, but the environment also plays a unique role in defining how practices, policies and procedures can be used toward similar ends. While the vision and mission can shape the definition of policies and procedures, for example, in response to increased risk, threat or vulnerabilities, once the environment is rocked by an event, the same practices used to shape and define the organization can have a very different purpose—one of responding to or accounting for what happened or didn't happen given the event that was experienced and the organization's vision and mission.

To illustrate how key practices might be "reframed" by different organizations after a crisis event, consider the following scenario: Two mainstream organizations, an airline and airport security, are shaken by a marginal organization, in this case a terrorist organization's attack.

Consider how this event impacts the pre- and post-activities associated with each organization's key operational practices. For example, we can begin by examining the effects on the "communication practices" of the organizations involved. For the airline, before the terrorist event occurs it's business as usual. Communication is used to facilitate interaction among stakeholders, particularly passengers, and generally to promote the organization. Likewise, prior to the event, the security organization may use communication practices to facilitate interaction among its staff and sometimes to promote benefits associated with the processes it has in place. The terrorist organization also uses communication practices to manage its membership but it frequently uses communications strategically to promote the organization's vision and, in this instance, tactically for planning related to the upcoming attack.

After the event, communication has to and does change. The airline's first objectives center communication around reassuring stakeholders that the event is under control. These communications may involve describing what occurred, the effects of the attack and what's being done as a result. The security organization's communications follow a similar theme with one twist: while both the airline and security organizations are independent entities, post-event communications focus on the nature of the general "partnership" existing between them and, then, their collaboration in managing the event and, importantly, preventing future similar events. And what about the terrorists? Their post-event communications continue their pre-event format promoting the organization by focusing on the organization's success—that the event was yet another illustration that the organization is engaged in activities that help it achieve its vision and mission. The terrorists' communicate their success.

This type of orientation to operational practices continues with other key practices. Consider the effects of the event, or the attack, on different relationship practices. Prior to the event, the airline's relationship practices might have stressed the need to work as a team, to build harmonious interactions between unions and management or across different areas of their organizations. The security organization's relationship management practices were perhaps more specific to particular organizations and the individuals hired to help it achieve its mission given those organizations.

" 'Own' your station, your job but work together." "Be on guard." All of this is in contrast to a terrorist's pre-event relationship practices, which might be summarized as "trust no one, you own your own success."

After the event or the attack, the airline's relationship practices need to reassure stakeholders that their relationship with the organization is secure, that they are safe, that the organization is safe, that the organization is doing what it can to protect them. Security, on the other hand, closes its ranks. Relationship practices that assumed one should "be on guard" shifts to "trust no one." Meanwhile, our terrorist organization's relationship strategies turn to "selecting the next team" and preparing them for the next event.

Clearly this scenario oversimplifies a very complicated event and the behaviors of very complex organizations, but it does illustrate some important points regarding the event and the organizations involved. First, events like the one illustrated affect the participants in different ways and, in this case, across virtually all of their key operational practices. It's possible, for example, to continue to write this "before and after" script for these organizations in terms of each of their other operational practices. What, for example, might be the "before and after" descriptions of each organization's "evaluation," "information management" or "performance management practices" given the event that occurred? It's not necessary to outline these in detail in this book for the reader can easily, intuitively speculate on what might (or should) occur for each of these as well as for any other practices. (see Tafoya, 2010, 2013a, for a complete list and related discussions). Things have to change in response to an event like that described or, in all probability, similar events with similar negative effects will likely continue.

It's also noteworthy to point out that, like it or not, these three organizations are part of the same network. There's more on this in later chapters but for now, each are stakeholders in the others' networks—it's just that when they are in those networks, they are there as adversaries and not supporters of the organization. Constructing social networks without regard for the membership and role of adversaries, opponents or enemies is an incomplete picture of reality. A crisis like the one discussed demonstrates how different members of the network with competing missions are connected and, in terms of this immediate discussion, how the organizations in these networks use the same key strategic practices (although differently) and how those practices overlap as the organizations interact.

This discussion's salience increases when one realizes that while the defined practices for organizations in general are meant to be used to guide and shape behavior, they are actually used quite differently by marginal and mainstream organizations. Use and application of operational practices are not uniform and balanced for the two types of organizations. In this instance, a marginal's fluid, flexible environment amplifies the use of practices as guides: invention is left to the agent performing a particular task. Mainstream organizations, partially because of their nature, and often, perhaps especially because of their relationship and links to stakeholders, don't have the same measure of autonomy. So while the practices for both marginals and mainstream organizations are defined as very similar, they are used differently for marginals and mainstream organizations. Practices in the mainstream link strongly to events; they are discrete tools for event management, for the ways things are done or have to be done. But practices serve a different role for marginals. A marginal's practices always refer back to the organization's mission and have a particular emphasis on the individual's role in managing or executing the event.

The mainstream's environment is of paramount importance to it and protecting it links directly with its image; protecting its environment is protecting virtually everything about its world; it can become the driving factor behind everything done by the mainstream organization. Since marginals don't make the same investment in an environment, their use of key practices rests with sustaining the integrity of the organization's vision and mission through its agents, those carrying the mission to the objective or event. Moreover, since the definition of a marginal's vision and mission rests with the stakeholders' operational practices, they can be interpreted and used in any number of different ways. What's important for the mainstream organization is that operational practices are followed and behavior is shaped by the practice. For marginals, practices are referents used to pursue the organization's vision and mission. Marginals use practices if they facilitate achievement of the event at hand and the organization's mission. When a practice isn't useful as designed, it's modified or discarded on the spot. Indeed, perhaps marginals add, use and rely on a collection of different practices in their efforts: those described as invention, innovation and creativity practices, policies and procedures.

So an organization's environment means something very different to marginals and mainstream organizations. Threats to a mainstream organization's environment can include its abuse or misuse, invasion by a competing organization, its contamination or, at the extreme, its destruction. Marginals take a more fluid approach to their environment largely because they aren't as likely to invest in a particular area as a mainstreamer may. However, this doesn't mean the marginal won't have to face territorial threats or challenges. Indeed, one can conclude two things about a marginal's environment in this instance. First, one might say that a marginal's environment is its mission, however defined, and ideas are very difficult to destroy, and second, a marginal's environment is, for all practical purposes, an extension of each member's "personal space" and, as a result, exists wherever the organization's members are at the moment.

Home Is Where the Hat Is (But If Marginals Aren't Tied to a "Home Base" Where Do They Hang Their Hat?)

Analysts studying marginal organizations can benefit from determining what happens if a marginal organization's fluid, mobile habitats are altered, degraded or ultimately lost.

Marginals may not invest in bricks and mortar as mainstreamers but that does not mean they aren't sensitive to location vulnerabilities or pressures. Food vendors have their trucks and particular parking places, prostitutes might "own" a particular corner and a drug pusher might have a special location or territory in which to sell drugs, even if it's only an open car window from which to make a transaction. Deny these locations to these marginals and they have to find different places, they have to create different environments to use as "selling" or "transaction zones."

In many instances, this loss of habitat can be more significant for the marginal than for the mainstream because again, the marginal cannot use operational practices to grow or promote their organizational habitats or the organization's transaction environments as a destination the way a mainstream organization can. For marginals, communication practices are dependent on word of mouth behavior; they can't put up a website or sign broadcasting "where we'll be next week." Evaluation practices are largely reflected in "repurchase" patterns with the only paper tracking the sale the currency used to buy the product or service. Relationship practices are a face-to-face exchange of money and or service and, performance management practices may be as simple as "being there" to make the sale. Being "on the run" or simply moving to avoid capture by a police officer are among the factors leading to an organization's fluid, movable organization habitats. They can also strain and sometimes drain organizational resources; they can impact the organization's image as a reliable and consistent provider of goods and services and its sheer capacity to deliver any goods and services.

Describing the operation, decline and subsequent end of an organization's functional environment from the outside is always difficult but this is particularly true when the subject is a marginal organization. On face value, marginals seem to operate as free spirits. Their characteristic organizational profile is often summarized as internally regulated, flexible and ready to use any number of channels to distribute their goods and services. It's a profile that relies on the ability to master skills and competencies needed to adapt to changing situations and settings. But overshadowing this profile is the realization that this way of life or operation is always at risk of being permanently terminated. Mainstream organizations, in contrast, don't typically face such ongoing "all or nothing" threats to existence. The differences between the two organizations in this instance may seem subtle but they are far from insignificant.

Since it's the nature of marginal organizations to be mobile, sometimes elusive and often transient, one is tempted to dismiss the value of isolating and accounting for the makeup, structure and role they play in society. Their mobility makes them hard to isolate or find, their closed systems can be difficult to penetrate and the nature of their business or activities can make even the casual encounter dangerous. Yet even an informal review of the literature illustrates that there is a lot to gain from micro- as well as macro-level analyses. Each can be essential contributors when seeking to understand the systemic nature of these organizations, their overall health and well-being and their vulnerability and susceptibility to decline or loss. Marginal organizations may be transient in nature but their role and contribution to any society is significant, observable and traceable.

For example, as one begins to examine marginal organizations in terms of their stipulative, emergent and operational functions, it is possible to isolate three key roles all marginals play in a society. First is their role as an alternative when a "best" choice is not available or is out of reach. Employment is a classic illustration. Many mainstream organizations are closed to undocumented aliens, people with prison records or some simply perceived as incapable of working because of physical, mental or emotional disabilities. Marginals don't screen employees in terms of those criteria. If you're willing to work, and a marginal needs the help, it'll often do what it can to work with you.

Second, marginals fill a gap or void when what is desired is missing and/or not serviced by existing mainstream organizations. Marginals can open doors for individuals who desire training or experience needed to work in society; they provide a means for transportation for those seeking to come to the United States but unable to enter the country legally; and, of course, they offer sources of recreation through drugs, sex and gambling that is not sanctioned by the mainstream. People may not want to admit it but there is a level of mischief and sometimes even evil in all people, be it a tendency to violate rules of the road, to cheat, to avoid taxes, to use illegal drugs or to engage in illegal sex. If a marginal can, it will try to meet the needs of people regardless of who they are, their stations in life or their interests.

Third, marginals can and often do challenge societal norms or the status quo. Some marginals operate "in the face of" established society as a means for setting new thresholds of acceptance, new standards or new practices.

Shifting attitudes toward marijuana use, same-sex marriage or the legalization of prostitution are examples of marginal activity successfully moving into the mainstream and then moving the mainstream's orientation to these activities. Finally, marginals offer a retreat, a sanctuary, a safe place for individuals shunned by the mainstream or who don't feel they have a place of their own in a rule-driven, pejorative, sometimes discriminatory, society. Undocumented aliens are an example. For years, mainstreamers have used these people as tools to clean toilets in their offices, restaurants and hotels, to mow their lawns or to pick their fruit and vegetables, all the while not letting them live, play or sometimes even shop among the privileged mainstreamers. Society's margins become a place for these people to meet their basic needs. The margins aren't just a place to go home to, they offer a place to avoid the mainstream's pressures and prejudices.

Whatever the reason a marginal, three things are clear. First, in most instances, the marginal's simple existence means it is often different from what an acceptable mainstream organization is and that sets the stage for stress, confrontation or conflict to become a feature of the marginal's character in society. Second, marginal organizations add a level of diversity and complexity that the parent society feels it must manage. The marginal's management is not without issues, however. Since many marginals operate illegally, they must be discovered, monitored and contained and these efforts require time, money and staff resources.

Finally, there is a notion that marginals impact mainstream organizations by competing for the same stakeholders or sometimes threaten a mainstream organization's well-being by simply operating in the same location. This fear was touched upon in chapter 4 regarding the emergence of trauma-related states and the real or perceived actions of marginals. These fears are unique because, in contrast to the others mentioned, their effects may be more psychological that real. Here the mainstream sees the marginal organization's presence as having a negative effect because of "who they are or what they do." It's a "they're not like us" mentality.

Now, in some instances, fear, or at least worry, can be a justifiable derivative associated with marginals. Few organizations want to see prostitutes or drug dealers working the streets outside their business and most restaurants don't want a food vendor to park a food truck near their operation. But the reality is that these marginals are not directly competing with anything the mainstreamers are offering. The marginals are after their own stakeholders; it's just that sometimes the marginal and mainstreamer share stakeholders whether either wants to admit it or not while other times the issue is that the stakeholders share the same geography and that's what draws mainstream and marginals into contact with each other.

An organization's social networks are seldom tightly closed or restricted but rather they are linked in some way or fashion with other networks and their respective stakeholders. Sometimes the links that make a network's walls or gates are artificial, like the media or Internet, which allow information to pass back and forth from one network to others. Other times, stakeholders who are members of different networks (organizations) are the links that challenge walls, gates or other seeming dividers.

These features (some might read "shortcomings") of networks can trigger the emergence of some marginals or, in other instances, lead to the collapse and disappearance of others. Well-bred, well-meaning, well-heeled, well-whatevered members of the mainstream cross over and choose to interact with marginal organizations. In fact, without them, some marginals might not be able to exist and certainly not at their current scale. Consider the plight and stress currently experienced by religions, drug cartels and breweries as women are allowed to become priests, marijuana is legalized and bootlegged basement beer is legitimized. What were once conceived of as strongly defined, discrete networks have melted and given way to the pressures of network ecological succession. The networks surrendered to the pressures of changing times, interests, needs, wants or desires.

Yet, despite weaknesses in marginal and mainstream organizations to control their own populations or destinies, or the fact that what was once taboo is somehow now legal, the potential for ongoing dissonance between marginals and the mainstream will continue. It's both a role and function of society to seek equilibrium, and most often (and sometimes self-appointed) caretakers in this effort are mainstream organizations or their membership. As a result, some mainstreamers somewhere will always find a way to demonstrate their objections to people with opposite needs and interests, or those who won't fit in and just want to "march to a different drummer." For these mainstreamers it's "their way or the highway" and they'll sometimes do what they can to demonstrate their disgust or disapproval by raising standards for respectability, loudly protesting when they feel that their integrity, capacity to be influential or their very way of life is threatened or, simply, when they feel the world would be better off if those who don't fit in were controlled or removed altogether. In other words, sometimes it's the mainstreamers who create the sector or need for a sector we've defined as the margins of a society.

Survival, the Marginal's Way

If one were to ask the leadership of organizations why the organization exists or its purpose, you'd likely hear responses such as "to meet customer needs" or to "achieve a particular vision or mission"; some have even said "to manage events" (Tafoya, 2010). Each of these is true but conventional responses have a way of covering up more pragmatic reasons why organizations exist, like they "exist to protect and preserve themselves," "as a shell, to launder money" or "to ensure the heir's kids have a job." Mainstream organizations attempt to preserve themselves in many ways, sometimes by attending to their own business, maybe by doing it better than others do, by improving the quality of their work and sometimes by attending to the business of others.

Now most societies have learned that it's not prudent to let private organizations take matters into their own hands when they find they object to others or other organizations. So in their wisdom, they have created an entire infrastructure of organizations devoted to the task of monitoring, policing and sometimes even punishing organizations that get out of line with what local communities and sometimes whole countries see or believe is appropriate. Some of these are national, state and local police organizations, various organizations devoted to "homeland security" or criminal justice and, of course, various branches of the military. Each of these exists, we're told, to preserve, protect and, to a certain extent, defend a particular way of life.

Now it should come as no surprise that many activities aimed at preserving, protecting and defending a particular way of life are devoted to organizations that are connected to the society's mainstream and follow the society's laws, rules and regulations. After all, as pointed out earlier, these organizations pay the taxes used to fund the society's protectorate.

Marginal organizations also seek to protect themselves and their way of life. Sometimes their protective efforts surface in strategies used to avoid contact with the mainstream or its agents and, other times, if it's at all possible, they might even build their own protection networks. A key difference here, however, is that, in contrast to the mainstream, whatever means a marginal organization uses to protect and provide for itself comes, almost exclusively, from the marginal sector. In many instances, there is/are no broader protective shield or services available to marginals from the mainstream. Protection is a major trade-off and loss for being a member of society's margins and not the mainstream.

But marginal organizations do manage to survive and, in many instances, prosper. They do this in many ways and one of the most reliable is by carefully managing environmental issues associated with their organization, just as a mainstreamer might. For example, size contributes to a marginal's capacity to survive, but for marginals size always must be interpreted vis-à-vis other key factors. Large marginals such as criminal or terrorist organizations manage their size through organizational diversity. Terrorist organizations disperse stakeholders across vast geographic regions with those affiliated with the organization linking to it via the organization's mission, rather than some physical structure. The mission carries the membership in these instances, not structure, a flag or uniform.

When structure is important, as for criminal or certain religious organizations, large size can be managed through the use of offices or business centers. These serve as a channel for resources, usually money and people, to be moved back and forth between the parent organization and areas where they are needed. These organizational structures are little more than distribution points for the organization's resources and mix of products and services.

Size also plays a role for small marginals seeking to survive and/or protect their habitat. For small marginals, small size can be used as a defense ("why bother with the small pusher when the big drug manufacturer is what we really want"), a strategy (blend in rather than be different or imitate rather than be unique) or a tactic ("use our small size to hide, to be invisible"). In these instances, the marginal, perhaps because it is small, does what it can to avoid detection while still operating or serving stakeholder needs.

Of course, the nature of the marginal's mission often attracts attention to the organization, so in these instances survival often depends on how well the marginal can manage the mission's profile, perhaps to make it less obvious. For example, some marginals disguise the mission under cover of another, often acceptable profile. Organized criminal groups often buy legitimate businesses as a way to both hide from law enforcement and to spend or launder the large amounts of money they may be earning illegally. Other times the only way to protect the organization and its resources is to hide major production centers in desolate parts of the country or deep in the boroughs of a large city. Gangs, drug manufacturers and those in the sex trade frequently use this strategy.

Focusing the organization's business on a single product or process is another useful means for limiting one's risk to exposure or vulnerability. Drug manufacturers who focus on making the cocaine and not distributing it significantly reduce their exposure while also ensuring revenue from the sale of their product. In these instances, the distributor accepts the risk associated with transporting, distributing and selling the product on the streets. Likewise, the pimp may "manage" a number of prostitutes but the pimp's exposure is small in comparison to the prostitute's, who is the distributor of the organization's product.

Each of these examples also illustrates another useful strategy for protecting the organization: managing the volume of goods and services sold. A pimp with five prostitutes draws less attention than one with twenty-five, and a bookie who takes bets from ten known clients has less exposure than one seeking to make a lot of money by taking bets from a larger number of clients or from those he doesn't know. In these instances, it's not just the number of exposures related to different transaction points that increases visibility, it's the potential for added overhead associated with increased volume of business.

Almost all marginals have a unique feature: a proprietary operational feature defined by the organization and typically stemming from the nature of the products sold or services provided. These marginals can reduce risk exposure by acting in terms of these key features or products and then knowing who they sell to, who they allow into the organization and who they trust. Even the food truck selling Greek food knows those coming to the truck are coming for that type of food. In each of these instances, the marginal's survival is linked to the way it manages its network and, in particular, how it controls those who enter and operate in the network. One reason government sting operations are successful is that they pierce an organization's proprietary operational features and, at least to the criminal marginal, become one of their own.

Care of a marginal's safety and security often extends to the makeup of its stakeholder set. Poorly performing or unreliable stakeholders draw attention to the organization. For example, unreliable stakeholders who can't be expected to do their jobs right or to ensure the quality, safety and security of their work or products can add unexpected levels of risk exposure to an organization's operations. Imprudent stakeholders who are careless about knowledge and information about the organization or its products and processes can draw attention and add risk, all of which increase the organization's vulnerability. Marginal organizations, more so than mainstream organizations, often find it necessary to use stakeholders who meet one critical characteristic: they must "think and act" like they are members of the organization. These stakeholders, while on the outside, must still buy into the organization's mission, its purpose. This seems an obvious prerequisite for those who are part of the organization's core, and certainly its customers. But this precept even extends to those on the outside who want a professional relationship with the organization—provided they "support," even nominally, the organization and its efforts.

Finally, some marginals are forced to "buy into" the security needed to survive. This may translate as "pay offs" to mainstream organizations like law enforcement for protection, to purchases of protection from marginal organizations who sell protection as part of their product mix or through the payment of special fees or kickbacks to the bureaucrats who provide needed licenses or permits. Like the strategies and tactics described above, these efforts are among the many things a marginal organization must do because its chosen path or the path it was forced to take prevents it from becoming a mainstream organization. Marginals by their nature are vulnerable to threats and pressures most mainstream organizations don't have to worry about—unless of course they do things that threaten their mainstream status, like breaking the law, disregarding rules and regulations or generally failing to meet the performance standards prescribed by society. Consider what it's like for marginals who often live by avoiding rather than seeking the society's limelight.

Being "Number One" Isn't Necessarily Good for Business

Marginal organizations are not measured by the same standards as those used for mainstream organizations. Some services provided by marginals are clearly necessary or preferred. Food trucks provide a quick place to get lunch on a busy street, lawn care workers and housekeepers are proven labor savers for the busy homeowner and cottage industries supporting manufacturing devoted to the clothing, automobile or construction industries seem to be part of every community. But just because the marginal provides a useful, perhaps even needed, service doesn't mean it will be overlooked or will be accepted by mainstream organizations or society in general. "Favoritism" usually isn't a perk available to marginals.

That is, unless the marginal gets preferred or favored status assigned to it by mainstream organizations associated with law enforcement, the justice department, special interest groups or even politicians or elected officials. Any of these and other agents may find a marginal organization a convenient means for promoting or galvanizing citizens around a cause or movement. Marginals have often been used as footstools by the politician needing to boost poll numbers in a close election. In these instances, it isn't the marginal per se that's the target, but rather what the marginal represents or is perceived to be doing that serves as the focal point of attack. The marginal is a "symbol of what's wrong, what's not working, what needs to be done."

Crime, "contamination of our youth," loss of "safe places," threats to our schools, disruption or abuse of social services or processes are among the rallying points for many interested in curtailing the activities of some marginal organizations. At other times, marginals may be tagged as an economic burden on society's schools, health care or criminal justice systems because of crimes they are alleged to have committed, taxes they have failed to pay or other similar marginal-based characteristics.

Since many affiliated with marginal organizations represent minority or other disenfranchised groups, such as the poor or uneducated, these become a familiar target for the social elite or racists that seem to be part of every society. Profiling, hazing, harassment and stalking by mainstream stakeholders bring the two organizational types into confrontational positions, with the mainstream at the obvious advantage because the "law" is on their side. These confrontations set the stage for marginal organizations to see virtually every aspect of their operations affected by the unfolding events.

Raids, inspections, document checks can, at a minimum, disrupt business processes or operations or, worse, send a message to customers and other stakeholders that they, too, may be at risk for interacting with the marginal. Claims, whether true or false, regarding the safety of products or services can result in demonstrations, boycotts, and legal battles further straining a marginal's capacity to operate. At the extreme, marginals and their staff can find their businesses closed, property confiscated, product destroyed, equipment disabled and staff arrested and sometimes deported. To aggravate matters, sometimes there's a seasonal nature to these mainstream interventions. Economic downturns, slow news seasons and the approach of elections often trigger attacks or increased aggression toward the marginals and their membership.

Any Resource the Marginal Can Use as a Recourse?

Ultimately, there are few ways to mitigate the stress on marginals and those engaged in purely illegal operations have fewer options. Farm workers have the advantage of doing critical work during particular times of the year. Need (and the fact that others won't do the work) is their shield. In other industries, particularly those with tight profit margins, like food production and textile and clothing manufacturing, only the disadvantaged are willing to suffer through pitiful working conditions or the small wages paid to these workers. Need for a job buys their silence and willing exposure to abuse.

Other times, laws can change thus legalizing a marginal organization's activity. The legalization of gambling has made it a widely accepted recreational activity to the extent that states that once carried laws to restrict gambling now freely reap the benefits of the sale of lottery tickets and the profits of gambling casinos. More recently, the legalization of marijuana in parts of the United States has had similar effects. Marijuana can now be openly possessed, used and freely grown and distributed in certain states.

Sometimes the penalties attached to an illegal or illegitimate activity can be reduced. This doesn't shield marginals or their patrons from legal entanglements but it can reduce their "value" or attractiveness as a target for the official looking to advance a career at the expense of another. Reducing the penalties associated with a "crime" has the added benefit of potentially reducing the caustic, confrontational and sometimes dangerous interactions between law enforcement and the alleged wrongdoer. Many on both sides benefit from this.

An improved economy frequently has a positive effect on the stress some target marginals face, if only by default. Full employment not only means more money is in circulation but can also lessen or divert criticisms leveled against migrants or undocumented aliens who, it is claimed, are doing work "legitimate" citizens might do. Indeed, in some instances, the need for workers to do time-sensitive work such as the harvesting of crops or for workers with the skills and competencies needed to complete complicated tasks does open doors often closed to stakeholders. But neither the marginal stakeholder nor the marginal organization can expect that these will be predictable or reliable alternatives for the needy marginal.

Finally, although not a desirable mitigating factor from either the marginal's or mainstream's points of view, sometimes a catastrophe can enhance the value of marginals to the mainstream if only for a brief period. A natural disaster or terrorist attack can divert attention from some marginals as those in recovery or law enforcement concentrate their attention on the disaster at hand. The missed opportunity here is that while a catastrophe is a momentary diversion, it does add perspective to what's really a problem for a society to manage. Despite this, however, once the crisis passes it's relatively easy for those interested in harassing marginals to pick up where they left off.

Part II. Marginals and Their Stakeholders: How These Relationships Materialize into a Collected Network of Stakeholders

One way organizations improve their self-respect, sense of integrity and scope of influence is by building, nurturing and using, to mutual advantage, a network of stakeholders. For marginals, a stakeholder network can transform it from an isolated point drifting around society's mainstream into its own oasis. In these instances, the stakeholder network can become a source of sustenance and, when needed, a foundation, retreat or a useful reference point.

Tafoya (2013a,b) has identified four groups associated with the stakeholder network. "Supporters" and "feeders" have a positive relationship with the organization. Their efforts can contribute to the organization's capacity to operate, they may provide protection for the organization or may even fund its operations. Feeders contribute to the organization's resources and sometimes directly to its success. Feeders often have a particular bond with the marginal organization. These stakeholders may put up money, supply key products or services or the materials needed to make products and services. Without feeders, the organization would not achieve its mission.

A supporter's role is more tactical. Supporters can and often do affiliate with any organization. All stakeholders join a stakeholder network because they stand to gain something from participation and this is clearly the case for supporters. The marginal organization needs these stakeholders "to get things done." In contrast to feeders who enrich and empower the organization, supporters are enablers.

The two other members of the stakeholder network are the "demanders" and "reliers." Both of these groups draw on the organization's resources and, in some instances, its capacity to perform. Reliers are stakeholders the organization relies on to function but who, at the same time, draw on the organization's overall resources. Employees, subcontractors used to repair broken equipment or the stakeholders "bought" to protect the organization or its products and services are examples.

Demanders have a unique role within the stakeholder network. Demanders have the potential to place the greatest drain on the organization's resources—in some instances, even the power to shut the organization down or to force it to abandon the patch it established for its operations. Demanders are stakeholders that typically can't be ignored or put off. These are the authority figures who grant licenses, audit products and services to protect consumer health or safety and, of course, those who enforce laws, rules and regulations. The marginal literally responds to their demands or faces the consequences of not doing so.

It's also important to note that a demander's role in the marginal's network is often more visible than it is in a mainstream organization's network. Marginals have expectations regarding stakeholders; they know what they want from stakeholders that support them and, generally speaking, what to fear or to be concerned about from stakeholders that are not supportive of the organization. Stakeholders, too, have their own expectations vis-à-vis the marginal organization and often know the power they have in the marginal's network. Marginals are vulnerable organizations for a number of reasons and this works to the stakeholder's advantage.

Vulnerability is a meaningful feature of all organizations because it is a gateway linking the organization and its environment. The more vulnerable the organization, the greater potential risk will increase as the organization interacts with members of the environment or, at times, the environment generally. The need for money, the criminal nature of a marginal's activity, its image or credibility in society, the extent to which it interfaces with or within the mainstream and its physical size, all contribute to defining the marginal's level of vulnerability. In these instances, vulnerability is a measure of the organization's capacity to withstand the threats, challenges or attacks aimed at it; except in the case of accidents or a natural catastrophe, stakeholders are the most likely agents capable of taking advantage of an organization's vulnerability.

Perhaps the greatest threat to a marginal is the formation of a stakeholder swarm (Tafoya, 2013a), a phenomenon triggered by a crisis and characterized by the loss of provider and supporter stakeholders and an increased number of demander stakeholders. Stakeholder swarms can cause the marginal to expend more of its resources on efforts to defend itself or to fight off the swarm's effects. If the swarm is particularly well established, the power center of the emerging social network can be dominated by swarm members, further weakening the marginal. Finally, and again because of the marginals role in society vis-à-vis that of a swarm's demanders (e.g., a drug dealer versus a police officer), the swarm may so overwhelm the marginal that it is captured by the swarm or, more often, its operations simply terminate.

In chapter 3, figure 3.1 was used to illustrate a condition where a stakeholder swarm has enveloped a marginal organization. In that illustration, demanders and reliers outnumber supporters and feeders but what's not immediately obvious is that some original feeders and suppliers may have already abandoned the failing marginal in an attempt to avoid capture or association with the marginal. Here again, without the resources provided by key feeders and suppliers, the marginal's vulnerability is likely to further increase and the marginal faces greater exploitation.

On average, marginals do what they can to avoid demanders, partially because of their power positions and, of course, because a demander's emergence may aggravate an already weak or vulnerable condition. Added to this is the fact that when a stakeholder swarm forms any attack on the marginal, it is usually not uniform or coordinated. Swarm members have a tendency to pursue their own mission, to do what they can to meet their own needs or fulfill their own interests. This is true even if the swarm member has a positive relationship with the marginal. Stakeholders know their time, resources and interests must be managed, so the addition of stress or potential harm brought about by the emerging swarm means all stakeholders have decisions to make regarding the unfolding events and their own well-being. Stakeholders typically are not fools, so while a crisis may affect some stakeholders more than others, the overall effects are always systemic—the "evolving trauma, to a greater or lesser degree, touches all elements of the system" (Tafoya, 2013a,b).

Of course, the effects of a stakeholder swarm need not have only negative consequences. Some marginals "see the error of their ways" and reform, and many mainstream organizations can reap an array of benefits from the impact of a swarm on a marginal and its network. Table 5.1 illustrates representative tangible and intangible benefits and costs one might associate with a swarm's

Table 5.1 Representative Tangible and Intangible Costs and Benefits to an Organization Resulting from Stakeholder Swarms

Tangible		*Intangible*	
Costs (Draining resources)	*Benefits (Contributions)*	*Costs (Draining resources)*	*Benefits (Contributions)*
• Divert the hub's attention • Financial losses • Suppliers may leave • Disrupted operations • Loss of customers • Litigation • Missed deadlines • Operations terminated • Loss of influence • Criminal charges • Loss of licenses	• Exposes violations • Reveals "enemies" • Inquiries expose ills • Links the "like-minded" • Adds new stakeholders • Career benefits • Investigations improve • Research skills improve	• Damage to image • Damaged reputation • Work time lost • Increased supervision • Increased regulations • Creates division • Creates tension • Wider exposure • More special interests • Loss of image	• Opportunity to change • Gets the past "behind" • Exposes issues • Sends a message • Alerts the "public" • Rights a wrong • Broader exposure • Marginals are "off the streets" • Authority's image improves

activities. Information in the table is self-explanatory. However, it is interesting to add that both mainstream and marginal organizations are exposed to potential costs and benefits when a crisis swarm materializes, so while the well-meaning, perhaps self-righteous mainstreamers may think attacking a marginal is a good idea, it might be prudent to question what risks or exposures the mainstreamers' organization might face as a controversy unfolds. Conflicts have a way of spreading pain and injury across all involved.

Conclusion

Stakeholders are important to all organizations, and when it comes to the feeders and supporters in a network, they can be essential to the organization's very existence. Feeders and supporters are those who bring resources, aid and support to the organization. But an organization is also made up of those who don't support it. In fact, they may even seek to inhibit the organization's actions or even end its existence altogether. This is true for all organizations but for marginals, by their very nature, it's part of their existence.

Marginals often find themselves under constant scrutiny. In contrast, mainstream organizations are targets of stress, conflict or attacks when challenged by a competitor, after violating the law, when some events, like a crisis, trigger an investigation or, of course, when a marginal invades their territory, attacks them or is perceived as presenting a threat to the organization.

In this chapter, we've explored the nature of marginals by examining ways in which they construct an environment within and from which they can operate. In most instances, and despite the fact that those operating as marginals may own their own property, the marginal's environment often is loosely defined, partially because of its role outside of society's mainstream or because of the often illegal nature of the marginal's work or residency status. As a result, marginals are often forced to rely on a stakeholder network as their means for connecting with key customers, support services or the mainstream in general.

Relying on a stakeholder network is not a novel circumstance for marginals for these networks are a critical part of all organizations, marginal or mainstream. But, here again, the marginal's stakeholder network, because of the marginal's vague, often blurred relationship with its host society, means the marginal's network is, by definition, often affected by the shadow cast by the marginal. As a result, the marginal's network may never be as robust a resource for the marginal as a mainstream's network is for it and, perhaps worse, may not be a reliable source for assistance should a crisis arise.

These can be meaningful handicaps for the marginal organization and with potentially significant ramifications. For example, consider these features of a marginal's stakeholder network. First, the bottom line behind the emergence of a stakeholder network is action—stakeholders form or join a network to achieve a vision or mission that reflects their own needs and interests. Marginal organizations have their own, definable stakeholder network but it's not necessarily a place where all stakeholders share or are committed to the marginal's mission. Indeed, challenges to the marginal may result in all stakeholders abandoning the net for their own safety or security.

Mainstream organizations can't be kept out of the marginal's network. They may not be evident but mainstream organizations are part of a marginal's network by the nature of their own missions. Sometimes this is by design: the nature of the marginal's business or mission means it sells or serves in networks controlled by mainstream organizations. Other times, mainstream organizations shadow the marginal as part of their own mission. This is particularly true if the mainstream organization is in law enforcement and is shadowing a marginal that is engaged in illegal activities.

The potential for dissonance surrounds any emerging stakeholder system. Stakeholders are their own organizations and have their own networks. When they join or interact with other organizations, like the marginals we've been discussing, they often have to learn how to work with the marginals with which they are linked. When the network is in the grip of a stakeholder swarm, the initial, established system can confront new thresholds, decisions and tensions that permeate the environment and ecology for those involved. What contributes to the complications associated with a crisis is that the dissonance experienced is driven as much by greed and self-interest as it is by the evident crisis.

The network itself becomes susceptible to increased and ongoing inference and resistance from the stakeholders who populate it, complicate it and even comprise its operations. Every network has a hub but the possibility that other hubs will form or that the original hub will be abandoned as a crisis unfolds cannot be overlooked. As a result, it's not uncommon for a marginal's network to be defined by stakeholders with "one foot in the net and one foot outside."

The role and function of time is dynamic in stakeholder networks. Internal and external events can unfold in unexpected ways and marginals are especially "event sensitive." Their often tenuous rapport with society in general or mainstream organizations in particular means even minor events may impact the organization or network operations. Time constraints add complications to the emerging system's efforts when a crisis emerges. Solutions or remedies for problems must be handled immediately, if for no other reason than to avoid drawing attention to the marginal and its network. As a result, externally induced boundaries (time constraints, rules systems, sanctions) mark transition points that can influence the marginal's movement from ill-established collective to recognized entity. Some time constraints are warranted, like meaningful deadlines and due dates; while others are unplanned, disruptive or injurious barriers. Time is something marginals must work with, not play with.

One way time's role surfaces in emerging and established networks is through inherent design faults and the ever-present possibility for a random error to occur. As result, an emerging swarm can trigger dissonance or capitalize on existing vulnerabilities making marginal organizations unreliable tools to meet the network's needs and unpredictable partners or adversaries. Moreover, there's always the potential for stakeholder flight or abandonment when a crisis occurs. This is a critical issue for any network, but because of the nature of most marginal organizations, it's always a very real possibility that needs to be managed.

Network members, feeders (++), supporters (+) and reliers (–) all have special relationships with "their" organization first, and then the marginal's network. Demanders (—) have an almost exclusive relationship with their own organization. In addition, feeders and supporters might not share the marginal organization's risk but they can have their own as a result of their relationship with the marginal, so that can make them especially sensitive to an emerging crisis or threat from the mainstream. Reliers, too, because of the very nature of their relationship with the organization, need some measure of protection. Unfortunately, more often than not, most organizations forget about these important stakeholder group relationships in a crisis, and look to their own needs first. That may seem good in the short term but the long-term ramifications may be embedded in the memories of those who were injured and then were overlooked or, worse, ignored altogether.

Most marginals do not have the skills, time or resources needed to develop and manage key operational practices and procedures that could help them manage a crisis and sometimes even the business at hand. Additionally, few have learned the benefits that effective use of time, discipline or sense of urgency can contribute to their organizations or way of life. This translates into limited or insufficient competencies and only adds to the marginal's vulnerability for it and any network of which it is part. Why should a stakeholder believe that a marginal (1) can handle an emerging crisis and/or (2) is capable of protecting the network's stakeholders if the marginal can't even introduce and manage operational practices and procedures most organizations recognize as fundamental?

Those who own or manage a marginal organization always must keep one point in mind: control within a marginal's network is seldom assured. Sometimes the sheer number of stakeholders emerging in and around a network can be daunting. All the same, each stakeholder must be addressed and attended to whether for day-to-day matters or when attempting to develop adequate, long-term solutions for a crisis that materializes. Moreover, it is a mistake to assume that network members will "pull together" in an emerging crisis or that the apparent hub is the affirmed leader of the network. The same foibles that plague individual relationships, bias, egotism, self-centeredness, favoritism, neglect and poor competencies, can emerge in a network with equally damaging effects.

A second control-related factor marginals must address is that stakeholders are a fluid bunch, and regardless of their apparent affiliations, in the end they always seem to do as they want. This has been an ongoing theme throughout our discussion of marginals and their networks, but a crisis only amplifies this instability. There is something very personal about a crisis. When one emerges, it can challenge and sometimes threaten one's values, competencies, expectations and even one's sense about what is right or wrong. So, in addition to the likelihood that the organization's stakeholder network will pull in different, self-centered directions in a crisis, it is also important to remember that there are individuals within those organizations who are also pulling in directions they see as most important and/or valuable to them. These points may become clear in chapter 6 as features associated with ways a crisis can impact organizations and their stakeholders are presented. For now, it is offered as another illustration of the layers of chaos those in a marginal organization must be prepared to confront as they handle problems that arise.

Finally, a marginal's network is a less-than-reliable way to mount a defense against any attack. This doesn't mean one can't draw on the network, but as we've seen, stakeholders in a marginal's network have their own needs and concerns to address—and that's typically their focus. In chapter 6, we'll examine how marginals work at defining their organization despite the range of challenges they face. The fact that marginals are a ubiquitous part of all societies and have been for thousands of years illustrates they can survive significant challenges, but how and why they survive is important and merits particular attention.

CHAPTER 6

For Marginal Organizations within a World of Mixed Certainty, Surviving May Be Just Enough

Marginal organizations are ubiquitous; they are part of all societies and have been for thousands of years. But mere survival is hardly an adequate measure of success or, as we've seen, a progressive way to plan for the future. Consider, for example, the legacy of mainstream organizations, those properly linked with the parent society of which they are a part. Mainstream organizations tend to be distributed throughout a community or country and often function within them regardless of either's size or location.

They are well established and less susceptible to extinction not only because of their size and value to the community but also because they serve functions that are of mutual benefit to themselves and the mainstream at large. Symbiotic relationships are possible and not uncommon. Mainstream organizations are networked throughout every facet of a society's political, educational, social, religious, industrial and artistic arenas.

Mainstream organizations also are seldom "stand alone" organizations. They work with, bond with and collaborate with other mainstream organizations. They are responsible for establishing, maintaining, funding and protecting the status quo. They can form cooperatives, buying groups or fully functioning market communities like shopping centers or malls.

Other times mainstream organizations form close bonds among themselves, specifically to restrict or inhibit emergence of unwanted organizations, movements or change on individual or systemic levels. Bonds among mainstream organizations serve as conduits for the exchange of information, ideas and general notions regarding what's good and not, healthy and not, wanted and not. This may not seem a "fair" way to manage a free-market economy, but it's the mainstream that also usually decides what's fair and not fair.

When acting as "defensive agents" protecting the mainstream or society (as they see it) in general, mainstream organizations prove to be powerful adversaries for marginal organizations. Their tactics against marginals can include attempts to diminish their size, to break up individual marginals or any relationships they may have with others. Mainstreamers will, if they think it's necessary, attempt to grind down, dismember and, of course, destroy any marginal targeted.

Marginals, in contrast, don't have the potential to build the range of advantages mainstream organizations possess to protect themselves because they are often encumbered by very powerful constraints. Marginals operating illegally or engaged in illegal activities create the subjects for continued scrutiny and surveillance and, at the extreme, investigation, assault and attack. More than distractions, such conditions force these marginals to be constantly vigilant of matters in their environment, to be less than trusting when dealing with those they don't know and, in some instances, to make quick, disadvantageous sales of products or goods simply to rid their inventory of ill-gotten goods or, worse, just to get the funds needed to maintain operations.

Marginals, then, can find themselves living in a world defined by anticipation and suspicion. For many, the issue is not if an encounter with mainstream authorities will occur, but what type of encounter will occur, with what intensity and when? For example, profiling and subsequent "stop and searches" have become such a significant occurrence for marginals and some disenfranchised members of society that some feel these mainstream behaviors are routine and to be expected. In other cases, it's sometimes possible to outline "disruption patterns" for certain marginals that reflect how often, how extensively and how intensely their routines are affected by the intervention of mainstream agents (Anonymous, 2009; Dickson-Gomez et al., 2008; Green, 2009; Ryder and Turksen, 2009).

But marginals survive and in many instances thrive in the shadows of the dominant mainstream, and in this chapter we explore how and why survival is possible and what it can mean for both segments of a society. The chapter begins with a look at the ways marginals negotiate and sometimes manage the flow of their operations and subsequent interface with the mainstream of society. Material in this section illustrates an ongoing dilemma for marginals: simple survival is seldom sufficient when growth and expansion are what's needed.

Second, change, adaptability and invention are key survival tactics for many marginals but these tactics often collide with efforts aimed at keeping a low profile, not drawing attention to one's self or generally trying to be out of sight of those who may not support the marginals' efforts and activities. In other words, marginals often must develop ways to cope with both "ways of being different" and the "effects of being different" by inventing and managing carefully crafted techniques and methods to preserve the health and well-being of their organization and its components. Many marginals, again often because of the nature of their business, don't have many "friends" and this can promote levels of defensiveness and self-management that are prudent on one level and excessive at another. Some marginals even take pride in claiming that "joining" makes someone a "member for life" without necessarily noting "how long" a life one may have as a member.

Finally, the culmination of survival strategies and tactics may reveal the unique ways marginals develop for managing stakeholders and stakeholder relationships. Mainstream organizations, as described above, may work with, bond with, collaborate with, sometimes even merge with different stakeholders but these options are not typically part of a marginal organization's management profile. Marginals almost always approach stakeholders from a functional perspective as tools either for achieving or for obstructing efforts toward a desired end. Stakeholder relationships also may not be public matters, but rather relationships in name only—and this is acceptable among all involved. Survival is the name of the game explored in this chapter, and for many marginals there is really only one player of any importance.

Survival at the Stream Level: Nurturing the Organization by Managing Money, People and Goods

Money may be the fuel that drives an organization but the organization's supply stream is its engine. The organization's supply stream serves as a conduit linking the people, processes, material and equipment needed to produce the organization's products and services. However, supply streams are more than a mechanism or linear collection of bits and parts, people and processes. For example, like any natural river or stream an organization's supply stream is subject to various flow rates, disruptions, twists and turns. These variations influence every part of the organization. A heavier flow can mean more work is available creating a need for more people to build products or deliver services to interested customers. For most organizations, this would be a plus, but that's not necessarily true for marginals.

More work may bring more money but it also means more exposure for the organization, overall an undesirable condition. In addition, more flow through the stream also means that increased volume may reveal or stress weak or vulnerable points in the organization. If the organization has a widely distributed supply stream, increased flow across weak or vulnerable points may add even more risk as these points may not be able to carry the same flow levels as healthy, strong process points.

A stream's flow volume isn't the only issue of concern for marginals. The variability in stream flows can trigger problems for a marginal that a mainstream organization wouldn't experience. Increased flows can mean the organization needs to hire more people, but there may not be extra people able or willing to do the work a marginal needs done and, also, since a marginal's work often borders on illegality, it may not be possible or prudent to recruit someone quickly to fill a needed position.

Timing of flow changes can pose other problems. If increased flows come when labor is unavailable, or if laborers with particular skills are needed but not available, the impact on service delivery and production can be dramatic. The same is true if the flow slows. Marginals can't afford to have people sitting idly and waiting for work to pick up. These people need to be paid and, moreover, workers just sitting around create another exposure point for an organization interested in maintaining a low profile.

Sales have a direct effect on a marginal's flows, and sales, in turn, are dependent on a number of other factors. Marginal organizations, for example, often operate with two types of "sales windows." The first are those sales that are tied to a particular event, like the vendor trying to work crowds at a special sporting event or a numbers runner working a particular horse race. If it's a one-time event, the vendor needs products for the event before the event—not after the event ends. A week or even a day late doesn't help the vendor. The same is true for the numbers runner. Bets placed after a race don't count. A second window is the type associated with a particular product/client relationship. Drugs for the addict are an example. This customer doesn't want to hear that the product will be late or is on the way. If the product isn't available, this client will try to get it from someone else. Timing is critical in these sales relationships.

The length of the flow also affects the marginal's capacity to manage its supply stream and ultimately production or service delivery. If demand is off and the flow is slow, should the marginal keep staff around hoping the flow will increase? Many marginals operate with low profit margins, so carrying a larger than needed staff can stress any organization. Keep in mind, too, that those who work for marginals may have "issues" of their own. Some may have criminal records or are illegally in the country, and this makes them attractive to mainstream organizations that like to look for or watch out for people with these profiles. The marginal that hires people like these may be getting cheaper labor but the organizations are also creating additional exposure for their operations.

Flow variability can also impact supply issues. Stakeholders who supply raw goods or materials to a manufacturer have their own supply streams and production processes to manage; not knowing if or when a marginal needs its products can force a supplier to deal with unsold goods and perhaps even question the marginal's reliability as a customer. Poor flows are seldom good for anyone involved in the supply stream, to say nothing about what it does for their relationships with each other.

Finally, unpredictable flows can add warehousing to those involved in a production process, and while this is one way to handle an overabundance of goods and material it also has its own risks. Warehousing can stress both parties. The supplier has to inventory unsold goods, find someone else to buy them and, sometimes, even sell them at a loss. Each of these conditions can draw unwanted attention to the supplier who wants to maintain a low profile. Finally, engaging in warehousing means extra facilities and often extra staff to manage the warehouse and sometimes skills and equipment to handle the goods being stored. All of this can place a drain on cash flow, and money tied up in warehoused goods is not money working for the organization's profits.

Sometimes warehoused goods spoil or rot or simply disappear. Beyond the expense associated with warehousing, storing certain goods can also affect their value or use. Clothing can fall out of fashion and consumer goods like beer, cigarettes, or drugs have a shelf life that can't be altered. Spoilage is a real problem in these instances. Moving goods around in storage or from production to storage can result in damage, and if the marginal uses damaged or inferior materials, the final products may be affected. And what about the goods that "disappear"? Then what's the marginal's recourse? Those engaged in an illegal activity can't run to the police to report, say, stolen cocaine. Finally, using a warehouse means the marginal has another "visibility point." A smooth, seamless supply stream has goods coming from suppliers to the production center. A type of "Just-in-Time-Drug Make." A warehouse puts another stop in the stream and this can be a risky exposure point.

Ultimately, any examination of supply or production streams factors should incorporate the role the stream has on a particular type of marginal. This analysis can approach stream effects from the perspective of the type of marginal organization (enterprise, community, team or individual contributor), its operational profile (active, passive, proactive) or some combination of the two. A religious cult (a "community" organization) reflects an active profile through its missionary work, a passive profile if the community lives the life of hermits or recluses shut away from society or a proactive profile when engaging in evangelical activities. There are different levels of potential exposure depending on the profile the organization follows. This becomes particularly clear when looking at marginals that operate as enterprises.

A marginal engaged in selling pornographic material (an enterprise) maintains an active profile if it operates a store to carry its goods, a passive profile if it markets and sells its products on the Internet and a proactive profile when it not only sells but also produces pornographic materials. Now, not only are the potentials for exposure increased, but so too are the potentials for different levels of prosecution.

Table 5.1 in chapter 5 sketched possible costs and benefits an organization might experience if a stakeholder swarm emerges because of a crisis. This is easy to see when one looks at the activities of two particularly malicious marginals, the teams that smuggle undocumented aliens across the border and the individual contributor who operates as a drug dealer.

For example, when the smugglers operate as casual traffickers the passive profile doesn't draw as much attention as when they are actively involved in frequent and extensive attempts to smuggle aliens from one point to another. Here the smuggler with an active profile isn't interested in trying to sneak one or two people across the border but rather trucks 15–20 at a time. There may be little effort to disguise the activity; the smuggler simply risks capture against earning a lot of money quickly. Compare this to the smuggler with a proactive profile. Here creativity and inventiveness can dominate smuggling activities. The smuggler may experiment with new devices (e.g., using submarines or ship containers), new routes by going around the American border in the southwest and attempting to enter the country via the east or west coasts or may try pooling, where the smuggler carries more than one product in the same trip, for example, aliens and drugs or cigarettes.

Individual contributors can demonstrate similar characteristics across the three profiles. A drug dealer with a proactive profile might concentrate on using sales plans that target primary, secondary and tertiary sales markets This expands the dealer's options so that if one sales area is closed or too risky, he simply moves off to another. A more passive profile, in contrast, might have the dealer selling the drugs at a discount to others who, in turn, become the dealers. This reduces the drug dealer's revenue but also avoids potential risks associated with handling every part of the drug-selling stream. Finally, an active profile is the one most often associated with a drug dealer. This profile has the dealer approaching potential buyers and simply asking if they want the drugs or not. This individual canvasses an area, a party or a function, like a concert.

Each profile reshapes the marginal's supply and value streams. What makes a focus on the marginal's operational profile most useful, however, is that it recognizes the potential diversity associated with a given marginal organization. So the focus isn't just a "cult" but rather a type of cult or, in a more thorough analysis, the three types of profiles that might be associated with a cult. The potential insights gained after comparing and contrasting organizations in this way give rise to potentially interesting perspectives; the approach is no longer a simple, one-dimensional study.

A stream analysis can also mix different elements of stream dynamics into examination of a marginal's activity. Some flows can be examined in terms of their predictability. Can a flow's magnitude, frequency and duration be predicted, and if so to what extent? In what ways do product type, time and production requirements impact flow rates and what bearing do these have on production costs? Answering these types of questions can provide specific information, in this case regarding supply stream flows, as well as a broader picture of a marginal's operation and the challenges it may face.

Finally, it's possible to manipulate these and other approaches to compare and contrast marginals with competitors or the mainstream organizations with whom they may interact (or want to avoid). How do society's constraints (e.g., laws, rules or regulations), agents (e.g., legislators or law enforcement) or cultural biases impact marginals vis-à-vis their supply streams? The border between the United States and Mexico illustrates a significant supply stream factor for those smuggling illegal aliens or drugs. After all, even if production runs smoothly and the product is available on time but it's not possible to move it across the border, what good is it? Moreover, impacting the supply stream in this manner also disrupts the vital "value stream" discussed earlier. The value stream runs throughout the organization connecting all stakeholders to the design, development, product and distribution of goods and services. Indeed, value streams, in contrast to other streams (e.g., supply, design, distribution), simultaneously cover all of those streams while serving as the "value center" as value is created (e.g., through product design or production), purchased (e.g., in the exchange of skilled labor for a finished product) or realized as a result of business transactions. So a food vendor's value stream includes various elements, from the purchase of a higher grade of meat for meals over lesser quality meat, the transformation of a patron's order into a delicious meal and, of course, the receipts for the sale of sandwiches.

All marginals, Cyber Spies, terrorists or gunrunners, have value streams that can be attacked and disrupted as part of the mission of a proactive mainstream organization. Mainstream stakeholders regularly incorporate strategies to disrupt a marginal's value streams as ways to achieve their own missions when pursuing their adversaries in the margins. The Federal Bureau of Investigation (FBI), for example, regularly targets the value streams of marginals it is tracking as part of its mission to neutralize threats to the economic and national security of the United States. According to Michael Morehart, section chief of the Bureau's Counterterrorism Division, one border-like barrier they use involves investigations into the financial information related to a target marginal and its operations (Morehart, 2006). When pursuing marginals engaged in criminal activity, this is a two-step approach designed "to deprive the criminal of the proceeds of crime. The first step involves aggressively investigating the underlying criminal activity, which establishes the specified unlawful activity requirements of the federal money-laundering statutes, and the second step involves following the money to identify the financial infrastructures used to launder proceeds of criminal activity" (Morehart, 2006). Compare this with Morehart's description of the approach used to tackle terrorist organizations.

According to Morehart, in the counterterrorism model, the keystone of the FBI's strategy against terrorism involves "countering the manner in which terror networks recruit, train, plan, and effect operations, each of which requires a measure of financial support." Here, again, targeting the organization's value stream permeates multiple areas: "The FBI established the Terrorist Financing Operations Section of the Counterterrorism Division on the premise that the required financial support of terrorism inherently includes the generation, movement and expenditure of resources, which are oftentimes identifiable and traceable through records published by financial institutions" (Morehart, 2006).

Disruption of an organization's operational and value streams can be achieved in more ways than targeting the organization's financial affairs. The Dickson-Gomez et al. (2008), Potok (2009) and Green (2009) articles referred to earlier illustrate that disrupting stakeholders' living environments, their employment opportunities and even where their shop is set up can impact an organization's streams.

Concentrating on challenges to a marginal's operational streams is only one facet or level of analysis of marginals and their efforts to survive given the trials they can face. Streams can be vulnerable to a variety of phenomena, from overt attacks by an adversary to naturally occurring disruptions. Since the streams are critical for the organization's survival, their disruption can create significant hardships for marginals. In the next segment of this chapter, we'll look at value streams again, but the focus of that discussion will be on exploring why money, beyond the obvious, is such an attractive target for both the marginal and its adversaries.

Streams May Be a Marginal's Engine but Money Turns the Engine on and Keeps It Running

Once one takes both a marginal and a mainstream organization into consideration, a very unique picture emerges regarding the contact between or among organizations with different and often competing supply or value streams.

In chapter 4, figure 4.1 illustrated how the streams of two organizations might come into contact. It's a useful model given the current discussion, too. Imagine that instead of two organizations there are three or more. For example, if there are three organizations and we're looking at the cyclical streams of those three organizations as outlined in figure 4.1, then the point of interest becomes that area where these streams meet. Consider a model of, say, a "drug bust." Now the point of intercept is where the drug deal is culminated between the pusher (A) and buyer (B), only this time consider what happens if we add a third circle reflecting the value stream of a police officer (C), about to arrest both of them as the money changes hands.

This is a simple model with only three players. Add more players, more marginal and mainstream organizations and the simple model appears as a network engulfed in a mix of stakeholder activity. If we continue our example of a drug bust, the network might reflect a large drug sale, perhaps among different gangs. Members of these groups might include those offering protection to the process, the specialist testing the drugs to make sure they are what they claim to be (we are talking about a deal among thieves after all) and, of course, there are the product and money handlers. The third circle is particularly unique for in addition to including members of the marginal sector it can also include different mainstream agents that might be involved, say representing local police and federal agencies, such as the FBI or Drug Enforcement Agency (DEA), and, of course, the media. So supply and value streams serve a critical purpose for the organizations involved, but they also carry their share of risks.

As attractive as money is to acquire and have, it can present real problems for marginal organizations, particularly if it's not claimed or taxes aren't paid. For example, as indicated above, mainstreamers like the FBI know that money can be traced or tracked and that large amounts of money, for example, the earnings associated with the drug industry, can result in a lot of volume to hold, manage and "get rid of." Money is an attractive target for thieves, so it needs to be stored somewhere, but where? Put it into an American bank and again it is traceable.

Strategies for Handling Money in Streams with a Lot of Players

Money management is a critical aspect of any organization; without sufficient money, an organization cannot continue operation. As a result, organizations often do what they can to ensure that more money comes in than goes out, and this is true whether it's a mainstream or marginal organization. Because marginals often (1) get money illegally and/or (2) fail to report the funds they do receive, everything about the way money is managed by marginals is interesting and notable, including one particular guiding theme: keeping money invisible. Take compensation strategies, for example.

Compensation strategies are a fascinating and sometimes very complex aspect of any organization. This usually isn't the case within marginal organizations. For example, funding operations by covering wages, buying goods and materials for production or generally covering expenses is one way to spend money but virtually everyone involved in these money exchanges has something to hide from authorities: Cash rules and paper trails don't. Paying employees illustrates this theme. It's difficult to track how marginals pay workers. It's not clear if their pay follows minimum wage standards or not, but given they are notorious for not adhering to other state and federal regulations (like paying taxes), it's doubtful they comply with compensation rules and regulations. In some cases, like drug smuggling, compensation is tied to particular activities such as production, transporting the product or sales.

Apart from the payment of wages, there are not a lot of other employee-based expenses. Medical care and health insurance isn't usually offered nor are typical retirement benefits. In most instances, you work until you no longer can. It's a unique form of exchange theory: employees live, get needed support, however defined, and job security, in exchange for work. The issue isn't growth or advancement; it is being of service, of meeting a need.

And, of course, there's equipment to purchase and that can be a different matter. One of the advantages of using a supply stream as a way to examine marginal organizations is that we have an opportunity to see where people, materials, equipment (including cars and trucks) come into the process of making a marginal organization work. For example, consider two rather simple but different streams, one for a standard, sit-down restaurant (Ramaswamy, 1996) and the other for a food truck operating outside an office building. The two streams are outlined in table 6.1.

Just looking at the stream illustrates that there are three steps less in the "Food Truck Stream" than in the "Sit-down Restaurant Stream" but it's the overall differences that are most dramatic. For example, food must be delivered to the customer in the restaurant, the restaurant's kitchen may have several different people working in it, more than just one or two people may

Table 6.1 Sit-Down Restaurant Versus Food Truck Stream: You Experience What You Pay For

Sit-Down Restaurant Stream						
Greeting	Seating	Menu delivery	Order-taking process	Meal delivery	Billing and settlement process	Departure process
Food Truck Stream						
Greeting	NONE	NONE: the menu is posted	Order-taking process	Meal delivery	Billing	NONE

interact with the customer (to greet, seat, take orders, deliver the food and take money) and there's the eating area's equipment (tables, chairs, reception area, etc.).

Our marginal organization has few of the elements one finds in the sit-down restaurant. In fact, the only employee may be the "proprietor/greeter/order taker/cook/bill handler" (who's also the one who drove the truck to the eating site). There's money involved in both production processes but usually less, and often much less for the average marginal. It's also easy to see why mainstream organizations with their potentially heavy overhead object to marginal organizations, particularly if they are operating nearby: both the loss of business and the fact that operating expenses must be paid regardless add insult to (perceived) injury.

A second money management strategy for the marginal is to buy toys. Lots and lots of toys. Lists of the items retrieved after drug arrests offer a revealing look into some marginals' operations. Houses or mansions, various luxury cars, property of all sorts demonstrate the potential income derived from this segment of the society's financial activities. But the items are just that. Indeed, they may be more interesting when viewed as attempts to demonstrate status, position or power than simply what one was able to purchase after the sale of illegal drugs. Considering the adage "pride goes before a fall," it's hard to maintain a low profile and not draw attention to oneself when driving (or being driven) in cars that cost $100,000 or living and partying in multimillion dollar mansions. Still, these are ways to spend the income derived from your business, and after all it's just money or, to paraphrase another old adage "you can't take it with you"—wherever you're headed.

Some owners and operators of marginal organizations have relied on patronage, the buying of support, affinity and/or affiliation as a way for distributing some of their excess monies. Many of these efforts are almost noble, like giving money to the poor. This may truly help the disadvantaged but in many ways it is little more than another attempt to create a pool of people dependent on the illegal organization. Other strategies are not noble. Attempts to buy protection, favors or help from those in authority undermine the fabric of the mainstream. When the police, members of the judicial system or other government agencies take bribes or kickbacks, it's not just the influence of marginals that expands, it's the number of stakeholders in the marginal environmental network that grows, too.

If I Can't Have You as a Friend Can I at Least Buy Who You Are?

Still, buying affiliations in this manner has its advantages. This can increase the number of eyes and ears working on behalf of the organization. Bribes and kickbacks are a means of extending the organization's range of security; now the organization has artificial boundaries that extend beyond main operation centers and sometimes even its satellite operations associated with distribution of products and services through to the markets it serves.

Care must be taken when buying favors, however, for while not actually adding people to the ranks of the organization, this still increases its potential exposures or confidants the police or authorities may use to gain access to the organization. On the other hand, buying a lot of little people, minions, can be a noteworthy tactic should law enforcement attempt to attack the organization for these people also have to be rounded up, held, processed and, if necessary, tried for their involvement, and this can be a significant burden for the judicial system processing the organization. In other words, the complexities associated with the management of marginals are not insignificant.

Processes related to a marginal's operation also can cloak its activities with levels of complexity that make investigations complicated, cumbersome and expensive. Money laundering is a sophisticated process conceived to help "criminals to do what they do best—commit crimes—with greater resource at their disposal and with less chance of detection" (Alasmari, 2012, p. 141). Money laundering is an example of an illegal operation used to facilitate another illegal operation. The principles are straightforward. Generally, an organization, say one involved in the manufacture of illegal drugs, takes its profits and sends them to the money-laundering organization, which then, for a fee, redistributes the money as far and wide as needed in order to make it difficult to trace the origin of the money. Different financial rules and regulations make this the most vulnerable part of the laundering activities (142).

Finally, the money is integrated into the environment using a number of otherwise legitimate tactics. According to Alasmari, this can involve (1) shifting from the use of different financial money management strategies and actions to the laundering of the original money so it can be used in legitimate channels; (2) making financial investments in legitimate enterprises (e.g., in the stock market); (3) purchasing other organizations to use as "fronts" or shelters for their illegal organization. Of course, any of these actions can create more money for the parent organization, but at least when that money is earned it's legally earned and, ideally, with proper taxes and fees paid.

Their Goods May Be the Root of Their Evil, But They're Also the Source for Their Income Stream

Marginal organizations are true examples of an entrepreneurial spirit. Owners and operators of marginals can be involved in the preparation and sales of food, have a cottage industry making sweaters, run an illegal liquor-making distillery or meth lab, sell dogs in a puppy mill or offer one's self as a prostitute. Just about anything animal, vegetable or mineral can be the basis of a marginal's product mix.

Some marginals may not have the resources or skills needed to develop and/or sell products and goods, so they look to the sale of services as the source of their income. Services in this instance can range from selling protection, smuggling, running the numbers in a gambling operation and, of course, selling fear or terror through murder or mayhem, hijacking or kidnapping. Service-based marginals have relatively lower overheads in comparison to marginals in the manufacturing business and may not require the levels of competence needed to operate in the marketplace, but there are common standards both must achieve.

Regardless of one's opinion of them as institutions or businesses in our society, they cannot succeed or, minimally, survive unless they accomplish two goals. Marginals must meet the needs of stakeholders in their network, and must also be prepared to change, adapt and invent who they are or what they do, or else the predictability associated with routines can be disastrous.

Regarding the first, the marginal must meet its stakeholders' needs—regardless of the product or service offered or the nature of their organization. This sounds obvious but even an addict knows the difference between good and bad drugs and prostitutes know who are "clean" or infected with a sexually transmitted disease. These points can be so important that the quality levels associated with some crimes are also of interest to regulatory and health agencies responsible for treating addicts suffering from drug overdose, the negative effects of tainted or bad drugs or alcohol or the spread of HIV. Indeed, some communities have incorporated needle exchange programs and disease screening as part of the services they provide, simply because of the presence and operation of some illegal marginals. Many police departments, too, offer training to their staff who work and patrol areas that may bring them into contact with those potentially infected with disease or suffering from extremes associated with excessive drug use. In fact, it's not uncommon for a modern police officer to use, in addition to the latest weapons and body armor, plastic gloves as part of the "uniform of the day"—all as a result of a marginal's activity in and around a society's mainstream.

In addition to quality and service standards, no marginal can avoid offering an acceptable level of performance with the work they do or the products they offer. Their stakeholders usually won't tolerate anything less than an acceptable level of reliability, uniformity and, of course, on-time delivery, regardless of the product or service provided. Law enforcement and others have been quick to recognize the impact delaying or disrupting the arrival and/or distribution of illegal products can have on that segment of the marginal economy. Disruptions of product delivery can create shortages, drive up prices of available goods or force customers to seek alternative ways to meet their needs. Challenging the reliability of a provider to deliver goods and services is another effective tactic. Keeping drug dealers, numbers runners, prostitutes or even the food vendor "on the move" by denying them access to the same "point of service" makes it hard for users to find them when needed. They become unreliable and, as a result, less useful as a means for needs fulfillment.

Moving Money in a Marginal's Supply Stream Meets the Marginal's Needs. Moving People Is Designed to Meet Stakeholder Needs

Apart from those who buy the marginal's products and services, people enter the marginal's supply stream in three ways. First, a marginal needs people to do work, to produce a product or to perform a service. These are the people who manufacture the products sold, make the drugs or rob the stores. These people are central to the organization; they are at its core.

A second group includes those involved in the organization's distribution process. They are the "middle force" that may or may not be directly linked to the organization. On the production side, these provide raw or finished goods and materials for the organization to include in its product mix. On the distribution side, these are the people who "fence" the stolen goods, move or smuggle goods to a sale point or sell the product. They may be employed by the organization or be subcontractors or people who work for subcontractors. What matters is that they move the product. Incidentally, it makes sense to mention that these people may be compensated for their work but the compensation plan isn't always built around money. The use of compensation in this instance may parallel uses in the mainstream, that is, it can be a means for keeping needed "employees" on the job. But, as is often likely to happen, various forms of compensation are also control devices, sometimes used to keep people in line or to "guarantee" their loyalty. For example, some are paid and some, in the worst cases, engage in their roles because they or their families are threatened or otherwise held hostage.

Finally, there are the people who are part of the product mix itself. They may be entertainers, the terrorist wearing a bomb, assassins or part of a multifaceted sex trade. Sometimes they are compensated for their work and other times it's the individual's family that receives the compensation, a frequent plan for the suicide bomber. These can be the most vulnerable of the organization's population mix. These people are not only at the transaction point, but also some *are* the transaction point. For stakeholders on either side of the transaction, these people are only important to the extent that they serve a purpose and are useful delivery systems. They are of trivial utility because they are so far downstream that they have little useful information about the marginal's core or, worse, they are handled by subcontractors and so aren't directly linked to the marginal per se.

Do I Know You? Are We Related? A Second Key Ingredient for Survival: Cleansing, Sanitizing and Decontaminating the Marginal's "Family"

The second notable survival goal is as important as meeting customer needs. In this instance, however, the marginal must be able to change, adapt and invent ways to run its operation and also adopt new ways to introduce people into its organization. The challenge here, however, is making sure change and adaptation efforts don't collide with efforts aimed at keeping a low profile, not drawing attention to one's self or generally being out of sight of those who may not support the marginal's efforts and activities. In other words, marginals often must develop ways to cope with both "ways of being different" and the "effects of being different" by carefully managing the health and well-being of the organization and its components. This is particularly true when problems arise because the marginal is being scrutinized or is under attack from mainstream organizations.

Many marginals, again often because of the nature of their business, operate in isolation and some, again because of the nature of their business, don't have many "friends"—some even have defined enemies whose objective is to do whatever is necessary to terminate the marginal's activity and sometimes the marginal organization itself. These outsiders are typically linked to the mainstream and can launch pressures that, while often expected, can be so destabilizing to a marginal's supply and operational stream that new levels of complexity emerge to address and manage.

The impact of interventions on the marginal's stakeholders illustrates this point. Raids by the Immigration and Naturalization Service targeting whole segments of a marginal's production stream can make it all but impossible to produce needed goods or services. These types of disruptions can overload a marginal's supply stream and completely disrupt its value stream. In these instances, pressures are successful because they don't target the marginal per se but the people who comprise the organization's stream activity. It's a clever strategy because the focus is on those most vulnerable in the stream and among the stream's weakest links.

Other times, pressures are exerted on the subcontractors, particularly those who hire undocumented workers—stakeholders at the end of this production stream. These attacks use the workers as the ones to follow when setting up raids on manufacturing and agriculture industries, whose businesses need a reliable labor source to meet production or seasonal needs. These farms and factories often are in the mainstream and they use marginals by incorporating them in their own supply streams. Attacks in these instances pressure the mainstream organizations directly involved in the now comingled supply stream of marginal and mainstream organizations.

Other threats target the marginal's image as a "relatively" safe place to work. These interventions target the marginal's workers but they also put indirect pressure on the potential marginal worker. For example, marginal organizations that seek to smuggle people, usually undocumented aliens, into the United States can charge a lot of money for their services with few promises of success. In these ventures, there are several targets to choose from: the smuggler is a target, the alien is another and, often, the factories and farms where the alien hopes to work. In these instances, systemic interventions communicate systemic threats or fear throughout the illegal immigration stream, raising risk levels for all involved.

Finally, mainstream organizations can put extra pressure on a marginal's production stream by targeting stakeholders who make up the organization's customer mix. Contributing to the pressure on the marginals in these instances may be sanctioned government agencies or unofficial special interest groups. Whichever, their interests are the same: affect the marginal's operation by drawing unwanted attention to its customers. These organizations use a variety of tactics to achieve their goals. Some publish the names and faces of people caught buying illegal drugs, alcohol or sex videos, or of those who use prostitutes. Having one's picture in the paper or on the Web in the middle of an illegal act can effectively disrupt a marginal's value stream where the important exchange of money occurs. When this happens, the marginal is in a particularly vulnerable position because it may have spent large amounts of money and/or owe other monies to those involved in the production process, and now needed sales or revenue-producing transactions cannot take place Other times, the targets may be mainstream organizations that while not working directly with the marginal rely on it to meet customer needs by operating as vendors selling food, goods and services. In these instances, the targets may be the sponsoring organization but it's often easier to pressure those who buy from the illegal vendors, those attending the festivals, sporting events or concerts. What parent would want to be entangled in a police action for buying a scalper's tickets, or bootlegged or counterfeit merchandise?

We Don't Like You Either

So, marginals can face threats from the outside but sometimes it's the internal issues that creep to the fore to create problems for the organization. One potential dilemma for the marginal organization is that while it needs people in different roles or capacities, each person ultimately represents a latent vulnerability point, particularly in the organization's efforts to maintain levels of secrecy or privacy regarding its operations or very existence. The assassination of Bin Laden illustrated that, just like money, people who operate on behalf of the organization can be traced and followed.

Added to this, some marginals already recognize that those who work with or for the organization don't necessarily maintain any particular allegiance to it. It's a job they need to have or need to do, but not necessarily an organization they want to work with, or for, or even care about. So the organization has stakeholders who are natural adversaries and whole sets of conceivable adversaries or who work for it but have no vested interest in the organization per se.

In the end, choice of survival strategies and tactics a marginal uses sometimes reflects the fact that the marginal operates outside of the society's mainstream. Mainstream organizations are expected to behave, to adhere to and to follow policies, practices, rules and regulations stipulated by society and introduced as safeguards in matters related to people, products, services and customers or patrons. Failure to do so can result in penalties, some of which are particularly harsh. Marginals, in contrast, often disregard or duck these safeguards and one thing that truly separates a marginal organization from a mainstream organization is the care and handling of the poor or non-performing member. Many mainstream organizations might attempt to assimilate, to reeducate or retool a troublesome employee for no other reason than that they may have a lot invested in the person's training and development or the person's knowledge and skills may be critical to the organization's operations.

Marginals, on the other hand, are not likely to risk retooling a poor performer; they simply don't have the luxury of time to do so. A marginal's approach to exposures and vulnerabilities associated with a poor performer might best be described as an effort to cleanse their operations—to decontaminate or disinfect vulnerable or under-performing areas.

It's Not That We're Defensive, It's That We're on the Defensive

Responses to the pressures of being under attack, scrutinized, investigated or just watched can materialize in discernible levels of defensiveness and self-management aimed at protecting the organization. Some of these self-imposed responses are particularly harsh and excessive. Anger can culminate in eruptions of violence or retaliatory attacks, particularly by marginals engaged in illegal activities. Other times, the ones who suffer are the system's weakest—the workers. In these instances, marginals may pull back, away from perceived threats or danger, through the use of a number of defensive moves aimed at containing or sometimes eliminating the troublesome person, process, product or service. Smugglers are willing to drop their cargo, whether goods or people, as soon as a threat is perceived. Loss of goods, in these instances, is one thing, but the loss of the lives of those just seeking to enter a country to find work or freedom is something totally different.

A marginal's nominal response to a crisis may reflect attempts to divert the pressures or attention it is experiencing. The diversion might be accompanied by increased activity in another area or a general reduction of activity throughout the organization; it can go underground. When advanced warning is possible, the organization can even attempt to intercept and, ideally, redirect investigations away from sensitive areas before they go too far. Shifting an investigation to areas or people the organization considers to be safe can have a dual purpose: it may remove suspicions regarding the marginal's activities and it may even give the impression that the marginal is a legitimate organization—after all, no problems were found and what was observed looked fine. Some organizations build and use sophisticated informant networks solely to augment their defensive profiles.

If the apparent vulnerability is associated with a particular person inside the organization, for example, an undocumented alien, that person's exposure might be reduced or, in the extreme, the individual might be removed from all activity until pressure is removed. If the individual doesn't serve a critical function, more extreme tactics may include removing the individual from the organization altogether. The latter is an often relied on strategy when an individual is not considered trustworthy.

Care in hiring is always preferred but sometimes when production or distribution needs are pressing, chances are taken. At the center of hiring activities in these instances is the employee's orientation. People with no history or who are new to the marginal's organization may find they have limited employment options and that their movement within the organization is restricted. It's nothing personal; it's just a precaution. A second focal point during the orientation is the performance review process. This is another discussion that doesn't take a lot of time; in fact, it may be quite casual, even unobtrusive. Some marginals are notable for claiming that joining makes one a "member for life" without necessarily also noting that it is the marginal that can define "how long" a life one has as a member. The emphasis behind all of these activities is to intercept internal problems before they happen.

Surviving via Relationship Management Is Just "Getting It Done"

Earlier, when discussing a marginal's stakeholder network, we outlined the four principal types of agents that define the network. These are the feeders, supporters, reliers and demanders. They are presented in chapter 3 and illustrated in figure 3.1. Mainstream and marginal organizations often work with and approach these agents differently. Regardless of their different approaches, however, both mainstreamers and marginals understand one salient point: while managing relations with the agents in one's stakeholder network can be difficult, doing so is critical for survival.

A primary difference between marginal and mainstream organizations vis-à-vis these four stakeholder groups is the way "demanders" are managed. Demanders play a key role for both types of organizations but they usually are in the background for those in the mainstream, as long as these organizations stay within boundaries, rules and regulations prescribed by the society in which they operate. Demanders usually surface in mainstream organizations when they are needed for procedural reasons (e.g., to secure a license or permit), when a rule or regulation is violated (e.g., the police or a regulatory agency) and if there is a crisis or accident and an investigation ensues.

In contrast, demanders can have an ongoing presence in a marginal organization's life, particularly if the marginal is engaged in illegal activity or otherwise operating in violation of the law. Demanders in these instances may not wait for a problem to arise, but rather either shadow or confront the marginal on an ongoing basis. Regularly surfacing controversies regarding police behavior such as the use of "search and seizure" tactics is an illustration.

Operators of food trucks and street vendors need licenses; undocumented aliens need, well, documentation; and, of course, those engaged in the sale of illegal drugs, pornography or the slave trade need the personal attention only law enforcement demanders can give. The role of demanders in the marginal organization's business can be so prominent that, from a relationship management viewpoint, marginals will often go to great lengths to improve the quality of the relationship they have with those in this stakeholder group. For example, one obvious way some marginals choose to work with demanders is to make them part of the organization—to put them on the payroll. Society doesn't condone this approach but it can work as a survival tactic for the creative marginal and willing demander.

Sometimes an especially inventive marginal may find something negative about the demander that can be used to blackmail or to "persuade" the demander to look the other way when encountering the marginal's activities. This tactic has its limitations, particularly if the demander in question is removed from a position of authority that is important to the marginal. Other times, bribes, kickbacks and the distribution of perks is a familiar relationship management tactic used by some marginals. These have proved useful for getting the demander to "look the other way," to offer protection, to lose key information or simply to stop harassing the marginal.

Relations with Other Stakeholders. Who Wears a Name Badge in a Marginal Organization?

Marginal organizations are not usually recognized for excellent customer relations. The *Seinfeld Show*'s "Soup Nazi" illustrated this flawlessly: it's process, process, process or "no soup for you." In many instances, marginals take this orientation because of their place, role and function in society. Marginal organizations, particularly those engaged in criminal activity, often prey on their customers. For them, the customer is a mark, a target or, more progressively, an economic or strategic objective and neither time nor circumstances will permit a different approach.

One result of this approach to the customer is that different labels are used to categorize marginals or their behavior. Words akin to parasite, exploitation, scrounger or freeloader and predator are used as descriptions for marginals and their relationship with stakeholders. To be fair, in some instances, particularly when the owner/operator is the same person making and selling the hamburger, there may not be a lot of time to engage in the kinds of social interaction one experiences in a mainstream organization. With some transactions, it's necessary to move on or away from the transaction point as quickly as possible. Drug sales can occur at a curbside, under a table or on a park bench. All the time that's needed in these events is what it takes to exchange the drugs for the money needed. Drug sales are not like wine-tasting events and don't need overt greetings or salutations, either.

The private versus public nature of marginals transcends every aspect of their economic, social and political systems. Consider, for example, the sheer number and types of professional organizations that exist solely for mainstream organizations that couldn't possibly exist for marginals. Mainstream organizations can belong to the Better Business Bureau, to Rotary or to a local Chamber of Commerce. If marginals come up as a topic of conversation in the meetings of these organizations, it's probably not for good reasons or in a good light.

There is no National Organization of Illegal Drug Manufacturers (NOIDM), no National Organization of White Slavers (NOWS) and certainly no International Organization of Child and Adult Pornography (IOCAP) for marginals to join. Mainstreamers have a plethora of organizations to represent their national and international interests but none exists for marginals. If a marginal has a complaint or an issue with the mainstream or society, it's up to the marginal to manage the issue as best as it can.

Finally, the range of similarities and differences between mainstream and marginal organizations is perhaps most significant in the type and amount of influence each can exert in society. For example, both mainstream and marginal organizations can define and claim a global presence. A recreational drug's life might begin in Afghanistan and end up in Toronto, London or New York, and money made from sales of guns in New York can be laundered in cities around the world. So, at least in terms of simple geography, some marginals can talk about global relationships much like mainstreamers do.

Influence among stakeholders manifests itself in other ways, too. Mainstream organizations can have nominal, accepted relationships with, or at least the support of, a mix of law enforcement organizations if they need them, and these are relationships marginals almost never have. Local and state police can respond to a phone call and sometime patrol areas where the mainstream operates. Other times, particularly in border areas and large cities, national militia (e.g., the Coast Guard) or other federal resources are available (the FBI, DEA or Bureau of Alcohol, Tobacco and Firearms) to protect the interests of the mainstream.

Conversely, however, some marginals have relationships with their customer stakeholders that mainstream organizations can only dream about. Drug addicts, sexual deviants, criminals and terrorists in need of guns or other weapons have a dependency relationship that only marginals are usually able to fulfill and both sides know this. These customers need the services offered by the marginal and the marginal can use its influence over these stakeholders in unique ways. The dependent stakeholder can be an informer, a transporter of smuggled goods, a laborer in a manufacturing facility or a prostitute in a sex house.

Conclusion

The nature and role of a marginal's influence as an organization is explored in greater detail in chapter 7. We conclude this chapter by taking an indirect look at influence with a quick review of the role size plays in relationship management for marginals and mainstream organizations. Size is another variable that favors mainstreams over marginals in several different ways.

First, there is size as a simple factor. Mainstream organizations have the capacity and, in some instances, seek to be as big as they possibly can be. Most marginals shrink away from size; being big can mean being visible. Mainstream organizations like size because it provides them with an economy of scale that can be used to drive down costs throughout their supply and production streams. Indeed, some mainstream organizations seek to control every facet of the product process from design and engineering through manufacturing, marketing, sales and distribution.

Such a long and hefty supply stream may only bring risk of exposure to the marginal organization. Consider the drug trade. A product may be grown in Mexico by independent farmers, processed by "the" organization and then passed on to others for the transportation, distribution and sale of the product. Clearly there's more money if one organization owns the entire stream but there's also more risk—it's riskier to move and sell the final product than to merely make it. If greed or visions of empire can be held in check, the marginal manufacturer can reduce both risk and exposure.

Mainstream organizations can capitalize on size in yet another way—through the formation of cooperatives and joint ventures. In these instances, different mainstream organizations combine their efforts, expertise, people and financial resources to produce and distribute a product, often globally. These kinds of cooperative ventures can be risky for marginals. After all, if your potential partner is a criminal, that may or may not be a good trait for you. Remember, sometimes "guilt by association" is just as damning as actually participating in criminal activity. The prudent marginal knows that just because they want to partner with you doesn't make them less of a criminal or potential threat.

Cooperative ventures also have rough spots that marginals may not have the experience to manage. Global ventures bring together organizations with different supply chains, timelines, material and resource needs and, of course, cultures. Mainstream organizations that enter into multi-organizational ventures typically have staff with the competencies needed to pull off these ventures. Marginals typically don't have this level of depth or experience.

Consider, too, that the mainstream organization in a global joint venture can and does work out in the open. It moves goods through international ports, across borders and onto foreign shores following protocols established by the countries from and into which they are operating. This level of legitimacy not only facilitates the overall cooperative process but also removes layers of risk a marginal must at least tolerate if not manage.

Perhaps because mainstream organizations don't have to waste a lot of energy looking over their shoulders, there's a level of efficiency in their operations that marginals, particularly larger marginals, have trouble matching. This is not meant to imply that marginals are not experienced or sophisticated organizations. Some are especially exquisite operational entities. It's just that the frustration of continuously being scrutinized or pursued means the marginal usually cannot devote all of the time, energy and money they'd like, for example, to maximizing the quality of their products or the efficiency of their service delivery. These are routine objectives of the mainstream organization but often only a luxury for marginal organizations.

Last, while organizations, mainstream or marginal, can expect challenges from competitors, those in the mainstream usually don't have to worry about a competitive challenge ending in a firefight or gun battle. Whether a small food truck or a large organization engaged in illegal drug, sex or other trade, many marginals have to be aware that threats or violence can be a very real part of their organization's life cycle. Territory, customers, and/or products can trigger wars among marginals or threats demanding payment for protection or even the "privilege" of operating a business. Marginals live in a different world with different rules, expectations and standards. Sure, there's the glamorous image often reported in the literature promoting marginals as examples of the entrepreneurial spirit and invention that provide employment opportunities and the possibility to run a business without the bureaucracy that can nag at a mainstream organization. All of this is true on the written page but on the streets the issue is survival, and that script often produces a different tale.

In chapters 7 and 8, the question of survival is raised in two different ways. Chapter 7 explores underlying sentiments regarding a marginal organization and its operation as a means for explaining how their capacity to operate and to influence the public to support them can be undermined by bias, prejudice and resentment. The study illustrates the complex set of feelings and sentiments that can be associated with a marginal organization even if it is not on the frontline of public opinion.

In chapter 8, survival is explored as a long-term matter. In this instance, survival for the marginal organization is a commodity, something that may be bought and sold—if there's a market for it. Mainstream organizations often don't have to raise the issue of succession for discussion. If there are members of the family who want to operate the business, some arrangements can be made, if not, and it is a viable concern, then sell it and its owners can move on. When one considers the marginals we touched on to this point, it's clear to see that it is not always possible to offer a drug trade, sex shop or even a food wagon as a "family business" and it's fairly safe to say they're typically not advertised as "business opportunities for sale" on the Web or in local newspapers. So what are the long-term options for marginal organizations and how do these fit into a survival discussion?

CHAPTER 7

Mapping the Decline and Loss of Organizational Influence in the Marginal Economy: A Case Study

Introduction to the Case Study

Mainstream economies don't exist in isolation; they are part of a larger social system defined by a variety of organizations ranging from the religious and political to business, the arts, cultural and even criminal. It's systemic diversity at its best. Apart from approaching organizations in a social system as a mixture of diverse entities, they can also be described in terms of two segments. Our focus has been on one of these segments, the marginal economy. This dynamic subsystem often comprises facsimiles of the mainstream economy, however metamorphosed as street vendors, backroom shops, legal or illegal labor, corruption or any number of other organizations. Taken at face value, these organizations might be described in ways that make them seem like vanguards of a liberated mentality. Indeed, one researcher described the marginal economy as a "low cost, grassroots and potentially revolutionary way to create jobs in the context of overregulated states" (Henken, 2008). In the absence of such grand sentiments, however, pursuits that are more mundane motivate organizations in the marginal economy—collectively earning money, avoiding taxes, dodging social security payments and generally skirting, where possible, labor laws—are recognized drivers of these organizations (Hart, 1973, 1990; Williams and Round, 2009; Andrews et al., 2011).

Two recurring themes in this book, one methodological and the other theoretical, are revisited in more detail in this chapter. First, a study is outlined to illustrate one means for examining a marginal organization. Marginal organizations aren't the easiest organizations to study. They are often private, sometimes hidden from view. In many cases, the owners/operators are reluctant to provide information about their organization and for obvious reasons. If the organization were engaged in otherwise illegal activities, no one would want to create a paper trail documenting this. In fact, documenting illegal activities has become a point of contention in many parts of the United States, in some instances, resulting in proposed legislation to prevent investigators from documenting alleged violators (Berg, 2013; Gray, 2013; Hauser, 2012; Keierleber, 2013).

The nature of a marginal's operations also makes them potentially dangerous organizations to study. Those in law enforcement are perhaps best prepared to study criminal organizations, yet there are roles for professionals to play in these investigations. Modeling, simulations, case studies and interviews conducted with former hostages, those in gangs or members of an organization (Howell, 2007; McFeely, 2011) are a means for safely targeting issues associated with even the most dangerous organizations or settings.

Studies like the one presented in this chapter illustrate another way to safely collect useful information regarding marginal organizations, their operations and stakeholder network. This study examines a key theoretical issue, the role of influence on a marginal's capacity to shape stakeholder sentiments. In the study, the influential nature of organizations in the marginal economy is examined by exploring the complexity of attitudes, opinions and beliefs associated with stakeholders who have no stake in an organization, yet who may, given the right conditions, side with or stand against the marginal.

Influence is not a new subject for study vis-à-vis marginals; in fact, the influence of marginals was the focus of a recent management conference sponsored by the American Academy of Management. Our slant on the topic is different from the Academy's, however. In this study, influence is approached as a dynamic feature of an organization that on the one hand can serve to draw stakeholders to the organization and on the other shape the behavior of stakeholders drawn to it. Influence, then, is an attractor that defines an organization's image or credibility and can lead stakeholders to believe that if the influence level they are seeing is valid, the organization is likely to be able to meet their needs, wants or desires.

The study also addresses another aspect of influence: the use of influence as a tool to shape stakeholders' behavior so that participation in the organization, their purchase of its products or services, becomes a means for meeting the organization's most fundamental needs. Influence is an organization's most valuable process attribute. With it, the organization achieves its vision and mission. Without it, it drifts and fades into oblivion.

The study examines three questions in turn. It begins by sampling a group of individuals who have no vested interest in the marginal examined. In this case, the marginals are "puppy mills," which raise dogs for sale to any of a variety of customers, from an individual to a retail pet store. In most cases, these marginals do not offer dogs with any pedigree—the marginal's mission is to turn out and sell as many dogs as possible without necessary regard for the breeding animal's health or well-being, a common complaint of those who wish to see these marginals shut down or at least regulated.

Research Questions and Methodology

Three issues are of particular interest in this study. The *first issue* examines the role influence plays in shaping the behavior of a key stakeholder group: those interested yet uncommitted citizens who define the potential membership roles, customer groups or, in the worst case, adversaries or opponents. Table 7.1 illustrates the overall social network of interest. We chose to focus on the interested citizens segment because it comprises stakeholders who might support or not support the marginal organization. In particular, we're interested in getting an idea about what might cause members of this segment to shift their posture from a passive to a proactive nature, either for or against the marginal.

The "interested citizens" are the most interesting of the five segments because while the sentiments and motivations of the other four groups are typically a foregone conclusion that's not the case for this segment. Members of the other four groups are where they are *because* of their position or sentiments vis-à-vis the marginal organization; they either support it or don't. Analysis for this and other issues examined in the study will focus on one type of organization operating in the marginal economy—the local sale of animals for pets, typically dogs, commonly referred to as puppy mills. We examine this segment of the marginal society because it clearly reflects all of the characteristics one expects to associate with marginal organizations plus one especially unique feature. This marginal illustrates the geographic dependency associated with some organizations operating in the marginal society (figure 7.1).

Unlike marginal organizations that tend to serve a broad customer group, for example, illegal drugs or gambling that can have national and even international scope and scale, puppy mills tend to be regional in nature. In this sense, they're a lot like smugglers who operate only in one region of a state or country ("Cigarette-smuggling," 2012). Finally, while the study is limited to marginal organizations that operate for a profit, its analysis can be extended

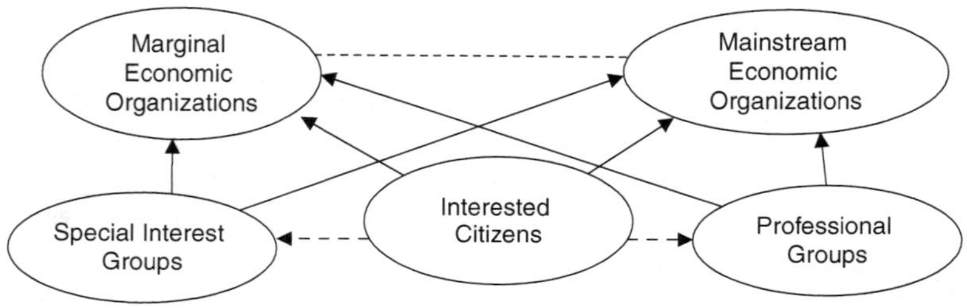

Figure 7.1 Stakeholders Defining a Marginal Organization's Social Network.

to include nonprofit organizations in either mainstream or marginal sectors of a society.

The *second question of interest* examines a different facet of the nature of influence: the emergence of a crisis can damage an organization's influence overall and, in particular, in its social network. Influence can be a fragile commodity. At the center of this issue is the role of stakeholder collective action toward a marginal organization. In this instance, swarm theory is used to describe how a marginal organization's network can be affected by the positive and/or negative influences it creates given its stakeholders and their own needs and capacity to be influential. Swarm theory has been used in organizations in different ways, typically to improve operations. Gloor and Cooper (2007a,b) and Gloor (2006) use swarm theory to improve business operations or at least standard operating procedures. Others use swarm theory to design algorithms to improve crowd control or public safety (Batty, 2007) or for better ways to generally route people or ideas (Kennedy et al., 2001). In this study, the focus is on those instances when an organization is in a crisis—a crisis fueled and sometimes exacerbated by the swarming of other organizations, a phenomenon we refer to as a "stakeholder swarm" (Tafoya, 2013a).

An organization engulfed in a stakeholder swarm struggles to be influential, to hold onto existing influence and/or to regain lost influence. A positive influence occurs when the organization successfully manages the swarm or its participants. A negative influence has an opposite effect. For this analysis, influence or the results linked to the organization's actions are examined in terms of three particular features: the products, outcomes and impacts associated with the influence observed (Tafoya, 2010).

Here *products* are the observable results of the organization's efforts. They are the things done or produced by the organization; they are the ways one behaves while delivering a service, making decisions, taking actions or displaying behaviors associated with a task, assignment, job, etc. Products may be tangible or as intangible as a process (e.g., service or information exchange) or effort (delivery of a product).

Outcomes result from products. In many ways, outcomes materialize along the lines of a classic stimulus/response or causal model. "The organization did 'x,' a product, and 'y' is an outcome." There may be more than one outcome associated with a single product and, like products, outcomes can be good or bad, desirable or not. Outcomes are defined in terms of verbs: for example, to increase, to fear, to purchase, to follow, to behave. Outcomes indicate a potential to direct or shape stakeholder attitudes, opinions, beliefs and/or behavior, particularly given the organization's mission.

Impacts are the end result of the products and outcomes. Their presence can be long-lasting and can unfold in other areas (i.e., not originally associated with the products or actions taken in the first place). Impacts are the *real* payoff, either good or bad results, of the organization's efforts. A desired impact is one that benefits the organization in a conscious, meaningful way. Attempting to produce a desired impact is the cause, basis, antecedent, motive or rationale for activity, action or effort. Impact may be tangible (e.g., market share, defeat of an opponent), or intangible, or abstract (image enhancement, creation of an emotional state—fear, satisfaction, happiness) (Tafoya, 2010). There are several ways to explore the results, products, outcomes and impacts associated with a marginal organization's influence, and in this instance we will do so by examining influence vis-à-vis changes emerging as a result of the organization's stakeholder network.

The *third question of interest* probes the nature of influence in organizations. *Influence* is a measure of performance and this is true whether the influence results in positive or negative responses by stakeholders. All organizations have the capacity to be influential; the distinction is that some organizations are more influential, more likely to promote a response from stakeholders than others. A restaurant is "popular" because it "influences" people's behavior, so that they seek it out as a place to eat when they are hungry. A restaurant with a bad reputation, in contrast, does not have a strong capacity to influence people to eat its food. What does a marginal organization's spectrum of influence look like? Where is the threshold that marks the transition from having little to increased influence among stakeholders? From being a positive to a negative influence?

The descriptive nature of the information provided with issue two provides the foundation for a third question: Is it possible to forecast the likelihood that performance perceived as unwanted or negative will have a negative effect on an organization's capacity to be influential? In this instance, four levels outlining the range of effects associated with a crisis stipulate possible negative conditions for an organization under attack, in a crisis. For this study, the "crisis spectrum" discussed in chapter 4 is used in conjunction with data collected regarding puppy mills to measure the respondents' perception of the seriousness or the extent to which the presence of the marginal organization (i.e., the puppy mills) reflects a problem or issue needing to be addressed. Once established, that benchmark becomes the focal point for a discussion of features related to the emergence of a stakeholder swarm and subsequent effects on the marginal organization's capacity to be influential.

The Puppy Mill Study

Subjects

Individuals representing one of the five stakeholder groups presented in figure 7.1, labeled "Interested Citizens," volunteered to complete a survey designed to measure their impressions and sentiments regarding the target marginal organization. These participants were selected at random and each completed the same questionnaire. Steps were taken to ensure that those in the sample were in the segment defined as "interested citizens" and were not affiliated with any of the other four segments.

The Questionnaire

One way to observe the impact that an organization in the marginal society has on its environment and its relationship with organizations in the mainstream is by examining its "attention factor"—the visibility thrust on it by organizations and particularly competitors in the Special Interest Groups or Professional Groups noted in figure 7.1. Mainstream organizations that are members of professional associations often use these groups to pressure law makers, regulators or others to manage marginal organizations (Anonymous, 2012b; Price, 1999), to change laws governing a marginal's mobility (Flaim, 2007; Price, 1999) or to prevent the marginal organization from operating at all (Anonymous, 2012a; Cohn, 2009; Gilbert, 2007; Worden, 2006).

But where are the stimuli or points where the marginal's influence is triggered and how is it observed? The questionnaire used in the study examined five areas where a marginal might extend its influence. These include the organization's impact on *policy*, for example, that leads to rule changes or policy reform, rule enforcement, the enactment of rules or legislation and, in some instances, the formation of watchdog agencies to oversee the marginal's behavior and/or performance. It also includes the marginal's effects on the general economics of the business environment, effects on market share among competitors, competition for customers and/or the extent to which the marginal was associated with crime or criminal activity.

A third factor examined was the perception of the marginal's impact on values or cohesion within the society in which it operates. This impact may extend to the creation of conflict or turmoil, division and, in some instances, breakdowns in social and/or cultural patterns or norms. Finally, the marginal's perceived influence on two other areas—the extent to which its activities contributed to occurrences of suffering, injury, pain or loss, and the likelihood interventions might be triggered—were examined.

The first of these, occurrences of suffering, loss and the like, included examination of incidents of injury, harm or cruelty, the belief that infection or disease might occur because of the marginal's activities or that the marginal and its operations reflect poor working or operational conditions. Finally, questions were added to gauge the likelihood that the marginal or its operations would elicit interventions by competitors, special interest or professional groups.

Questions related to these "impact areas" were developed from a content analysis that examined the conclusions contained in several articles and studies or the results of investigations of different crises and charges brought against various marginal organizations. In addition to questions related to these categories, an important set of questions was included to identify the nature of a threshold that once crossed would lead individuals in this group of "interested citizens" to shift from an interested but passive role to one of a more proactive nature. Finally, four levels of negative effects were included in the survey as questions to see how the respondents would react to these effects given other options.

The survey contains 27 items, scored using a 10-point scale. The first 21 items asked respondents to indicate how likely the statement reflected something that might occur (e.g., "I'd tell someone about this . . . ," with a range from 10, a "strong likelihood," to 1, "little or no likelihood"). Responses to the 21 items revealed perceptions of ways the existence of this marginal organization (puppy mills) influenced their behavior or sentiments. Six other items were introduced at the end of the survey to measure the depth of the respondents' sentiments regarding these puppy mills. Respondents indicated the extent to which they agreed with the statements presented, again along a 10-point scale. (For example, "Existence of puppy mills is a significant problem" or "Existence of puppy mills is dangerous; they must be stopped.") Table 7.1 lists the survey questions and the scoring by respondents.

Study Results. Question One: The Characteristic Makeup of Stakeholders Described as "Interested Citizens." Describing the Nature of a Marginal Organization's Capacity to Be Influential

The responses of 20 people served as the basis of the analysis in this study. Each voluntarily completed the paper and pencil measure designed to tap categories described above. All of the subjects reflected the category of stakeholders described as "interested citizens," that is, none was a member of the four other groups making up the network defined in figure 7.1.

Table 7.1 contains the results of the survey. Emerging patterns are strong and evident. Organizations in the marginal economy are, by definition, typically looking for a "work around." They are often looking at ways to avoid taxes, paying benefits to employees and sometimes even paying them fair wages at all. This orientation casts a shadow that can strike people at their most visceral level. For example, even with this small sample, two sides of the issue begin to emerge. First, puppy mills are perceived as influential: the items receiving the highest mean score, items 9, 15 and 27, do appear to capture the notion that puppy mills affect animals (item 9: "they cause injury"), those who encounter these organizations (item 27: "they make me depressed") and there is a level of resentment against those who operate these businesses (item 15: "they think they can get away with this"). These types of sentiments seem to point to the conceivable foundation for the levels of resentment and seeds of discontent associated with organizations that operate outside the boundaries of acceptable conventions or standards.

On the other hand, however, the data also indicate that there are limits to what one might do on one's own or that there's any likelihood people will be punished for their actions or even that anything meaningful will prevent these organizations from operating. For example, item 7 ("I'd confront the owner") illustrates that while the subjects don't support the operation of puppy mills they're not likely to act on their own, probably a wise move particularly when the marginal is engaged in criminal activities. Additionally, item 12 ("someone will be disciplined") and item 20 ("all this talk will won't make things happen") suggest that the respondents don't see anything preventing these organizations from operating in the future.

A secondary analysis provided more revealing data regarding the subjects' sentiments. A correlation analysis measuring the relationship among the responses to different questions revealed two strong clusters, both of which add insight into this marginal organization's capacity to influence the behavior and/or sentiments of these participants. The first cluster defined by items 1 ("I'd tell someone"), 3 ("I'd do something"), 6 ("This can hurt

Table 7.1 The Puppy Mill Study—Descriptive Statistics

Survey questions	*Mean*	*SE*	*SD*
1. I'd tell someone I know about the existence of this puppy mill.	7.36	1.02	3.38
2. Puppy mills hurt business for professional dog breeders.	8.182	0.807	2.676
3. I would do something about this.	6.64	1.08	3.59
4. Laws should be enacted to prevent puppy mills from operating.	7.818	0.644	2.136
5. I'd report this to someone who could put a stop to this business.	7.000	0.842	2.793
6. This kind of operation can hurt our culture.	7.273	0.964	3.197
7. I'd confront the operator of this business with my objections.	4.64	1.07	3.56
8. This type of organization can't be allowed to continue operations.	7.091	0.868	2.879
9. Puppy mills can result in injury to animals.	9.091	0.436	1.446
10. Puppy mills probably do well as a business.	6.545	0.718	2.382
11. If not addressed, operation of puppy mills will spread.	7.455	0.888	2.945
12. Someone involved will be disciplined.	4.909	0.768	2.548
13. Existence of puppy mills can lead to conflicts with professional dog breeders.	8.000	0.405	1.342
14. Some government agency should monitor this type of organization.	8.364	0.592	1.963
15. Those involved will think they can get away with this behavior in the future.	9.000	0.330	1.095
16. No one will be punished for operating this business.	7.091	0.547	1.814
17. The public will ignore the existence of puppy mills. They'll learn to live with it.	8.000	0.302	1.000
18. Existence of operations like puppy mills signals a breakdown in our society.	7.000	0.831	2.757
19. Law enforcement is viewed as ineffective.	6.455	0.578	1.916
20. All the time spent talking about the problem will make things happen.	2.818	0.423	1.401
21. Allowing organizations like this to operate will create divisions in our society.	6.727	0.764	2.533
22. Existence of businesses called "puppy mills" is a problem.	8.727	0.557	1.849
23. Existence of puppy mills is a significant problem.	8.091	0.756	2.508
24. Existence of puppy mills is dangerous; they must be stopped.	7.727	0.843	2.796
25. Puppy mills are a tragedy. They can result in harm and can't be allowed to continue.	8.636	0.472	1.567
26. Existence of puppy mills is one of those things that just happens.	7.818	0.711	2.359
27. Coming across a puppy mill is depressing.	8.909	0.392	1.300

Note: The closer the mean score to 10, the greater the agreement with the statement.

our culture") and 11 ("They'll spread if not stopped") might be defined as outlining the organization's role in influencing the participants' "urgency to act." However, given the previous discussion, it seems clear that while there's a motive for action it doesn't look like the subjects would act on their own. Joining or supporting a group, perhaps like those Special Interest or Professional Organizations given in figure 7.1, or even boycotting the marginal organization by supporting only "legitimate" organizations in the mainstream economy may temper emerging risk, however.

The scoring of the second cluster amplifies the marginal organization's influence on the respondents' sentiments. Four variables define this cluster: item 21 ("Allowing them to act will create division"), item 22 ("Puppy mills are a problem"), item 23 ("They're a significant problem") and item 24 ("They're dangerous and must be stopped"). This cluster is particularly interesting. The items that define it were added to the survey as a way to examine the underlying nature of the participants' sentiments, and the high mean scores of their responses suggest that regardless of their feelings about how or why this marginal organization is of concern, they are convinced it reflects a problem that needs attention. But if a marginal organization is a cause for concern, how does sentiment translate into action for the stakeholders in this particular network? Clearly, individuals can take action into their own hands but wide-scale change is most often when a large group or movement emerges, and when this occurs, the nature of influence around a marginal organization can increase to dramatic proportions.

Results Question Two: Nature and Likelihood of Influence as Measured by Stakeholder Response and Behavior

The questionnaire described above is a useful way to measure the unique nature of a marginal organization's influential potential in terms of the products, outcomes and impacts associated with its different features, behaviors or the general impression stakeholders have of it. Collectively, an organization's products, outcomes and impacts tell us a variety of things about an organization. We can get a sense of the organization's intentions, what it values, its image, how it might affect us or what it thinks its stakeholders need and sometimes the relationship between the organization and society as a whole. For example, it's possible to use the data from this survey to prepare for subsequent studies of the same marginal, only in those studies we'd seek to understand the "causal" relationship among key themes suggested by the results we've just discussed. This type of analysis will help us understand the relationship between the products, outcomes and impacts of puppy mills from the point of view of the interested citizen.

For example, Question 2 ("Puppy mills hurt business for professional dog breeders") has a mean score of 8.1 indicating strong agreement with the statement, and Question 25 ("Existence of puppy mills is a tragedy. They can result in injury, harm or loss. They can't be allowed to continue") has an even higher level of agreement with a mean score of 8.6. The question with the highest agreement score among these was Question 9 ("Puppy mills can result in injury to animals") with a mean score of 9.0. If we interpret the response to these questions as the "products" the respondents associate with puppy mills, what then would be the outcomes for each or all of these collectively?

Is there a causal link, for example, between these "products" and the response to questions like Question 1 ("I'd tell someone I know about the existence of this puppy mill"), which received a mean score of 7.2? Perhaps response to Question 4, for example, is an outcome associated with the feelings indicated in the first set of questions. Question 4 ("Laws should be enacted to prevent puppy mills from operating") had a mean score of 7.8. And then there's the response to Question 14 ("Some government agency should monitor this type of organization"), which had a mean score of 8.3. These results could be possible outcomes, but given the only moderate scores questions 1 and 4 received, these responses appear to tell us more about the respondents than any possible outcomes associated with the perceptions raised in the first three questions we just looked at. Indeed, looking at the responses to these and similar questions in table 7.1, one gets a sense that (1) these respondents don't see themselves as getting involved beyond expressing their opinions and (2) there's not a great deal of interest in seeing any outcomes that might add to the bureaucracy or local tax base—but then these respondents represented a largely conservative group of people.

For our purposes, however, the products, outcomes and impacts associated with a puppy mill give us an idea of how secure it is as a member of the marginal economy. The results tell us something about this marginal's vulnerabilities, exposures or crisis potential, that is, the likelihood it may be engulfed by a crisis associated with its operations. Examining the nature of the products, outcomes and impacts associated with an organization can provide real insight into the influence of an organization in the marginal economy at different points in time.

For example, Tafoya's (2013a,b) illustration of the emergence of stakeholder swarms around a crisis provides a useful framework for exploring the role and vulnerability of a marginal organization's influence vis-à-vis its stakeholder networks. The network in figure 3.1 in chapter 3, for example, illustrates a marginal organization's capacity to be influential as it develops, maintains or negotiates its relationships with the members of its social network, its primary sphere of influence. But figure 3.1 is a network in distress. Its actual makeup shouldn't be dominated by so many "demanders." The value of the study described in this chapter is that it illustrates just how a network like that given in figure 3.1 can materialize.

Those "neutrals" that we surfaced may not become members of a swarm such as the one in figure 3.1, but they certainly may be the "voices in the background" urging demanders, special interest groups, legislators and regulators to get involved. Indeed, the negative influences created by a marginal may motivate some to form their own special interest groups, thus adding to the swarm of activity engulfing the marginal.

There's nothing neat about a swarm engulfing a network. Influence in a swarmed network is shared by the numerous organizations making up the swarm. This, in fact, is part of the challenge for a marginal caught up in this type of situation and another illustration of why marginals like to keep such a low profile. Swarms wrestle control from the marginal; it's forced to explain itself, to answer questions, to justify actions, behaviors or claims.

As mentioned in chapter 3, one doesn't usually see stakeholders who are angry or dissatisfied unless there's a reason for them to enter the net, and this is particularly true for an organization operating in the marginal economy. These are the emerging stakeholders one often sees when a stakeholder swarm materializes: regulators, the media, special interest groups, professional organizations like doctors and lawyers and, of course, law enforcement (Anonymous, 2011a,b; Johnson, 2012; Tafoya, 2013c).

Tafoya (2013a) labeled that point when an organization's social network gives way to the increasing activity of outside influences like that reflected in figure 3.1 as a "stakeholder swarm." His research illustrates that when a crisis occurs, an organization's typical network can swell to unmanageable sizes and complexities as new organizations enter the network expecting that their needs or issues will be met or addressed and often with little concern for the needs or interests of the marginal organization at the network's hub. The size of the emerging swarm isn't the most pressing issue for the target organization experiencing a stakeholder swarm. As the swarm forms, the makeup of the new social network seems to comprise different organizations, each having a potentially different vision and mission, goals, objectives and, most importantly, the capacity to affect the marginal organization's operations, stakeholders in its network and, often, even the marginal's capacity to be influential in its own right.

Moreover, when a swarm forms in response to a crisis, stakeholders who may have been supportive of the marginal organization often find it expedient, for their own sake and image, to abandon their support of and subsequent position in the network. Throughout the book, we've suggested that marginals often start with one strike against them. In fact, it is sometimes difficult to find people who might be sympathetic to the existence and operation of, for example, a puppy mill; they may not want to be associated with it once the crisis breaks and swarms emerge. It's not a socially desirable position to maintain. Marginal organizations involved in illegal drug sales, gambling or the like regularly experience this level of rejection or disdain.

Figure 3.1, indeed all of chapter 3, illustrates this point. The figure contains the five components associated with a typical network. At its center, the hub, is where communication and information management are controlled; it's the area where the organization's mission is centered, presented and managed for the network and stakeholders. Feeders (++) are primary suppliers for the organization. Sometimes they are sources for financial assistance or external guidance. Feeders have a strong, positive valence for the organization; without them, it may be impossible to achieve one's mission.

Supporters (+) also have a positive effect on the organization. Supporters are a generic collection of individuals and groups. They provide the overall foundation for the organization. Two other network components, however, "demanders" and "reliers," draw on the organization's various resources. For example, puppy mills incur expenses when they subcontract veterinary work and basic repairs for buildings or cages. Other reliers can put a non-monetary draw on the organization's resources. For example, once a crisis breaks, reporters, special interest groups and sometimes law enforcement may demand time to answer questions, time that the marginal would otherwise devote to its business.

Again, reliers divert an organization's resources, such as staff time, away from regularly expected responsibilities. "Demanders" place the greatest drain on the organization's resources and demanders are stakeholders that one doesn't ignore or put off. This is particularly true if the puppy mill is being investigated. Then a typical group of demanders expands to accommodate lawyers or similar authority figures associated with professional organizations expected to act on behalf of the public or, in this case, the defenseless.

Every member of an organization's stakeholder network fits one of the four roles: feeders, supporters, reliers or demanders. The plus (+) and minus (–) signs (figure 3.1) illustrate the potential capacity for them to contribute to or draw on the organization's resources, to be influential in their own right. The challenge a crisis presents is that as a crisis unfolds and the number of stakeholders increases, the hub's (in this case the organization in the marginal economy) capacity to be influential may be diluted as more stakeholders enter, some of whom may be significantly more influential than the marginal organization.

For example, the simple fact that a crisis is usually an atypical or extraordinary event means there is likely to be an increase in the number of "demanders" in the net and a possible loss of "feeders" and "supporters" as a crisis unfolds. A fire in one of the marginal's buildings, for example, might mean that demanders like the police, fire department or health care organizations become part of the organization's network and, in turn, shift control of the network away from the organization so that they can better perform their roles as "crisis managers." In moments such as these, the marginal organization's influence may be so limited as to be virtually nonexistent as it becomes subject to the influence of these stronger organizations.

Results Question Three: In What Ways Is an Organization's Influence Affected by Negative Events and the Organization's Capacity to Manage Them?

Another issue underlying our interest in the nature of a marginal organization's influence is its vulnerability to change, particularly when loss of influence affects an organization's overall equilibrium and general capacity to function. Marginal organizations already operate on the fringe, so demanders and reliers, characterized as naturally drawing on an organization's resources, can create a greater burden for the organization in a crisis. Matters are only aggravated when the number of demanders increases, the nature of their roles become exaggerated or they simply are angry, have a desire to retaliate or are generally agitated after being asked to do extreme, undesirable tasks (as when emergency teams are called in to handle sick or injured animals that haven't been cared for by the puppy mill's operators).

Imagine what's going through the minds of those in the marginal organization illustrated in figure 3.1. Here the number of demander and relier stakeholders has increased such that the burden of their actions, needs and interests can overwhelm even the most sophisticated organization. The marginal organization's influence in this instance may have shifted to such an extent that it may find itself completely vulnerable to the needs and interests of its new, emerging adversaries. Add to this the fact that the number of supporters and feeders may have decreased and/or their potential to be influential also compromised and the marginal organization may feel it is in a network defined by dissent and distrust and in a role that may be less than secondary to those now in control.

What's at risk is not just the marginal organization's capacity to be influential, it is that the marginal organization may lose any influence whatsoever; in the worst case, it may have to turn all of its capacity to be influential over to new agents, such as the lawyers who represent it. When a stakeholder swarm materializes, new stakeholders join the existing network segments (i.e., feeder, supporter, relier and demander) for the same reason as the initial network members: because they get something in return for their participation. In the original network, this usually makes for a classic two-way street with all members receiving something in return for being part of the network. The difference is that when a swarm forms, swarm members not only pursue their own mission and goals (and not the swarm's, per se) but also the added number of stakeholders almost immediately places a burden on the hub's resources. When the requirements or burden of "demanders" and "reliers" outweigh those with a positive agenda, the drain on the marginal organization's hub can be dramatic, sometimes even detrimental to the organization's performance and existence; it's no longer a two-way street. Finally, it is also interesting to note that one of the benefits these new members to the stakeholder network gain is more influence for themselves, for their organizations or their membership. For example, advocates for animal safety who successfully terminate an illegal puppy mill stand to gain stature or add to their influence quotient among members, affiliates or even adversaries. Understanding the needs and motives of the network participants is a valuable means for plotting how the network will perform over time.

The capacity to be influential is on one hand a measure of the organization's credibility and on the other a metaphor for its image, perhaps the strength of its brand. One way to understand a marginal organization's capacity to be influential is to examine it in a crisis, when its potential to be influential is threatened and possibly lost. Table 7.2 presents the ways in which the emergence of a crisis can shape an organization's influential nature. Use of a format like that in the table allows us to examine possible effects a crisis can have as it progresses from a mere incident or challenge to the full-scale attack described. For example, the products directly associated with the crisis emerge and these then contribute to observable outcomes, which in turn, have a particular level of impact on the organization, its stakeholders, its network or environment. Moreover, this analysis also allows us to speculate on how a crisis, and more importantly the poor handling of a crisis, may affect a marginal organization's capacity to influence others.

For example, in table 7.2, one can't help but notice how this organization's influence, in this case, attractiveness to its fruit-buying customers, seems to be slipping away as it moves from a legitimate pursuit in the marginal economy (i.e., selling fruits and vegetables) to one that has negative connotations associated with it (i.e., selling puppies). But what does it mean to the operator of an organization in our marginal economy as challenges to the organization escalate from Level I, a predicament, to higher levels on our crisis scale? Maybe the nature of the organization's influence-as-attractor

Table 7.2 When Stakeholder Swarms Emerge: Puppy Mill Products Trigger Outcomes That Trigger Impacts

	Representative products trigger →	*Representative outcomes trigger →*	*Representative impacts*
Level I— A predicament: jam, pickle, mishap mess, confusion, chaos, disorder, disarray. Scope: Typically within the capacity of the organization to address.	You operate a fruit stand to get extra money for the farm. Your collie, said to be neutered, gives birth to 12 of the cutest puppies	You decide to sell the puppies (along with the fruit and vegetables)	Someone may complain. Damage may occur but will likely be local, containable. Potential damage rating: PDR 1–2
Level II— A dilemma: impasse, problem, misfortune, adversity, hardship. Scope: Ideally addressed in the organization, possibly with external assistance.	The money from the collie's pups came in handy. She's pregnant again. Let's sell those, too.	Someone claims it is a puppy mill. "Didn't you sell pups just a few months ago?"	Focus: Damage is possible. Sale of fruits and vegetables falls off. Potential damage rating: PDR 3–5
Level III— A disaster: debacle, cataclysm tragedy, blow, adversity, danger, deluge, wreckage. Scope: External assistance needed; organization must support.	We're getting a reputation. People know they can come to us for dogs. This is profitable. No attempts to prevent the dogs from breeding.	Complaints are made. Special interests enter. Stakeholder swarm emerges at this level.	Focus: Damage and loss are probable, possibly extensive. Potential damage rating: PDR 6–8
Level IV— A catastrophe: devastation, destruction, calamity, ruin, upheaval. Scope: External assistance required and leads the effort.	Large-scale breeding and sales are recorded. This is a primary source of income. Lots of dogs taking up lots of space.	Can't keep up with kennel repair. The place is a mess. Complaints are made. Some dogs are ill. SPCA is called in.	Focus: Damage and loss are likely, extensive. Need immediate action. Manage effects and recovery. Consider future plans. Potential damage rating: PDR 9–10

rating may actually increase if the sale of the first litter is a one-off event: "This won't happen again. That dog's been neutered."

The probability that damage results in influence loss and costly resolution is an open question. (To see a more detailed analysis of this question, visit our website at www.compcite.com.) However, it seems likely that there are negative exposures at each level beginning with a warning at Level I, the arrival of special interests and a possible investigation at Level II, the emergence of a stakeholder swarm, possible injury to animals and the requirement that an investigation be launched at Level III and, at Level IV, the media arrive and begin covering the events, production shuts down, key feeders and supporters leave and there's a strong likelihood that litigation and penalties will occur.

Finally, the impact that delaying or simply a failure to act on an emerging crisis can have on an organization's capacity to be influential is always problematic given the four crisis levels described. In other words, how is an organization's capacity to be influential, its credibility, impacted as a crisis escalates out of control? When a crisis progresses, that is, when it is not resolved at any of the first three levels but progresses through each level, the likelihood for disaster increases.

An organization in a crisis is in its best position if the crisis does not progress beyond Level I, "A Predicament." This is obvious for most for organizations but keep in mind that there's also no guarantee that this is a likely outcome for organizations operating in the marginal economy. At Level I, organizations often receive a warning, a "slap on the wrist." If this marks the end of the crisis, the probability of "influence loss" may be negligible given certain caveats.

As we've seen, organizations in the marginal economy may already be tainted as less than desirable, and they frequently have fewer resources needed to manage or weather a significant crisis. Moreover, if they are operating a business that has established negative connotations associated with it (e.g., illegal drugs, animal cruelty, gambling), public sentiments and the influence of special interest groups may not let "no fault" be an acceptable conclusion. Indeed, as we observed, when an organization is operating on the downside of the marginal economy, public opinion may not tolerate leniency in any form. The controversy regarding the Philadelphia Eagles football player who engaged in "dog fighting" is a case in point. Some wouldn't let the popular college star with a promising career at Philadelphia off the hook even after he broke away from the negative activity. Rather, they were not satisfied and continued to want to use him as an example for others (Tamari, 2010).

The potential for damage resulting from a crisis increases as the organization moves through subsequent levels. An unchecked or uncontained crisis can have cumulative effects for those associated with it and, in addition, the likelihood for harm to stakeholders can increase as a crisis progresses through its life cycle. Guilt by association is a real phenomenon that is not easily dismissed.

Since the organization's capacity to be influential is at the heart of this discussion, it is prudent to address anything that has the potential to damage the organization's image, credibility or capacity to continue operations. This is particularly true if there's potential for a threat to harm the organization's capacity to be a positive influence for key stakeholders like customers, suppliers or feeders. An organization can better manage its losses if it successfully manages each of the four levels, and while there is no single best way to do this for every crisis, it would be wise for organizations operating in the marginal economy to follow practices already familiar to many organizations in the established mainstream economy. Developing and maintaining key competencies, critical operational practices and a sense of urgency regarding the potential for a crisis to do harm are among the steps those managing effective organizations have learned to benefit from as they guide their organizations (Tafoya, 2010).

Final Observations Regarding Organizations in the Marginal Economy as Examined in This Case Study

Whether a mainstream or marginal organization, stakeholders perceived as influential gain patrons, members, affiliates and the like, because they're viewed as a credible means for meeting the stakeholders' needs. Moreover, and as illustrated in this study, whether approached as credibility, image or status, influence is a fragile commodity, particularly for organizations in the marginal economy. Influence for marginal organizations doesn't appear to stem from the content area in which the marginal organization operates. A drug dealer operates in one of the most dangerous and least respected marginal economic industries, yet a successful drug dealer can be perceived as highly influential if he/she is a *reliable distributor*; the drugs must be safe, but quality among many street drugs is otherwise a highly variable feature ("Lo Hsing Han," 2013). So it isn't the field of operation that necessarily defines the influential nature of an organization; rather, it's the marginal's standards of performance that define its scope of influence for stakeholders. Those in the mainstream, however, may judge the marginal solely on the nature of its operations. Mainstreamers just know that a terrorist is a terrorist, a cult is a cult, a drug organization is a source for illegal drugs, etc., whether these organizations are operational or not.

Unfortunately (or fortunately, depending on your orientation or bias), marginal organizations typically function with fewer resources and often greater risks than the same organizations in the mainstream economy. Their level of influence is exposed and vulnerable to continuous scrutiny and frequent challenges or attacks. Organizations in the mainstream economy, unless operating in a regulated industry like a pharmaceutical company, typically don't experience this measure of pressure. Marginal organizations are often expected to meet minimum performance standards of organizations operating within the established mainstream economy, yet without necessarily sharing the same perks as those on the mainstream side.

The public isn't likely to give some organizations operating in the marginal society a break or at least the same amount of slack other organizations might benefit from having. People, from concerned citizens to members of special interest groups or professional organizations, are quick to take up the cause for human or animal rights, to prevent substance abuse, gambling or related activities that often define organizations in the marginal economy. So a word of warning to some marginal organizations, toe the line or be prepared for the worst. Make sure animals are well cared for, your office betting pools are legitimate and your drugs... at least out of sight and don't operate a sweatshop.

Without the resources needed to manage the emergence of phenomena like a stakeholder swarm or even a simple challenge or complaint, marginals are often forced to handle their problems themselves—another disadvantage. A challenge to a food wagon's health and safety practices is difficult or at least inconvenient to argue since most public officials who oversee these organizations only meet during the day, typically when the food wagon needs to operate. Other times some marginal operations are so precarious that challenges to their operations typically result in an attitude best defined as "let's shut them down and investigate and only let them open if we don't find a problem." Backroom clothing manufacturers, puppy mills, food wagons, dog and horse race tracks are among the types of organizations with this kind of exposure. Shutting them down even for brief periods can have a severe impact on continued operations.

Some marginal organizations will always be considered "second class" or be subject to the scrutiny of those higher up the food chain. There's often a legitimate or acceptable competitor for the organization functioning in the marginal economy. Our oft-cited example of the local food wagon is a case in point. We like the food, the entrepreneurial spirit displayed and the freedom of choice it provides, but local restaurateurs may not share our sentiments. Marginals in this instance can be viewed as competitors who have the potential to interfere with profits and an established customer base. Even organizations on the deeper, darker sides of the marginal economy are subject to these types of pressures. For every drug dealer, numbers runner, gun and cigarette trafficker, there's a competitor within that business segment ready to raise a challenge, be it a health organization offering drug substitutes, legal gambling operations or someone selling cigarettes at a discount.

Having established policies, procedures and practices in place so that emerging crises or challenges are contained says a lot about the way an organization is being managed or what its operators care about or think is important. What bureaucrat wouldn't be impressed with the food wagon or dog kennel that has safety, health and hygiene practices and procedures in place? These practices may appear to be more than precautions; they may give an air of respectability to the organization and its operations.

Operating an organization with these types of fundamentals in place can make a statement about the organization's credibility, its desire to do the right thing, its sense of order or priorities in the likelihood of a crisis. It's a good idea, but for the marginal organization operating on a shoestring or with limited time available to do anything but get the product out to make a sale, such paperwork may be viewed as little more than a nuisance or, at best, something beyond the skills or resources to develop. So, having a well-organized operation may prevent a crisis from dominating the organization and can convey a sense that the organization is well-managed, but don't expect your local food truck to have one or the local drug dealer or gambling ace to construct anything that may look like a paper trail. This is simply not the way these organizations operate.

Finally, when possible, attending to each of the last points may help not only the marginal organization in times of crisis or stress but also help move it from its current position in the marginal economy to a more established role in the mainstream economy. This move may bring more benefits than costs and, ultimately, greater security overall, but it can be an expensive trip. This type of change can require expenditures of both physical and monetary resources as well as dramatic changes in an operating culture defining a free and easy life. Some marginal organizations may dream of running with the "big boys" but for most that desire is, at best, a dream.

Conclusions

Obviously, many aspects of the study presented, from the small sample size to the limited capability to use more sophisticated mathematics and statistics, limit its "academic" push. However, despite the study's obvious (and rectifiable) limitations, it is noteworthy that the observations just presented emerged as plausible without the use of a large number of subjects or carefully controlled experiments. In other words, certain features of the marginal economy and/or organizations operating in this economic subset are revealed without a great deal of effort.

Information exists that explains the impact of different stakeholders on the marginal organization's capacity to be influential over time and conditions. For example, should special interest groups whose mission includes the promotion of a particularly disturbing value, norm or ethic be allowed to operate freely and without some boundaries? Does an organization operating in the marginal economy that doesn't have the resources to fight a battle against a well-heeled special interest group or government agency have any recourse when its economic well-being is a target or is disrupted because of groups operating as little more than modern vigilantes?

The relations among all members of the marginal organization's social network also merit more attention. We only collected data from a small sample of one segment "Interested Citizens," but how would data collected from that segment compare across different types of organizations operating in both the mainstream and marginal economies? Would the same sentiments expressed by stakeholders in this study surface for other members of a marginal organization's social network? What do a marginal's stakeholders look like? What are their profiles, spheres of influence or operating characteristics, and how might they differ across different types of marginal organizations or between organizations in the marginal and mainstream economies? Studies that explore or draw attention to organizations operating in the marginal economy stand to reveal a great deal about these dynamic environments.

For example, we often know why marginal economies form, but what more can we gain from examining the stakeholders who comprise the marginal organization's network? In some ways, any organization's stakeholders exist on two planes simultaneously. The first is the obvious; it's the plane that's the basis for the day-to-day activities that define the organization as a functioning entity. These are the customers of the food wagon or restaurant or the members of the religious community, political or social movement, the drug or gambling addicts. The second level, still a very real part of the organization's social network, is a very different plane, however. Here stakeholders are defined by those with both official and unofficial responsibilities to observe, monitor or act on the organization if required to do so.

Any number of factors may motivate these stakeholders: workplace abuses or conditions, mismanagement, poor decisions or general shortcomings associated with the marginal organization or its actions. The key point is that these stakeholders can quickly mobilize and become part of a dynamic new network described here as a "stakeholder swarm" and their potential for influence can extend well beyond an attack on a local puppy mill or drug pusher. These stakeholders influence public opinion, shape media coverage, drive or prevent efforts to increase legislation or punishments for violations of industry, social and sometimes even moral standards and values.

There are few rules associated with the formation of marginal organizations. Once formed, they can find their organization and activities scrutinized if not regulated by particular organizations or individuals that feel they have a right to "be involved." Those engaged learn to rely on local information to guide them and their efforts. Indeed, local issues, local information and, social communication phenomena like rumors or information grapevines drive the process if for no other reason than what's emerging is typically counter to the expectations or desires of the parent organization. Indeed, the entire effort may appear as a giant work-around motivated by the parent organization's established structure, people, processes and procedures. Issues, in the form of gripes or complaints, play an important role in the formation process for involved stakeholders. Individuals use issues as part of a concept optimization process to identify the processes and ultimately the significance of what matters to them (Martin, 2007; Eaton and Voos, 2004). Few organizations, either mainstream or marginal, have little control over factors that motivate stakeholders to act.

What they do recognize, however, is that these interlopers can influence their value streams and this can be a long-term issue for them to manage. Stakeholders become a burden when their roles and affiliations with a particular issue or cause serve to define an underlying "current of urgency" for them and their affiliates. As a result, a stakeholder's singular focus means it and its membership can mobilize quickly in response to an issue but it also means there is little capacity or willingness to alter the special interest group's mission in any meaningful way. Given the overall subject of this study presented, we can see that the role of influence vis-à-vis the marginal organization gains traction from the moment the marginal organization begins its first transaction. After that, however, a marginal's influence is shaped by an array of stakeholders; some support the organization and some don't, but they all seek to define, develop and utilize their own influence, sometimes at the marginal's expense

CHAPTER 8

Conclusions: Strategies for the Management of a Society's Marginal Organizations

When researching for and writing this book, I expressly wanted to avoid writing from a particular academic orientation typically associated with the subject. Researchers in disciplines such as economics, sociology, anthropology, political science etc., have and continue to make significant contributions to our understanding of the marginal sector. Our contribution was to be an examination of organizations within the sector using tools commonly found and used in studies of business or organizational theory. Our hope was that taking this different approach would provide new insights or at least complement some of the research that already exists. It seems this objective is accomplished. Building off existing literature and using various tools and methods in business or organizational theory have illustrated how organizations in the marginal sector operate, why they operate as they do and, in turn, what this may mean for these organizations and the mainstream generally. That much seems accomplished.

Now, in this conclusion, I aim to do three things. First, I summarize the use of business and organization theory tools to describe or compare marginals with mainstream organizations to illustrate their usefulness and limitations. The exercise was instructive; it provided new ways to look at, think about and research marginal organizations as well as the sector itself.

Second, I want to take a shot at describing what I believe marginal organizations can do to maximize their operations and, in turn, contribute to the societies with which they are associated. I do this from the marginal's perspective vis-à-vis the mainstream. Several researchers have recognized that the marginal sector comprises a variety of organizations operating, as some have concluded, in "different degrees of illegality." These researchers recognize that treating all organizations in the marginal sector the same way is to say the least unfair and ultimately unproductive. The suggestions offered here separate the good from the bad and may benefit the former.

Finally, I draw some conclusions regarding what the mainstream can do to improve its approach to marginals. In contrast to the last section, the emphasis of this section might be described as ways to approach "good" marginals and to treat "bad" marginals." Those who are expected to manage or otherwise produce solutions to address marginals might find this of use.

The Use of Conventional Business and Organizational Theory Tools to Describe Marginal Organizations

To say that marginal organizations are different from those in the mainstream seems obvious, but it is not a distinction usually made. Most writers seem content to refer to marginals as Thomas (2001) has described them. Marginals, for Thomas, are organizations that are, from their processes to output, engaged in illegal market transactions. Distinguishing marginals from the mainstream because of the legality of their operation is important because that factor shapes everything else about marginals and their operations, but it has its limitations.

Indeed, claiming that marginals occupy the lowest rung of society's ladder isn't because of the nature of their work in illegal drugs, smuggling, or petty crimes like pickpocketing, prostitution or gambling. Marginals occupy the lowest rung because that is the best place to occupy when an organization seeks to avoid the attention of adversaries, particularly those in law enforcement. Marginals have an operational lifestyle defined by secrecy and stealth combined with a mixture of suspicion, mistrust and defensiveness. It can be a brutal, sometimes violent way of life where the marginal's agents do what they can to avoid leaving a traceable paper trail that might give away their location or associate them with a crime or act.

To maintain a profile like the one described means that many of the accoutrements one associates with mainstream organizations don't exist for the marginal. Planning is reserved for the task at hand, so few marginals consciously think in terms of vision or mission statement or plan—key elements for many mainstream organizations. Product design is seldom a complicated affair since the best products for a marginal are the easiest and most convenient to produce, to transport and to sell.

Some of their core products, like marijuana, are grown in backyards, in containers in a back bedroom or on the roof if the building is tall enough or out of the way. Talk about low overheads and production costs! Cocaine is a time-consuming, somewhat complicated product to make, so some criminals look to less complicated products to produce: meth labs, for example, have been set up in garages or even cars, the latter a twist perhaps borrowed from another marginal, the mobile food wagon, which has the facility to make and deliver food from the same vehicle.

Marginals also don't engage in elaborate organizational programs designed to market or sell their products. They don't have annual sales meetings or professional conferences to meet and exchange ideas on new product designs, production methods or even products. In fact, marginals can also be distinguished from mainstream organizations in that most have a very limited product mix. Even the pimp with a string of prostitutes doesn't mix the nature of the product with others, for example, drugs, illegal cigarettes or bootlegged liquor. The pimp may have more than one prostitute in the house but only one product line.

One benefit of maintaining a narrow focus is that the organization remains highly mobile, able to adapt to changing demands or situations—a particularly useful competency when avoiding the police is required. Apart from a quick escape, however, maintaining a flexible orientation has promoted a certain level of inventiveness and creativity among marginals. Invention and creativity may help the marginal avoid detection, dodge a pursuing authority or refine one's approach to the work at hand. Many pickpockets, for example, are especially inventive in the ways they can get money and materials from their targets. A more involved opportunity available to those with a narrow product mix is referred to as a "displacement" (Guerette, 2009). For those engaged in criminal activity, crime "displacement is the relocation of crime from one place, time, target, offense, or tactic to another" usually as a result of some crime prevention initiative (3). Displacement is particularly insidious because it can occur in various ways with each way having a different level of effects, making organizations like our marginals especially hard to manage or contain (Branton, 2009).

For example, members of a marginal organization may change the time when they commit a crime (temporal displacement). Unlike the predictable street food wagon that must be available when people want to eat their meals, the organization that is able to use temporal displacement disrupts the capacity of the organization seeking to track or control it by making it difficult if not impossible to predict when a crime will occur. This is particularly troublesome if the police, for example, have altered their staffing plans to correspond to times when they believe, based on past behavior, a crime will occur.

Equally disruptive is spatial displacement, where the marginal shifts from targets in one location to targets in another location. The effects of this move are obvious: with limited resources, the police cannot be spread too thin or be in more than one place at a time. In some instances, whole organizations can shift their area of operation from one location to another. For example, according to Richard McFeely, FBI Special Agent in Charge in Baltimore, gangs "are no longer limited to urban areas, but have migrated to more rural settings." Gangs have also infiltrated prisons and even the military and have diversified from drug running and petty crime to armed robbery, home invasions, mortgage and health care fraud and even human trafficking (Sassen, 2009, p. 34; McFeely, 2011). This shift of activity and location has multiple effects. Now under-resourced rural areas are faced with well-organized, experienced adversaries thus impacting the crime-fighting networks in those areas. In addition, emergence of gangs in mainstream organizations such as the military provides a level of training and development in armaments and technology the gang would have a difficult time getting elsewhere. This is an especially inventive strategy for adding to the marginal's skills and competencies.

Target displacement occurs when the marginal changes from one type of target to another as when the prostitute shifts from an off-the-street target to well-heeled executives attending a conference or the drug pusher shifts from his current customer base and moves to neighborhood schools to enrich his client base. Moving to schools has a dual benefit for the pusher for it not only adds numbers to the customer base, it adds younger users who may be with the pusher for a longer period of time.

As the marginal adds to its skills and competencies, it opens the door for tactical displacement, shifts in the methods used to deliver its products or services. Computers open the door for cyber crime; and just adding a microwave to a food truck can speed the processing and delivery of foods. Finally, offense or transgression displacement reflects a switch from one type of crime or activity to another. Drug runners who shift their efforts to smuggling of cigarettes (to avoid having to cross or to deal with borders) or who begin to traffic in illegal aliens because it is, perhaps, more profitable, are practicing transgression displacement. It, like the others described, demonstrates the ways by which marginals can enrich their organization's activities or performance by leaving themselves open to invention, creativity and flexibility (Bounds and Wilson, 2002).

Invention and creativity are often displayed in the ways some marginals source their "clients." The marginals use supply and value streams parallel to that of mainstream organizations but with some important variations. For example, since supply streams and value streams increase the organization's visibility, a negative feature for most marginal organizations, streams they use are often only an abbreviation of what one might see in a mainstream organization or, also to reduce risk, are broken into segments with the segments farmed out to others. So one marginal may make the product, say an illegal drug, and then another marginal distributes it, with yet another selling the product. Finally, money received from these activities that go back to the lead marginal is then turned over to another contractor who will "launder" the money so it cannot be traced back to the lead. These hybrid supply, distribution and value streams can be models in creativity and inventiveness brought about by the marginal's need for safety and security.

Frankly, creativity, inventiveness and resourcefulness are not restricted to large marginals or to marginals selling certain types of products or services. All marginals may find it necessary to create opportunities that improve the capacity to reduce risk, avoid detection or secure needed resources. The behavior of marginals in pursuit of their mark is often reminiscent of the ways insects forage for food (Camazine et al., 2001), fish school in order to avoid a predator or the ways other animals nest or find shelter to avoid capture (Dowling et al., 2010). Schooling and foraging in these instances are elements of harvesting processes marginals use, as discussed above.

Harvesting, when it is used by marginals as a strategy for collecting resources (money, materials, people and the like it uses in its trade), is of particular interest for two reasons. First, it is part of a marginal's value stream, where the supply, process and distribution streams collectively merge to add value for the marginal. What makes harvesting unique, however, is that the process brings the marginal into direct contact with a target organization or its membership. Harvesting is that point where the drug dealer sells cocaine, the prostitute pleasure, the pickpocket scores with his mark, the thief breaks into a store or the smuggler buys cigarettes taxed at a low rate for resale in a state with a higher tax rate.

When the act of harvesting occurs, the marginal's value stream meets the target's value stream, and if the marginal's timing is good, the marginal will not experience any ill effects from the harvesting process. Any number of potential ill effects can unfold if the marginal's timing is bad. For example, if harvesting overlaps the target's value stream at a point when the target is prepared or if the opportunity for surprise is lost, disaster can result. The same is true if the target's security system detects the marginal: it may attack the marginal, or if a third party (e.g., the police) is present to witness the harvesting process, those stakeholders may join in the attack.

Some mainstream organizations also use a facsimile of a harvesting model as part of their value stream. In contrast to marginals, however, since mainstreamers operate in an aboveboard fashion, the overall interface between their value stream and their customers' is coordinated. A mainstreamer's harvesting-like transactions are usually planned. True, the marginal operating as an enterprise selling drugs may plan an exchange of cash for the delivery of products, but that's a sale, not harvesting as we use the term. Harvesting is an inventive process, designed to be flexible and adaptive to changing circumstances. Planning may be behind a good harvesting model but it is different from the transaction model one typically associates with organizational interactions.

Marginals differ from mainstream organizations in a number of ways but one way in which they are similar is that organizations from both sectors can be described using the same classification system: Tafoya's classification of organizations as either "enterprises," "communities," "team/groups" or "individual contributors" is an illustration. Enterprises operate in terms of a for-profit model; that doesn't mean that the other three types don't need or seek money, it's just that the pursuit of money is a means not the end of the others' efforts. Enterprise organizations pursue a mission, for example, "to be the finest provider of quality cars," or "to provide excellent service to our customers," but these missions are always defined in terms of what they contribute to the organization's purpose, in this case to earn a profit. So a manufacturing organization, clothing retailer or professional sports team are examples of mainstream enterprises just as organized criminal organizations or manufacturers of illegal drugs or alcohol are examples in the marginal sector.

Community organizations, in contrast, operate almost exclusively in terms of a mission, often defined around key values, ideals or morals. Everything the community organization does aims at, in one way or another, supporting its ideological mission. Organized religions, schools and universities and charities are examples of community organizations in the mainstream, and terrorists, cults and political extremists are examples in the marginal sector. Teams/groups pursue a mission but these organizations have a designed, finite existence. Once the mission is achieved, the team organization disbands. Both enterprises and community organizations may use teams/groups in this regard from time to time as they pursue their own missions. Mainstream teams include the police swat team organized to capture a bank robber, the "skunk works" team organized to solve a manufacturer's quality problems or the team organized to plan for the company's annual employee picnic. Marginal teams are put together to launch a terrorist attack, to smuggle products across the border, to intimidate a group of merchants into buying "the security their organization offers."

The fourth organizational type, the individual contributor, is that person who operates in a largely "stand alone" capacity either as a singular agent (e.g., a self-employed doctor, lawyer, plumber or consultant) or in the same capacity within a larger firm (e.g., a surgeon, teacher or editor). These "organizations" are defined by their competencies; their capacity to make a contribution because they possess certain skills, capabilities or talents that others do not. Those just named are good examples of individual contributors in the mainstream but an assassin, a chemist in an illegal drug lab or a skilled pickpocket are examples in the marginal sector.

There is a good deal of value in being able to use the same tool to classify organizations in both the marginal and mainstream sectors. For example, there are many times when the same types of organizations from the two sectors come in contact with each other and being able to identify them by type can help in anticipating the outcome or at least the course their interactions might follow. For example, when a terrorist strike team encounters a police swat team. This is an interesting match, because we know, from our research, that each shares the same classification but each also operates using different supply and value streams. Other times, different types of organization from the marginal and mainstream sectors come in contact with each other, like a spy or an informant (individual contributors) infiltrating an organized crime syndicate (enterprise). Or when a radical special interest organization (community) launches a campaign to challenge a meat-processing plant's treatment of animals (enterprise) and uses an undercover infiltrator (individual contributor) to collect information in support of its campaign.

Using the classification scheme helps to describe and understand both the makeup of different organizations and their potential orientations to other organizations, to problems or to their work in general. Planners and researchers in both sectors could use this information to their advantage in improving their own organizations or when preparing for interactions with others. This last point is especially interesting, for while marginals and mainstream organizations use and maintain their own, separate operational networks both still may come into contact with each other as networks are invaded or collide.

Networks can be critical for an organization's success but sometimes they malfunction or even collapse. When networks overlap by plan, as when one organization enters into a business relationship with another organization, elements of their networks can interact for the benefit of the business relationship. Of course, the ideal situation is a well-defined network that operates for the organization's benefit. However, when a network isn't maintained or a crisis occurs, it can become imbalanced and dysfunctional, particularly if other organizations infiltrate the network, and especially if the infiltrators wrest the network's control from the parent organization.

Taken collectively, the tools used to describe the similarities and differences between marginal and mainstream organizations can reveal a good deal about the nature of their interactions, reasons for their interactions and, often, how those interactions might unfold. We collect this type of information because when looking at the similarities or differences between the two sectors, data collected can help the observer understand the strengths, vulnerabilities and/or weaknesses the organizations may have. Then, with that information in hand, it is possible to prepare organizational profiles or to map operational processes or interactions.

Interestingly, too, we can also see that some of an organization's strengths, vulnerabilities and/or weaknesses may be inherent to the type of organization and the sector in which the organization operates. For example, a marginal's need for secrecy may be a vulnerability while its capacity to adapt to changing situations a strength. However, many strengths and vulnerabilities and/or weaknesses are not inherent to an organization or its type but rather may reflect the organization's overall management, design or operation. The mainstream organization that overlooks the need for security may find itself vulnerable to attack or the marginal that's careless about the way it hires or recruits members may be vulnerable to infiltration by an adversary.

Solutions for What Good Marginals Need from Society Begins with the Mainstream and Its Approach to Marginals

The tools, methodologies and theoretical approaches used and described are helpful because they not only reveal something about particular marginals or mainstream organizations but also provide information regarding both sectors. This book's focus has been on marginals that operate outside a society's rules, regulations and laws. It's a functional dividing line but it can be a harsh way to describe the nature and makeup of all marginal organizations. For example, some organizations belong to the marginal sector because a society's infrastructure can't provide for its population's economic or social needs. Numerous self-organized enterprises form around the world because of these conditions. It's not necessary to read 100, 50 or even 25 articles related to organizations in a society's marginal sector to realize that active membership as either a worker or owner/operator is a poor substitute for a decent way to earn a living. True, some people in this sector do make a lot of money but it's a suboptimal situation for the worker (Sabatini and Farnsworth, 2006) and the marginal organizations are typically unable to grow and are "extremely unproductive compared with even the small firms" of the mainstream (La Porta and Shleifer, 2008).

Marginals often appear to emerge as options for the poor or disenfranchised when a society's rules and regulations are unevenly administered or ill defined. They are the responses of rational people when the state or conditions challenge opportunities for membership in legitimate organizations or simply stand in the way of efforts to fulfill one's needs, wants or desires. For some, the sector is defined by people operating outside the legal parameters of their society who, to paraphrase Thomas (2001), only differ in the degree of their illegality. It is as though the sector is part of the genetic make-up of all societies, and triggered by a defective gene in the society's DNA when times or the environment make it viable. Healthier members can manage the challenges facing them or have access to resources to help them, the weaker don't. In other words, marginals and those who rely on them have limited capabilities in societies whose political, economic, social or cultural conditions are not functioning properly and in complete equilibrium with all other key societal elements. This seems a plausible conclusion since few perfect worlds exist. In fact, after reviewing the literature, it seems the scale of a country's marginal environment appears to be a function of some combination of that country's administration, its regard for the poor, helpless and disenfranchised, and the country's overall capabilities to operate. Moreover, this seems true, regardless of whether one is looking at the world's developing regions or the established, wealthy developed countries.

The marginal sector exists as an outcome, a poor option that Sabatini and Farnsworth seem to have accurately described as "a two-way street, with both firms and workers calculating costs and making choices. Firms hire informally or extralegally in order to avoid the costs (financial and administrative) associated with formal, full-time employees" and where employment "is generally a suboptimal situation for a worker. Those who toil on the fringes of the formal economy all too often have limited access to even minimal job security or basic benefits and safety protections" (53–54). Then, their options gone or reduced, these people gravitate to life outside of society's norm.

Other times, marginals form not because people are forced out or simply not allowed to enter the mainstream. Prejudice, discrimination and fear deny or further remove options for these people, their organizations and the ways their organizations operate. Consider the mobile food trucks mentioned often in the book. Scanning the literature associated with that economic class reveals a whole group of enterprises that are valued by many because of their potential contribution to a local economy, because of the services they provide or, often, because of the quality of food served (Russell, 2006; Comas, 2008). Yet, other times, the literature suggests an undercurrent of racism or prejudice against those who operate these enterprises. In these instances, it is not the presence of a food truck or the food served, but who owns the truck or who's serving the food (Wilson, 1991; Montano, 2006; Brus, 2010).

Still other times, resistance comes not because of who's offering the service or where the operators are from but because they are viewed, by some in the "establishment," as unfair competitors for the same customers or market share (Radzievich, 2010; McCallum, 2011; Phan, 2012). However, here too, one has to wonder if it is "this" competition that the establishment objects to, or is *any* competition a threat? And, of course, there are those food vendors who are targets because they avoid paying taxes, don't have required licenses or operate eateries that may be unhealthy or unsafe (Gillette, 1999; Burt et al., 2003; Levine, 2006). But, here again, the literature doesn't support claims that these are in the majority of those operating in the marginal sector. In fact, a quick survey of retail enterprises operating in the mainstream suggests there are whole groups that are guilty of the same criticisms leveled at marginals. These operations may present themselves as upright and righteous mainstreamers but they avoid paying taxes, scheme to find ways around labor and tax obligations and harass, discriminate and treat employees as little more than second-class citizens.

What the Mainstream Can Do to Improve Its Approach to Marginals

Throughout the book, all marginals have been treated the same. That is, if an organization, by design, acted in ways that caused it to engage in illegal behavior of any sort, it is classified and treated as a member of the marginal sector. That's okay for this book but it's not a useful strategy for society in general: This book is not about politics, religion or economics, it is about processes. Societies benefit most when organizations function in ways that contribute to the overall well-being of society and its membership. Failing that, a society is obligated to pursue those organizations that commit illegal actions and those marginal organizations that are truly classifiable as marginals because they avoid paying taxes or other rules, regulations or laws of society.

The rub in the second instance is that there are organizations that operate in society's margins because they have little choice; our discussion of food wagons is an example. These organizations and others like them should be part of the mainstream and treated as such with the same rights and privileges. What makes misclassification of this group of marginals as important is that it is a double hit for the mainstream society as a whole and for those in the mainstream whose job it is to regulate and/or police *real* marginals. Society's loss is obvious: failure to let ill-defined, misclassified organizations operate denies the society of revenues and employment opportunities for those wanting to work. Once classified as a marginal, an organization and its members behave as criminals in order to avoid discovery or capture.

Being "on the run" doesn't help any organization that otherwise would pay license fees and taxes to do so. That said, there are individuals and organizations that are in the marginal sector and that is the only option available to them. These are the operators who can't get permits because they cannot afford to pay kickbacks, don't know what's required to operate legally or, simply, need to live, so they agree to create criminal acts to get the money necessary to survive.

The second "hit" is as dramatic. Misclassifying an otherwise legitimate (or conceivably legitimate) organization as a marginal means that someone has to pursue, track down and apprehend the organization and, with all of the bad marginals in society, chasing otherwise beneficial marginals is both a waste of time and money. Potentially good marginals employ more people in a society than do the bureaucracies that employee "marginal chasers."

There are ways to rectify the misclassification of marginals or those instances when otherwise well-intentioned organizations are pushed to the margins in order to survive. For example, among the first things a society can do is to view potential marginals as part of the society's legitimate organizational network. This classical approach views organizations as part of the mainstream until an organization decides it doesn't want to follow society's rules and regulations. The focus of this orientation shifts emphasis from challenges and police actions against "fringe marginals" to efforts aimed at the society itself. What society does or doesn't do contributes to an organization's decision to leave the mainstream for the margins or prevents it from entering it in the first place. Legalization of marijuana, gambling and "home brewing" of beer and wine are examples. Organizations in these areas, once a drain on society's police, justice and penal system resources, are now contributors to its tax base either directly or indirectly by providing employment opportunities and growth to secondary support services.

Rules and regulations meant to punish, biased in favor of protecting friends or outdated need to be addressed. Immigration, the legalization of marijuana and policies that allow aliens the opportunity to work are good places to start ("Drug legalization," 2013). Politicians who are little more than sycophants to business, religions or other special interests stand in the way of a healthy society. Drug clinics, needle exchange programs, employment training programs (e.g., Wodak et al., 2003) that both teach the casual laborers how to work safely and let them know that safe work is expected as the rule and not the exception accomplish two things.

First, they give marginals an opportunity to see and lock-into the change desired, to make them part of a larger "loyalty program." Organizations accepting this path become potential change agents working with society and its stakeholders. Hadfield and Measham's (2009) position that effective licensing can positively affect crime prevention is an illustration. "Licensing frameworks," they write, "serve to delineate certain forms of social and cultural activities by prescribing the times and places [in their illustration] in which nightlife can occur. Licensing also moulds the content of nightlife, being a key mechanism through which regulators—primarily the police and local government—facilitate and promote certain forms of leisure activity, while at the same time, adjusting, restraining or banishing other forms. Thus, licensing, through its processes of inspection and validation, operates as a little understood form of administrative governance, that exerts influence over urban spaces and the activities therein and that acts as a check upon the agency of businesses and consumers" (219).

Once legitimate, fair licensing is in place, the process can be administered so that those who comply are as easy to find as those who don't (Norton, 2008; Brus, 2010). Once licensed organizations have their licenses and their demographic information on file, the next step might include using technology to help monitor compliance. RFID chips attached to their site can be logged into a database and monitored even if their operations are primarily mobile. This benefits both the organization and the licensing agency. Moreover, equipment and vehicles with RFID chips can be located if stolen, thus benefiting business owners whose targets are thieves, extortionists or other illegitimate marginal organizations.

Deeper and perhaps more pervasive issues are prejudice and bias. Many who work in marginal occupations or organizations are members of different racial minorities. Some research (McLaren, 2003; Cox, 2011) suggests that simple physical divisions forced by ideology and nationalism or promoted by physical geography that keeps people apart are reasons that prejudice appears. McLaren (2003), for example, wrote, "One way to encourage more peaceful relations [among those of different races] may be to encourage friendships between members of the different groups... contact does have an effect on attitudes toward immigrants in the European context" (929). Ljujic et al. (2012) came to a similar conclusion in their study of Romaphobia, Islamophobia, anti-Semitism and anti-Chinese feelings. Feelings toward the four groups, they wrote, "were partially explained by social distance at work and antipathy in general" (141). Moreover, the "discursive representation of Roma has been somewhat ambiguous, oscillating between a sympathetic image of 'troubled' European minority and a pariah pan-European 'troublemaker,' prone to immorality and criminal behavior" (142). Clearly bias of this sort is in conflict with existing laws and cannot be tolerated. Worse however, is that sometimes prejudice or expressions of racial bias serve to traumatize people to the extent that they form preconceived notions of others without even having contact with those whom they mistrust or "dislike."

Profiling is an example (Tafoya, 2010). Profiling can occur at any time and by anyone, but when it is done by those in positions of authority who are expected to be objective if not bias-free in the administration of their duties, it's more than problematic, for it can send a message that such behavior is acceptable and, at times, socially reinforcing. Weizer and Tuch's (2005) examination of racially biased policing is an example. "In the U.S., white support for the police has traditionally been robust. At the same time, whites tend to see blacks as inclined to criminal or violent behavior." "For whites" they wrote "who subscribe to these views [that blacks are violence prone], there is a tendency to condone police suspicion and disparate treatment of blacks as 'rational discrimination'" (1010). King and Wheelock (2007) came to a similar conclusion. "We suggest group threat theory, and specifically the racial threat derivative, provides a useful framework for understanding state social control practices and popular support for crime control initiatives" (1256).

When the group that is in control acts against those who are not, the bias can become particularly insulting because friendship or affiliation, not competence or fairness, underlie actions and decisions: insult adds to injury. Consider how competition and fair play can be treated among friends and those who aren't. "Competition policy is intended to ensure a fair fight, not to punish winners or protect losers," wrote Shapiro and Varian (1999, p. 301). "The underlying principle guiding antitrust law," they wrote, "is the protection of competition as a process. If a single firm is victorious and gains a monopoly position based on offering low prices and superior product quality, the competitive process has worked just fine" (301). Unfortunately, this isn't how competitive policy has worked for many organizations forced to turn to the marginal sector in order to survive. Food vendors are an example. Montano (2006) found that vendors often felt threatened because city officials often worked hand in glove with local restaurant owners to prevent competition from the vendors. Brus (2010) and Wilson (1991) noted a similar trend when vendors fitting a certain profile were the targets.

Bias in these instances not only impacts the marginal organization but also can directly affect stakeholders who otherwise would work with, support or utilize the marginal to meet their needs. Unfair behavior by officials in this instance can create significant market inefficiencies as the favored organizations disregard benefits associated with economies of scale and gorge themselves on the captive customers who have no other alternative places to shop, eat, work or play and push an artificially manufactured demand-side response to the market. Indeed, favoritism and bias create another instance when no one benefits because creativity and innovation become needless expenses rather than useful performance strategies and tactics.

Maximizing a Marginal's Effectiveness: What "Good" Marginals Can Do

Solutions for people and organizations that feel pressured, discriminated against, harassed or the like doesn't rest just with the mainstream; marginals too have an obligation to do what they can to bring about needed changes to their own environments. Among the first things these organizations can do is to make sure their operations are legal, in compliance with local, state and national laws, rules and regulations. Obviously, this doesn't remove the potential for unfair challenges, requirements or prejudice and bias to surface, but it does give those who come to the well-organized marginal's defense a better foundation from which to work.

Some marginals literally create trouble for themselves. They may be unaware of laws, rules and regulations, and at other times they may not think before they act. Reilly (1988) noted a number of food vendors were sued because they were misrepresenting their hotdogs as Vienna sausages. On a more progressive note, Chanen (2007) and Wilson (1991) support the notion that some marginals can benefit from organizing informal unions among like organizations. This runs counter to a marginal seeking to stay out of the public's limelight but change can require that some risks be taken. Organizing may be an excellent strategy for transitional or "fringe marginals." These informal organizations can give them the "buying power" of a group, a place to get needed information or assistance, an opportunity to collaborate with those facing similar challenges. In fact, given the precedents established with the legalization of marijuana and online pornography ("At a XXX-roads," 2011) and drive through prostitution (Foulkes, 2013), these efforts can provide the opportunity to revolutionize even the most extreme occupational pursuits.

Some marginals can save themselves a lot of headaches and challenges by simply upgrading their operations. Cell phones, the Web and social media networks are ways to stay in touch with customers or like-minded stakeholders. Moreover, some marginals must upgrade their existing operations to bring them into compliance with health codes or safety requirements (Norton, 2008). These are the "little things" that not only are within the marginal's capacity to manage, but also are the "musts" that have to be in place if one ever hopes to be viewed as a serious, conforming member of society.

Finally, it might help some marginal's credibility if they worked on improving key processes and practices. Knowing stakeholder needs, operations and processes is one (Graham, 2000), and many marginals may benefit by taking a long view of their organization. Organizational succession plans help all stakeholders associated with a marginal to think about the organization beyond the present tense by incorporating a sense of the organization in their future and them in it. This contributes to risk reduction, overall planning, the design and development of products and product lines, in short the entire organization as dynamic entity. As importantly, however, sketching a sense of the future also can be a powerful way to present one's self as an organization that "intends to be around" in the future and is not just a means for short-term employment until something better comes along. What banker, for instance, would feel comfortable giving a 20-year loan to the owner of a business who is only thinking in terms of 1 or 2 years into the future?

And Then There Are the "Bad" Marginals: Ways Mainstream Can Approach Bad Marginals

The material in this book offers both analytical tools as well as prescriptive material. It can be used to improve the operations of most organizations described regardless of the type. For example, organizations whose role in the marginal's network is to evaluate its performance or to offer coaching or guidance, to gauge its operations or to isolate performance issues and, when possible, help rectify their problems may find it particularly useful.

Organizations, regardless of their levels of sophistication, always operate in terms of different activity streams. Some are supply streams, others for distribution or sales and, of course, the overall value stream. As indicated in the text, it's often possible to engage an organization at different points in its streams, so technology is a useful tool when this is an objective. Weisel (2004) demonstrated how closed circuit TV can be used to track the behavior of specific targets, and Radcliffe (2011) provided a broad view of the use of this type of technology. Technology in these instances is particularly useful when the observer wants to be as unobtrusive as possible, or in situations that might be dangerous to anyone trying to infiltrate the organization.

Other times, existing technology or resources can be redefined and used where they typically haven't been used. Web technology can be used to track illegal gambling (Assad, 2007), illegal sale of drugs (Eltis, 2008) or elder abuse (Liang and Lovett, 2012). The new use of the US Coast Guard's mission for border patrols and to fight smuggling activities (Truver, 2000; Felbab-Brown and Aho, 2010) illustrates how the mission of entire organizations can be amended to meet the demands of current problems.

The use of technology by itself is little more than a mechanical solution. A stronger approach to the management of marginal organizations begins with the design and use of appropriate methodological approaches to the problem at hand as the foundation for any well-conceived plan. Designing such an approach begins with a concerted effort to think systemically and is always grounded in terms of involved stakeholders and their needs, wants and desires.

One effective approach for dealing with undesirable marginals is to concentrate attacks on the organization's network, and in particular the supporters, feeders and reliers that make up the network's core players. Focusing on supporters, feeders and reliers is different from approaches that focus on the network's demanders, for example, by increasing the number of regulators, legislators or police or by enhancing their roles and/or capabilities. Think, for example, how an organization's supporters, feeders and reliers (e.g., employees) might react if they were provided security, educational opportunities or the health care or medical insurance they need to protect themselves and their families in case of illness or injury (Olivo, 2009). A prerequisite for health care is documentation, so making this resource available creates a true trade-off for the marginal: the marginal must recognize that to provide for the health and well-being of one's family, one must be willing to provide needed documentation to secure this resource. Using an approach that targets those the marginal organization needs to support or work for it can be very effective in challenging the marginal's very nature. Moreover, with enough of the right changes the marginal may become a candidate for membership as a mainstream organization, the ideal solution for all involved.

Klamm and Weidenmier (2004) suggest that organizations interested in improving their performance should link business processes with their customers' transaction cycles. We agree, with three amendments to their recommendations. First, more than organizational process, the key practices defined and discussed throughout this book should be included in these planning efforts. Looking at both processes and transaction cycles in the same context can reveal a great deal about an organization's strengths, weaknesses and vulnerabilities.

Second, rather than restricting assessment to just customers we suggest that the examination should include transaction cycles of all stakeholders and certainly major stakeholders. Customers are only a part of the organization's value stream, usually considered briefly at the beginning and most often only appearing at the stream's end. Systemic examinations of the transactions among stakeholders will provide real knowledge about what's happening in the organization.

Finally, Klamm and Weidenmier's plan could really benefit by expanding their analysis so that it includes the organizational typology presented in earlier chapters. This approach begins by approaching organizations as belonging to one of four categories: enterprises, communities, teams/groups and individual contributors. This allows the researcher the opportunity to explore organizations by focusing on their unique underlying nature and purpose vis-à-vis business processes and their customers' transaction cycles.

Once the best tools are selected and a plan is sketched, it's critically important that those doing the planning engage the organization's stakeholders in an exercise devoted to think about what happens *after* the plan is implemented. For example, one thing discussed throughout this book is that often marginals are "survivors" because they are skilled at adapting to changing situations. Many in law enforcement organizations have recognized this competency because it frequently surfaces along with strategies like "crime displacement and diffusion" (Guerette, 2009). "Crime displacement," writes Guerette "is the relocation of crime from one place, time, target, offense, or tactic to another as a result of some crime prevention initiative" (3). His treatment is very enlightening and extensive.

Displacement is a tactical move and that is one reason why it creates problems for those in law enforcement and related fields. For example, displacement can surface in a number of different ways. Temporal displacement describes those instances when offenders change the time at which they commit crime. Law enforcement organizations or businesses that are routine-dependent can be caught completely off guard when something as simple as temporal displacement occurs.

Spatial displacement occurs when criminals switch from targets in one location to targets in another location. This gives the criminal organization a type of fresh start to their nefarious activities. Just as when gangs move out of cities and into rural areas, the change of location doesn't hurt their skill set but it can catch their new targets completely off guard and leave the law enforcement organizations that were left behind wondering what happened and, of course, makes them think about what they should do to fill any extra time they may have on their hands. Target displacement is similar to temporal displacement, only in this instance the criminal switches from one type of target (e.g., the elderly) to another (e.g., children). As with the other forms of displacement, the criminal's skill sets, objectives, needs and interests don't change, only the circumstances do.

Displacement strategies are mechanical tactics, however. As some criminal organizations become more sophisticated or their activities are discovered, they switch from the reliance on simple tactics in their crimes to more strategic efforts. Indeed, some organizations go so far as to transform who they are or how they operate. These transformations can range from simply switching from one type of crime to another (e.g., switching to long-distance crime through the use of computers or the Internet) to changing one's role in a value stream (e.g., from manufacturer to distributor) to completely changing the organization's mission (e.g., from being the "best provider of illegal drugs" to being "the premier provider of weapons and armaments").

To counter the various strategies and tactics a marginal organization might use, those "demanders" who are crime fighters can also make changes in the ways they operate. Some in law enforcement might benefit from expanding their use of the strategic practices discussed earlier in the book. This is a two-part approach that begins with an audit covering the status of their own use and familiarity of the practices and then consideration of ways the practices can be adapted to address the profiles and activities of particular marginals.

Targeting strategic practices reveals important information about an organization and its operations, whether in the marginal or mainstream sectors. For example, with unchecked, changing conditions, a previously dominant organization may fail and create a vacancy in the environment in which it operates. If another organization emerges to fill the void created with the departure of the first organization, that's a great time for the law enforcement organization to act, before the new organization establishes itself and organizes its own policies, procedures and practices for action. This illustrates an advantage law enforcement has over most criminal elements: law enforcement is hardly ever the "newcomer" on the block while the criminal organization almost always is in that role.

Every organization/network has a set of natural, inherent conditions that, unless managed, can increase its overall risk exposures and/or vulnerability to threats. Failure to develop and use key operational practices is an example. Disrupt an organization's capacity to use communication management practices and strategies and not only is its ability to exchange information with stakeholders impacted, the stakeholders' relationship with the organization can literally wither. Likewise, failure in administration and use of evaluations can confuse stakeholders regarding the organization's commitment to quality and service. Commitment to evaluation conveys an image of authority and a dedication to rooting out bias, poor procedures, incompetency and substandard products and service.

Strategies, practices or procedures used to acquire, build, develop and maintain relationships between or among individuals, groups and organizations are essential and critical for marginals given the degree to which risk is embedded in their environments. Disregard for "people" values facilitates defensiveness on the part of stakeholders. Why should a stakeholder believe they have value in the organization if the organization so quickly devalues others? Even relatively poorly handled routine matters can lead one to question the competency and commitment of an organization. Careless hiring practices put everyone at risk in the marginal organization and relying on people to do good work when jobs or assignments are poorly defined can lead to wasted time, material and financial resources. Every organization has to focus on the "details" but for marginals operating so near to risk and danger, diligence is critical.

When dealing with the typical illegal marginal organization, those in law enforcement and related fields can use the fact that while most marginals have inherent vulnerabilities, particularly in their operational practices, they (1) may not be able to see these and (2) often do not have the skills and competencies needed to rectify their shortcomings. Here's a very simple illustration: running stop signs. Most people who don't stop at stop signs or who "roll" through them are both familiar with the sign and its purpose and, as importantly, the roads around the signs they run. More than running a stop sign, because that's part of their driving behavioral set, what they are really demonstrating is careless behavior. What the traffic cop has to do, given our discussion of operational practices, is to realize that (1) for this driver, running the stop sign is a routine part of traveling on a particular road and (2) it's also a vulnerability in the driver's *operational practices* that the traffic cop can take advantage of. These and more strategic operational practices are discussed throughout the book and in other resources (Tafoya, 2010, 2013a). One last strategy to use when attempting to manage or otherwise address an illegal marginal is to let its overall organizational profile reveal the organization's inherent and existing vulnerabilities. The typology was discussed throughout the book. Here's a scenario based on an attack on one of our favorite targets: a terrorist organization.

The Terrorist Organization (Community Type) Scenario

Both overt and covert efforts can destabilize an organization. In either case, the effectiveness of destabilization efforts increases when tailored to fit the particular type of organization targeted. For example, what works best to destabilize an Enterprise organization might be completely ineffective against Community, Team or Individual Contributor organizations. For example, in dealing with terrorists, the prudent strategist might begin by recalling the makeup of a community organization, then proceed to prepare a list of general conclusions regarding the organization based on the top-level assessment. Finally, the attack can begin in the third stage of his plan, keeping in mind that as the plan unfolds, it's only based on a partial view of the true nature of things. It's a limited view, but it's a way to begin. Here's an example.

Part I of Your Plan: Begin with the Fundamentals

Destabilize the Leadership. The "Community Organization" is often "leader-dependent" ("Zeta zeroed," 2013). Community organizations view some leaders as god-like, some as members of a royal family with leadership prescribed by tradition or rule; and, of course, there are the charismatic leaders. Destabilizing strategies for organizations with a leadership-dependent profile are most effective when the organization's structural makeup is poorly defined. What's the role of leadership in the organization you are examining? Who's in charge? How did the leader(s) get to become the leader? What's good or bad about this ascendancy process for *this* organization?

Can the Mission Be Destabilized? The community organization has one feature that tends to protect it from threats: the mission is critical to the community organization and people drawn to the organization's mission usually have a very personal, deep-seated affiliation with the organization *because of the mission.* In fact, a community organization usually exists because it presents the mission as though it is each member's personal, special interest. So, in addition to providing particular services that are otherwise hard for the individual to find (everything from training to warm clothes and food), everything becomes the mission and, through participation, the mission becomes the person. As a result, members not only invest in the organization, they can take a strong stance to protect the organization from attack or internal turmoil as well. Members may see themselves as the organization. Undermining the mission's salience for its membership is an effective strategy for some community organizations.

Community Organizations Rely on Three Distinct Developmental Phases. Can They Be Disrupted? The membership rites and rituals of community organizations typically reflect three phases. (Actually this is true for most organizations —i.e., enterprise, team, individual contributor, community— but the stages are particularly critical for community organizations like a terrorist organization.) Community organizations can be very dependent on the extent to which members successfully move through these phases. The phases make the member a part of the organization. Conversely, the more an organization is dependent on these phases, the more likely the rites and rituals are susceptible to emerging threats, risks and vulnerabilities. The phases outlined below are for our community organization, but keep in mind they can apply to all organizations.

Becoming a Member of the Community: Phase I—Pre-Community. Every organization has some type of joining process but the community's is particularly unique. Awareness of this process is important because a member's opportunity to participate may be limited during this period and dependent on successful completion of the phase.

Membership Phase II: Full Participation. The second phase is marked by full participation. Involvement increases and, typically, levels of mutual affinity, fondness, closeness, trust and congruence between the member and the organization increase. As importantly, levels of tolerance, responsibility and compatibility increase with all bonded by a general sense of harmony.

Membership Phase III: Immersion and Integration. Immersion and integration reflect heightened levels of maturity within the organization and evident increases in the range and diversity of a member's contribution and involvement. Ever-evolving order, standardization and uniformity among the membership define the phase. The individual's participation in community events can increase in scope and scale, perhaps to the extent that the one-time neophyte may now become a planner and designer of those events that are the organization's hallmark. Friendships, mobility within the network and dependencies are likely to increase as both the participant and others within the organization develop an overall sense of closeness, which, when necessary, can solidify in "them-not-us" or "we/they" sentiments toward those outside.

Part II of Your Plan: What Can You Conclude about the Organization Now That This Top-level Analysis Is Complete?

1. What are the organization's vulnerabilities? If you listed the top three what would they be and why? For example, can the organization handle an unexpected or unwanted economic burden? What if the economic burden came from competition versus say a breakdown in a key operational area? Would a breakdown in one area be worse than in another area? What's the nature of the organization's stakeholder network? What would it look like if diagrammed? How would the network change if the organization was under attack? Finally, how influential is the organization within its network? What rating would you give it? How about among competitors? Among adversaries?

Can the organization withstand disruptions that come from a loss of life? Loss of activity? Damage or loss of property? Which disruptions would be most problematic? Does it matter where disruptions occur in the supply or value streams?

2. How does this marginal contribute to vulnerabilities in the mainstream? How does it exploit these vulnerabilities? Does its activity lead to economic competition and/or loss? Does the terrorist organization create a physical, emotional, cognitive threat to mainstreamers? When and how? Does the organization weaken the social fabric of an organization or society? To what extent does the organization create complete losses to the mainstream organization?

3. Where do generic threats come from? Is the organization vulnerable to any competitors? From affiliates? From external organizations via its supply chain? Are there any "copy cats" or spin offs to contend with that might be a threat?

4. How are vulnerabilities and threats managed when experienced? Where are evident vulnerabilities in the supply, distribution, sales/promotional chains? What about the overall value stream? What about any key personnel? Who are critical people/positions? Which must the organization have in place? What about vulnerabilities in the core network? The extended network (i.e., those of stakeholders?)? Any particular "network needs"?

Part III of Your Plan: Build Off What You Learned to Launch a Strategy Like the One That Follows

1. Challenge the organization through its network. (Sustainability and Threats to Ecological Succession.) Some marginals are able to spawn "offspring"—spins offs with some of the parent's features. Sometimes these are planned, at other times they are not planned for but occur, and still other times, the opportunity for spin offs is possible but not recognized. Spin offs are hybrids, not true copies, so it's important to know how they are similar/dissimilar. This is important, for regardless of how the spin off emerges, keep in mind that the parent knows how to "do things" but the hybrid may not. Additionally, there may be a greater learning curve for the hybrid. Perhaps the work it does is particularly complicated or its staff untested and immature.

Some hybrids may be uncontrollable; they may not follow the organization's mission or rules. Perhaps the organization's mission is in conflict with the hybrid's. Continuity between the parent and offspring can increase the latter's "influential integrity." Does the hybrid command respect? How influential is it? How does it interpret the organization's mission (or its own?)

Some hybrids can play important "supportive roles" for the parent. Offspring can be an integral part of ongoing recruiting. They may be key tools when dealing with adversaries. The more hybrids differ from parents the more new and different models are needed to predict or describe hybrid behavior. Having hybrids that are different can demand more resources: time, costs, etc.

2. Target and disrupt the organization's equilibrium. What will immediately affect the organization's sustainability? How would new rules, regulations or laws and penalties affect the marginal? Use events like the legalization of marijuana or gambling as betas. What can be targeted in stakeholder alliances or the stakeholder network generally? What "poison pills" are threats to the organization? What about encouraging a "cowboy" mentality versus a more deliberate and planned approach to planning and

problems? How would strategies like this affect the organization? How could it/they be introduced? How could shifting the target's orientation from its business to addressing its rivals work on your behalf? What can be standardized in your approach to the target? Where are your process "economies of scale"?

3. Encourage and nurture new entrants, new challenges from technology, stakeholder needs and interests. Can the target handle them? What is the organization's "technology profile"? Does it have its own cyber specialists? In a world of constantly evolving needs, interests, changing morals and greed, is the target keeping up? Can it or its products become "old news"? What are the target's physical strengths, the strengths of relationships with affiliates? How many affiliates does the organization have and how loyal are they?

What can be said about the organization's enemies or competitors and its relationship to them? How many are there and what are their strengths and weaknesses? How does the organization respond to their presence? For example, does the organization get caught up in "Exponential Arming"—a condition marked by layering itself in armaments and weaponry? How does it target "opportunities"? Does it work from a plan or simply shoot from its hip? Does it target with impunity or is it flexible enough to target a range of vulnerable segments of society: the elderly, the young, women?

4. Work on morale and cohesion. Encourage greed. Hubris goes before the fall. Where might vanity or arrogance contribute to the organization's vulnerabilities? Where are yours? If the material offered above were applied to your organization, what would that picture look like? Is your organization ready to take on this target? How do you know?

5. Keep trying and good luck.

Final Thoughts

A simple conclusion to a study examining marginal organizations would break across two themes: marginals are illegal organizations noted for avoiding taxes, labor and employment laws and, in the worst case, predators who prey on a society's agents—its citizens and institutions. A second notion, one more romantic, would describe the same organizations—well, maybe not those with pure criminal intent—as examples of an entrepreneurial spirit, challenging the hardships and obstacles confronted to employ the unemployable, to feed the hungry, to generally serve as a means for a whole segment of society's disenfranchised to meet their needs, interests and desires.

In reality, neither orientation is completely correct; a final conclusion is probably a combination of the two, with a true emphasis on the fact that these organizations are, in the final analysis, illegal. The real issue seems to be one of discerning not what these organizations are but why they form and, subsequently, are forced into practices that lead people to classify them one way or the other.

Marginal organizations or, perhaps more accurately, those in marginal organizations accept their position in that segment of society; they resign themselves to the fact that they exist and operate outside of the mainstream society—in its margins. Over time they recognize that they are subject to prejudices, general disenfranchisements and/or simple bad luck, where things are not meant to "go their way." By their mere presence they are stakeholders in the larger society but they are designated to work and live on the fringe, which often restricts their employment opportunities and/or prevents them from enjoying the country's social and economic benefits. The solution for some is to meet their survival needs any way they can, which, as we've seen, can mean doing something that the host society considers illegal.

Now one could waft on regarding the nature and causes of these conditions, remarking on their legitimacy or fairness but that would be repeating what so many others have written. Ultimately, too, it would be of little help or interest to those good people who are captured in this sometimes dangerous and often insulting and deprived segment of life and society. It would do little good and would be of little use. Rather, we choose to end this treatment by suggesting that solutions to the wrongs of the marginal society, to the unfairness of the experiences those in the segment bear and the factors that contribute to the formation of marginal organizations or the segment in the first place are outlined in this and many other documents. These exist, but what's missing is the action that's needed to bypass the hypocrisy, laziness and incompetencies that stand in the way of either doing what needs to be done or at least letting those interested and willing to do the right thing take action.

Bibliography

Adam, J. 2003. *Mathematics in Nature: Modeling Patterns in the Natural World.* Princeton, NJ: Princeton University Press.

Alasmari, K. A. 2012. "Cleaning up dirty money: The illegal narcotics trade and money laundering." *Economics and Society* 5, no. 2a: 139–148.

Allport, G. W. 1958. *The Nature of Prejudice.* New York: Doubleday.

Andrews, D., A. Sanchez, and A. Johansson. 2011. "Towards a Better Understanding of the Marginal Economy." OECD Economic Department Working Papers 873, May 30.

Anonymous. 2006. "Lunch wagons can keep serving." *McClatchy—Tribune Business News.* http://search.proquest.com/docview/459774920?accountid=35396.

———. 2008. "Sen. Lautenberg introduces bill to stop illegal drug smuggling aboard elusive, low-cost submarines." *US Federal News Service, Including US State News.* http://search.proquest.com/docview/473226191?accountid=35396.

———. 2009. "Low-income Latino immigrants in the south often targeted for abuse, discrimination, new SPLC report finds." *PR Newswire.* http://searchproquest.com/docview/448128867?accountid=35396.

———. 2010. "Congress passes Representative Kirkpatrick's measure to help coast guard stop drug trafficking submarines." *Lanham: Federal Information & News Dispatch, Inc.* http://search.proquest.com/docview/755919041?accountid= 35396.

———. 2011a. *ABCNews.* http://abcnews.go.com/lotter/mcdonalds-dumps-mcmuffin-egg-factory-health-concern/storyid=14976054, November 18.

———. 2011b. "Sparboe farms face false advertising claims following undercover animal cruelty investigation: Animal rights group files Federal Trade Commission complaint citing egg producer's false and misleading animal welfare claims." *PR Newswire,* December 1.

———. 2012a. "Huntington beach bans sale of dogs from puppy mills." *McClatchy—Tribune Business News,* May 8. http://search.proquest.com/docview/1011566229?accountid=35396.

———. 2012b. "More than 2,000 pet stores take a stand against puppy mills." *Targeted News Service,* December 14. http://search.proquest.com/docview/1238451220?accountid=35396.

Ashby, W. R. 1962. "Principles of the self-organizing system." In H. Von Foerster and G. W. Zopf, Jr. (eds.), *Principles of Self-Organization: Transactions of the University of Illinois Symposium*. London: Pergamon Press.

Assad, M. 2007. "Private valley clubs may fold under loss of video poker play: Compromise sought as associations feel state's pinch over illegal games." *McClatchy—Tribune Business News*. http://search.proquest.com/docview/462506790?accountid=35396.

"At a XXX-roads: The adult industry is seeking respectability—and profits." *The Economist*. October 1, 2011.

Axelrod, R. 1984. *The Evolution of Cooperation*. Cambridge, MA: Basic Books.

Batty, M. 2007. *Cities and Complexity: Understanding Cities with Cellular Automata, Agent-Based Models, and Fractals*. Cambridge: MIT Press.

Becker, K. 2004. *Fact Finding Study: The Informal Economy*. Stockholm, Sweden: Swedish International Development Cooperation Agency.

Berg, L. 2013. "Ag gag laws really do protect animals, producers." *National Hog Farmer*. http://search.proquest.com/docview/1330830922?accountid=35396.

Bounds, A. and J. Wilson. 2002. "Arms and drugs trade booming in Central America." *Financial Times*. http://search.proquest.com/docview/248307909?accountid=35396.

Branton, J. 2009. "Illegal drug world evolving in county: Price, demand for meth sky-high as producers change tactics; no labs found locally this year." *McClatchy—Tribune Business News*. http://search.proquest.com/docview/457977580?accountid=35396.

Brus, B. 2010. "Health department cracks down on mobile food vendors in OKC." *Journal Record*. http://search.proquest.com/docview/744414475?accountid=35396.

Burt, B. M., C. Volei, and M. Finkel. 2003. "Safety of vendor-prepared foods: Evaluation of 10 processing mobile food vendors in Manhattan." *Public Health Reports* 118, no. 5: 470–476. http://search.proquest.com/docview/201515804?accountid=35396.

Camazine, S., J.-L. Deneubourg, N. R. Franks, J. Sneyd, Guy Theraulaz, and Eric Bonabeau. 2001. *Self-Organization in Biological Systems*. Princeton, NJ: Princeton University Press.

Castells, M. and A. Portes. 1989. "World underneath: The origins, dynamics, and effects of the informal economy." In A. Portes, M. Castells, and L.A. Benton (eds.), *The Informal Economy—Studies in Advanced and Less Developed Countries*. Baltimore, MD: Johns Hopkins University Press.

Chanen, J. S. 2007. "FOOD FIGHT." *ABA Journal* 93: 8. http://search.proquest.com/docview/194394827?accountid=35396.

Charles, Dan. 2012. "Who sent those sick cows to the slaughterhouse?" *Salt*. August 23.

"Cigarette-smuggling: The urge to smurf." *The Economist*, November 24, 2012.

Cohn, A. 2009. "E. V. pet stores pledge to avoid puppy mills." *McClatchy—Tribune Business News*. http://search.proquest.com/docview/457330839?accountid=35396.

Comas, M. E. 2008. "Hot dog pushcart first mobile food vendor in Tavares." *McClatchy—Tribune Business News*. http://search.proquest.com/docview/464899718?accountid=35396.

Cox, O. C. 2011. "Race, prejudice, class conflict, and nationalism." *Race/Ethnicity: Multidisciplinary Global Contexts* 4, no. 2 (Winter): 169–182.

Dickson-Gomez, J., M. Convey, H. Hilario, A. M. Corbett, and M. Weeks. 2008. "Structural and personal factors related to access to housing and housing stability among urban drug users in Hartford, Connecticut." *Contemporary Drug Problems* 35, no. 1: 115–152, 2–3. http://search.proquest.com/docview/233171791?accountid=35396.

Dowling, Z., T. Hartwig, E. Kiviat, and F. Keesing. 2010. "Experimental management of nesting habitat for the Blanding's turtle." *Ecological Restoration* 28, no. 2 (June): 154–159.

"Drug legalization in Uruguay. The experiment: Another blow against prohibition." *The Economist*, August 3, 2103, 31.

Eaton, Adrienne E. and Paula Beth Vogle Voos. 2004. "Managerial unionism: Prospects and form." *Labor Studies Journal* 29, no. 3 (Fall): 25–56.

Eltis, K. 2008. "A first step towards curtailing illicit cross-border I-Pharma: Drawing practical solutions from the regulation of on-line gambling." *Health Law Journal* 16: 173–205.

Elfrink, T. 2009. "South Florida cigarette smuggling funds terrorism." *Broward-Palm Beach New Times*. http://search.proquest.com/docview/370404723?accountid=35396.

Felbab-Brown, V. and M. Aho. 2010. "Narcotics International, Inc." *Americas Quarterly* 4, no. 2: 42–49.

Ferenchik, M. 2006. "Code enforcers crack down on food wagons: North side leaders concerned about spread of mobile food wagons popping up in parking lots along Rte 161." *McClatchy—Tribune Business News*. http://search.proquest.com/docview/465610761?accountid=35396.

———. 2007. "Food wagons an acquired taste: Mobile stands bother some neighborhoods; city considers regulations." *McClatchy—Tribune Business News*. http://search.proquest.com/docview/463473129?accountid=35396.

Flaim, D. 2007. "Newsday, Melville, N.Y., animal house column: Puppy mills need to be stopped at the demand end." *McClatchy—Tribune Business News*. http://search.proquest.com/docview/463134714? accountid=35396.

Foulkes, Imogen. 2013. "Zurich introduces 'drive-in' sex." BBC News, http://www.bbc.com/news/world-europe-23339358, August 26.

FSIS. 2012. "USDA suspends Central Valley Meat for humane handling violations." *News Release*. United States Department of Agriculture Food Safety and Inspection Service. August 21.

Garza, J. 2008. "Independent Catholic parish to ordain woman as priest." *McClatchy—Tribune Business News*. http://search.proquest.com/docview/462693283?accountid=35396.

Ghyka, M. 1977. *The Geometry of Art and Life*. New York: Dover.

Gilbert, M. 2007. "Bill targets unethical breeders of dogs: Oversight sought to end 'puppy mills.'" *McClatchy—Tribune Business News*. http://search.proquest.com/docview/462219644?accountid=35396.

Gillette, B. 1999. "State cracking down on side-of-the-road sellers." *Mississippi Business Journal* 21, no. 41 (Pre-Aug 20, 2012): 3. http://search.proquest.com/docview/206578771?accountid=35396.

Gloor, P. 2006. *Swarm Creativity: Competitive Advantage through Collaborative Innovation Networks*. New York: Oxford University Press.

Gloor, P. and S. Cooper. 2007. "The new principles of a swarm business." *MIT Sloan Management Review* (Spring): 81–84.

———. 2007. *Cool Hunting—Chasing Down the Next Big Thing*? New York: AMACOM.

Graham, J. 2000. "Successful selling: Learn the customer's buying cycle." *American Salesman* 45, no. 3: 3–9. http://search.proquest.com/docview/203361557?accountid=35396.

Gray, A. 2013. "Anti-farm photo bill altered." *McClatchy—Tribune Business News*. http://search.proquest.com/docview/1330984860?accountid=35396.

Green, L. 2009. "The fear of no future: Guatemalan migrants, dispossession and dislocation." *Anthropologica* 51, no. 2: 327–341. http://search.proquest.com/docview/751936748?accountid=35396.

Guarino, M. 2013. "Abercrombie & Fitch: What's wrong with selling just to 'cool people?'" *Christian Science Monitor*. http://search.proquest.com/docview/1354535617?accountid=35396.

Guerette, R. 2009. "Analyzing crime displacement and diffusion." *The Problem-Oriented Guides*. Center for Problem-Oriented Policing, US Department of Justice, Washington, DC, June, no. 10.

Hadfield, P. and F. Measham. 2009. "Shaping the night: How licensing, social divisions and informal social controls mould the form and content of nightlife." Supplement Special Issue: Violence and the Night-Time Economy, *Crime Prevention and Community Safety* A 11, no. 3 (July): 219–234.

Harford, T. 2008. *The Logic of Life*. New York: Random House.

Hart, K. 1973. "Informal income opportunities and urban employment in Ghana." *The Journal of Modern African Studies* 2, no. 1, 61–89.

———. 1990. "The idea of economy: Six modern dissenters." In R. Friedland and A. F. Robertson (eds.), *Beyond the Marketplace, Rethinking Economy and Society*, New York: Aldine de Gruyter, pp. 137–160.

Hauser, C. 2012. "Undercover videos. Work at slaughterhouse is halted after graphic videos." *New York Times*, August 24.

Henken, T. A. 2008. "Out of the shadows: Political action and the informal economy in Latin America." *The Americas* 65, no. 2, 283–285.

Holland, J. 1998. *Emergence: From Chaos to Order*. Reading, MA: Perseus Books.

Holt, D. M. 2008. "Unlikely allies against factory farms: Animal rights advocates and environmentalists." *Agriculture and Human Values* 25: 169–171.

Howell, J. C. 2007. "Menacing or mimicking? Realities of youth gangs." *Juvenile and Family Court Journal* 58, no. 2 (Spring).

International Labour Organisation (ILO). 1972. *Employment, Incomes and Equality: A Strategy for Increasing Productive Employment in Kenya*. Geneva: ILO.

Johnson, J. 2012. "'There's a reason the government is involved.' Readers write: Light rail, soda tax, animal welfare." *Star Tribune*, February 3.

Johnson, S. 2001. *Emergence: The Connected Lives of Ants, Brains, Cities, and Software*. New York: Scribner.

Keierleber, M. 2013. "Bill would shield farms, factories from cameras." *McClatchy—Tribune Business News*. http://search.proquest.com/docview/1312136346?accountid=35396.

Kennedy, J., R. C. Eberhart and Y. Shui. 2001. *Swarm Intelligence*. San Francisco, CA: Morgan Kaufmann.

King, R. D. and D. Wheelock. 2007. 'Group threat and social control: Race, perceptions of minorities and the desire to punish." *Social Forces* 85, no. 3 (March): 1255–1280.

Klamm, B. K. and M. L. Weidenmier. 2004. "Linking business processes and transaction cycles." *Journal of Information Systems* 18, no. 2: 113–125.

Krugman, P. 1996. *The Self-Organizing Economy*. Malden, MA: Blackwell.

La Porta, R. and A. Shleifer. 2008. "The unofficial economy and economic development." *Brookings Papers on Economic Activity* (Fall): 275–363.

Levine, C. 2006. "Hard to keep tabs when food vendor has wheels." *McClatchy—Tribune Business News*. http://search.proquest.com/docview/463420054?accountid=35396.

Liang, B. A. and K. M. Lovett. 2012. "Online elder abuse: Addressing senior safety risks." *Experience. The Magazine of the Senior Lawyers Division* American Bar Association 22, no. 2: 17–22. http://search.proquest.com/docview/1032808933?accountid=35396.

Ljujic, V., P. Vedder, H. Dekker, and M. Van Geel. 2012. "Romaphobia: A unique phenomenon?" *Romani Studies* 22, no. 2 (December): 141–152.

"Lo Hsing Han." *The Economist* July 27, 2013, 78.

Martin, A. W. 2007. "Organizational structures, authority and protest: The case of union organizing in the United States, 1990–2001." *Social Forces* 85, no. 3 (March): 1413–1435.

McCallum, K. 2011. "Santa Rosa restaurateurs decry mobile food vendor events." *McClatchy—Tribune Business News*. http://search.proquest.com/docview/849633256?accountid=35396.

McCarty, M. 2013. "Abercrombie controversy shows how easy it is to brand our fellow humans." *McClatchy—Tribune Business News*. http://search.proquest.com/docview/1355340847?accountid=35396

McCune, Marianne. 2013. "Go east, young marijuana dealer." Morning Edition, All Things Considered. National Public Radio, May 22.

McFeely R. 2011. "Information sharing efforts with partners span many FBI programs." Special Agent in Charge, Baltimore Office. Federal Bureau of Investigation. Statement before the Senate Judiciary Committee, Wilmington, Delaware. June 20.

McLaren L. 2003. "Anti-immigrant prejudice in Europe: Contact, threat perception, and preferences for the exclusion of migrants." *Social Forces* 81, no. 3 (March): 909–936.

Montano, R. 2006. "Mobile food vendors feel threatened: Restaurant owners, city officials seek to keep catering operations moving." *Knight Ridder Tribune Business News*. http://search.proquest.com/docview/465697513?accountid=35396.

Morehart, M. 2006. "Combating international money laundering operations." Presentation before the Senate Committee on Banking, Housing and Urban Affairs, Washington, DC, April 4.

Norton, J. 2008. "Unlicensed food vendors a health risk; Preparation, storage conditions are vital to food safety." *McClatchy—Tribune News*. http://search.proquest.com/docview/462167711?accountid=35396.

Olivo, A. 2009. "Illegal immigrants face life-and-death decisions without health insurance." *McClatchy—Tribune News*. http://search.proquest.com/docview/457734409?accountid=35396.

Phan, A. 2012. "New mobile vendor could create unfair competition, Kingston business owner says." *McClatchy—Tribune Business News*. http://search.proquest.com/docview/1169120516?accountid=35396.

Polanyi, Michael. 1974. *Knowing and Being*. Chicago: University of Chicago Press.

Porter, Michael. 1980. *Competitive Strategy: Techniques for Analyzing Industries and Competitors*. New York: Free Press.

Potok, Mark. August 2009. *The Second Wave Return of the Militias: A Special Report from the Southern Poverty Law Center*. Montgomery, AL: Southern Poverty Law Center.

Povich, E. S. 2013. "Cigarette smuggling cuts states' per pack tax revenues." *McClatchy—Tribune Business News*. http://search.proquest.com/docview/1357118809?accountid=35396.

Price, M. 1999. "Legislators groom rules to control puppy mills." *Journal Record*. http://search.proquest.com/docview/259328472?accountid=35396.

Radcliffe, J. 2011. "Video surveillance of public places." Problem-Oriented Guides for Police Response Guides for Police, Response Guide Series, Guide No. 4. August.

Radzievich, N. 2010. "Vendor clears first hurdle to sell hot dogs in Bethlehem: City board recommends Christopher Morales get the first mobile vending license under city's new laws." *McClatchy—Tribune Business News*. http://search.proquest.com/docview/506535771?accountid=35396.

Ramaswamy, Rohit. 1996. *Design and Management of Service Processes: Keeping Customers for Life*. Reading, MA: Addison-Wesley.

Reilly, L. 1988. "Firm sues vendors to stop sale of hotdogs as Vienna sausages." *Washington Business Journal* 7, no. 14: 5. http://search.proquest.com/docview/229512349?accountid=35396.

Russell, E. 2006. "Ellsworth: OKs food vendor for harbor." *McClatchy—Tribune Business News*. http://search.proquest.com/docview/463166467?accountid=35396.

Ryder, N. and U. Turksen. 2009. "Islamophobia or an important weapon? An analysis of the US financial war on terrorism." *Journal of Banking Regulation* 10, no. 4: 307–320. doi: http://dx.doi.org/10.1057/jbr.2009.10.

Sabatini, C. and E. Farnsworth. 2006. "The urgent need for labor law reform." *Journal of Democracy* 17, no. 4 (October): 50–64.

Sassen S. 2009. "Cities in today's global age." *SAIS Review* 29, no. 1 (Winter–Spring): 3–34.

Schneider, F., A. Buehn, C. E. Montenegro. 2010. "Shadow economies all over the world: New estimates for 162 countries from 1999 to 2007." Revised Version. Policy Research Working Paper 5356. The World Bank, Development Research Group, Poverty and Inequality Team & Europe and Central Asia Region Human Development Economics Unit, July, 19–20.

Schrodinger, E. 2006. *What Is Life?* Cambridge: Cambridge University Press.

Scott, S. 2006. "Chaplain praises women's ordinations: Minnesotan could be excommunicated after her symbolic recognition as priest, deacon." *McClatchy—Tribune Business News*. http://search.proquest.com/docview/4651238330?accountid=35396.

Seeley, T. D. 1985. *Honeybee Ecology*. Princeton, NJ: Princeton University Press.

———. 1989. "Social foraging in honey bees: How nectar foragers assess their colony's nutritional status." *Behavioral Ecology and Sociobiology* 24: 181–199.

Segel, L. A. and J. Jackson. 1972. "Dissipative structure: An explanation and an ecological example." *Journal of Theoretical Biology* 37: 545–559.

Shapiro, C. and H. Varian. 1999. *Information Rules: A Strategic Guide to the Network Economy*. Boston, MA: Harvard Business School.

Shaw, K. A. 1992. "Episcopalian priest breaks new ground: Privitera says women's time has come in modern church." *Telegram & Gazette*. http://search.proquest.com/docview/268464047?accountid=35396.

Sole, Richard V. and J. Bascompte. 2006. *Self-Organization in Complex Ecological Systems*. Princeton, NJ: Princeton University Press.

Tafoya, D. 2010. *The Effective Organization: Practical Application of Complexity Theory and Organizational Design to Maximize Performance in the Face of Emerging Events*. New York: Routledge.

———. 2013a. *Organizations in the Face of Crisis: Managing the Brand and Stakeholders*. New York: Palgrave Macmillan.

———. 2013b. "The emerging crisis and the phenomenon of the stakeholder swarm: Tracking the emergence brand trauma resulting from the decay of network order to network chaos." Paper presented at the Annual Swarm Conference, the University of Central Florida, July 6–7.

———. 2013c "Retail in the shadows: Mapping and describing sales transactions among those engaged in the informal economy's drug, prostitution and smuggling trades." Fifth Annual Complexity in Business Conference, University of Maryland, Reagan Conference Center, Washington, DC, November 7–8.

Tamari, J. 2010. "Animal rights activists mixed on vick move." *McClatchy—Tribune Business News*, September 22.

Thigpen, D. 2010. "Lodi crunching down on lunch wagons." *McClatchy—Tribune Business News*. http://search.proquest.com/docview/458476698?accountid=35396.

Thomas, J. 1992. *Informal Economic Activity*. Hemel Hempstead: Harvester Wheatsheaf.

———. 2001. "What is the informal economy anyway?" *SAIS Review* 21, no. 1 (Winter–Spring): 1–11.

Truver, S. C. 2000. "Recapitalizing the coast guard for the 21st century." *Sea Power* 434: 70–75.

Weisel, D. 2004. "Street prostitution in Raleigh, North Carolina." A Final Report to the US Department of Justice, Office of Community Oriented Policing Services on the Field Applications of the Problem-Oriented Guides for Police Project. August.

Weizer, R. J. and Steven Tuch. 2005. "Racially biased policing: Determinants of citizen perceptions." *Social Forces* 83, no. 3 (March): 1009–1030.

Wilson, K. 1991. "Vendors fight to keep city space." *Philadelphia Tribune*. http://search.proquest.com/docview/337780876?accountid=35396.

Williams, C. C., and Round, J. 2009. "Out of the margins: Re-theorizing the role of the informal economy in Ukraine." *International Journal of Economic Perspectives* 3, no. 1, 45–58.

Wodak, A., A. Symonds, and R. Richmond. 2003. "The role of civil disobedience in drug policy reform: How an illegal 'safer injection room' led to a sanctioned, 'medically supervised injection center.'" *Journal of Drug Issues* 33, no. 3: 609–623. http://search.proquest.com/docview/208840758?accountid=35396.

Worden, A. 2006. "Rendell is urged to fix puppy mills." *McClatchy—Tribune Business News*. http://search.proquest.com/docview/459738582?accountid=35396.

"Zeta zeroed." *The Economist*, July 20, 2013, 35.

Index

Numbers in **bold** indicate figures and tables.

Printed in the United States of America